My Foreign Country

Other books by the author

WALES AND THE WELSH

TALKING OF WALES

AMERICANS AND NOTHING ELSE

INDIA FILE

THE STATE OF AMERICA

OUT OF RED DARKNESS

My Foreign Country

Trevor Fishlock's Britain

JOHN MURRAY
Albemarle Street, London

First published in 1997
by John Murray (Publishers) Ltd,
50 Albemarle Street, London W1X 4 BD

A catalogue record for this book is available from the British Library

ISBN 0–7195–5228 1

Typeset in 12½/13½pt Bembo by Servis Filmsetting Ltd, Manchester

Printed and bound in Great Britain by
The University Press, Cambridge

For Penny

Contents

1

Landfall

Roused from sleep, I pulled on boots and oilskins and swung myself up the companionway to the deck. For a moment I shivered in the cold air. The vast night sky had a thrilling clarity. We rolled down the moon's bright beam, a silvery ship on a pewter sea, streaming a starry tail.

On the long marching swells, the tops rushing and breaking, the bow plunged and rose in rhythmic exhalation, as if the schooner were a living creature, a sea horse in harness. In these restless western reaches of the English Channel we moved in our authentically British element, our encircling, defining and inescapable sea.

By and by, the gleam of a distant lighthouse would prick the night. At dawn we would spy a mote of land upon the gauzy horizon and watch it rise slowly from the sea and gather substance. The mirage blur of distant blue serrations would drift into focus, sharpening into leonine capes and rampart cliffs, promontories of caves and fists of scoured rock, watercolour downs and wooded valleys stippled with spires.

An approach from the sea, the home-blowing wind on your neck, is shot through with expectation and hope. The smell of the land seeps into the imagination, caresses desire and teases appetite. To the eye wearied by the dishwash monotone of the waves, the coast in sunshine has all the dazzle of curtain-up in a theatre, the vividness of a newly-sliced melon. In this brilliant tapestry meadows glow emerald and marigold. Soil turned by the plough glistens as red as liver. Small ports, even those you know are as plain as slate and grubbily workaday, reveal themselves as picture postcards. Smoke drifts from cottage chimneys, streets wind their way from quay to pub to church, seagulls strut on rooftop sentry-go, sunlight throws harlequin spangles on the lazy harbour water and glints on the sign of The Anchor Inn. The intoxicant perfume of a port, pungent, kippery and tarry, is borne on the breeze.

The spirit quickens. Sailing ship men were tantalized by the prospect of these harbours, and – 'Western wind, when wilt thou blow?' – were impatient for breeze and tide to hurry them home to their families and women and roast beef, all the mingled joys and longing of their hammock dreams.

Channel fever, or 'the Channels', they called the anxiety of homecoming. Off the coast, among the free swooping seabirds, you sense the ache in it still.

A Decline in the Sales of Shoe Polish

I was setting off to fossick about in Britain, to walk cliffs and mountains, lanes and city streets, to visit fat land and thin, to drink a little, to be entertained, to poke into history's sediment.

I hoped that clues in my search for the spirit of the times would emerge not only from encounters along the way but also from the evocative land itself, and from its accretions, its barnacles and lichens, its churches, castles, pubs, walls, shrines, bridges and blank-eyed ruins; all the repositories of legends. Some countries wear their histories very lightly, but the British have theirs as a tortoise has its shell, not merely as armour, but as something organic and integral, a spine.

Britain is only six hundred miles long and three hundred miles at its widest. It would fit almost three times into Texas; and visiting Americans are instructed that England itself is the size of Alabama. Britain is small enough to be conquered by foot, and striding its length from John O'Groats to Land's End has been a fairly commonplace achievement ever since the foursquare brothers John and Robert Naylor pioneered the journey in 1871. They set off in hobnailed boots, vowing to abstain from drink and tobacco and promising to attend church twice on Sundays. Prudent Christians both, they carried heavily-ferruled cudgels, selected by their fencing master, to deal with any ruffians they might encounter along the way. They knew that such toughs were 'by no means uncommon'.

Although relatively small in its dimensions, Britain is a country too varied for any single person to get to know well in a lifetime. It is a most intricate jigsaw and each piece is compressed and dense, like pemmican or good fruit cake, the landscape intensively farmed by history; and although the country has formed a political whole, the jigsaw parts have resolutely and stubbornly retained their character so that the whole is not homogeneous and digestible.

The dispatches I read in the years I worked abroad described a Britain that lay under a cumulus of doubt. According to the news from home, the national rudder hung out of its gudgeon. Ragged-bearded prophets stalked the newspapers and other godless pulpits and complained of a national decline, moral and spiritual, a catastrophic dragging of the anchor. I wondered if they were observing change and mistaking it for decay; but the force of the reports was that Britain was in discontented middle age, morose, fearing ambush, easily alarmed, severely afflicted by mulligrubs. When cross-examined, people saw their country as John of Gaunt, in Shakespeare's words, saw his adored but sorry England – 'bound with shame, With inky blots, and rotten parchment bonds'.

Here, by all accounts, was a country of broken confidence, seized by pessimistic fatalism, relishing self-flagellation. I read that hope itself was threadbare, that when the British observed their country they saw gaping seams and prospects of weeds. On the threshold of the twenty-first century they felt less respected

and less influential in the world they so lately and so confidently
bestrode. A survey, seeking to measure the immeasurable,
showed that they were among the least happy people on earth
and that half of them longed to emigrate, though where they
wanted to go was not clear. A strange phenomenon, the feel-
good factor, emerged as a political consideration, but only
because it barely existed.

An enervating self-pity pervaded. The British had always
imagined themselves robust, and in their legends there was a relishing of risk, but robustness was in retreat. A headline in a
newspaper proclaimed: 'Nation's Morale Approaching A Crisis'.
A West End play was commended by critics as a properly gloomy
elegy for a Britain in decline. Editorials rued the 'torn fabric' of
'a sick society' and searched for the synonyms for rot and decay.
The death of England was announced. One newspaper asked
pitifully: 'Can The John Bull Spirit See Our Heartland Through
These Dark Times?'

As evidence accumulated in the fattening dossiers of decline
it was reported that the British gentleman, one of our chief
contributions to civilization, had become as rare as the okapi.
Foreigners, once much poorer than we were, journeyed to
Britain and remarked upon the dowdy women and unkempt
men scuttling through the litter of scruffy streets. Returning
expatriates shuddered to see what they had thought to observe
only among lesser breeds abroad: hollow-eyed young men and
women begging for loose change and sleeping rough. A decline
in the sales of shoe polish was cited as proof that the British no
longer cared for their appearance and that their self-esteem had
crumbled. A Japanese business study concluded that 'the British
are happy to settle for second-best'.

Looking to sport as a metaphor for the nation, the British
found evidence enough of malaise. The unshaved chin of
England's cricket captain was held to be emblematic of the
country's declining opinion of itself, the blokeish stubble of
shame; and failure at the wicket was, as always, damning evidence of a brittleness of national character. Commentators
chronicled a rabble's retreat from the Corinthian ideal and
sportsmen displayed their feet of clay. An editorial on sport was

headed 'The Era of Mr Nasty'. Footballers were seen as spoilt and vulgar. Their extremist supporters, spitting, vicious and as ugly as cockroaches, were condemned as barbarians. The funerals of old-time cricketers and footballers became national meetings of mourning for a golden age of chivalry and sportsmanship. Across the coffins of the old clean-cut warriors men reminisced about an age when terraces were full and stars were modest heroes: the era before television, big money, celebrity and hooliganism.

Many detected cultural impoverishment in a faltering grasp of the English language. More than half a century after the introduction of universal secondary education it was found that students emerging from schools and universities were unable to express themselves simply. They could not spell, their grammar was flaccid and their writing was pitted with the greengrocer's apostrophe. It was revealed that some new Royal Air Force officer cadets had not heard of the Battle of Britain, could not waltz and could speak only in grunts. There were fears that English was becoming a native gibberish to be cashiered out of gentlemen's houses. Hearing the language everywhere mangled, not least in the mouths of their own young, the horrified middle classes concluded that the oiks were at the gates. In response, a cabinet minister declared war on the glottal stop, the sort of action that reminded me of the thoughtless edicts that sputtered from the Kremlin in the anguished death throes of the Soviet empire in the early 1990s.

As part of a spreading sense of loss there was alarm at assaults on 'heritage' and concern at the withdrawal of distinctive British ornaments, like red telephone boxes and the navy blue British passport. This document was replaced by a paltry European thing, no better than a Frenchman's; but we ensured that it still carried the traditional imperious demand to foreign border guards, embellished with appropriate British cocked-hat majuscules: 'Her Britannic Majesty's Secretary of State Requests and requires in the Name of Her Majesty all those whom it may concern to allow the bearer to pass freely without let or hindrance . . .'

Nostalgia was the weft to melancholy's warp. For many of a

certain age a sunnier era had been reflected in the popular weekly *John Bull*. I grew up with it. It cost threepence, its telegram address was Heroically, London, and it portrayed a hopeful country which was being re-ordered and made better, a time when anything seemed possible. Its cover paintings celebrated a Britain of cake-baking mothers, pipe-smoking fathers and scampish small boys with fallen socks; a Merrie England of Pancake Day and the Dunmow Flitch, the village green, shire-horses, haymaking and country fairs; the modest Britain of Bile Beans and Ovaltine, Songster Gramophone Needles, Denis Compton's Brylcreemed hair, Billy Cotton, straight bats, permanent waves, friendly bobbies and cheerful cockneys; *Children's Hour*, 'The Teddy Bears' Picnic', 'The Laughing Policeman', and 'The Runaway Train'; thatched pubs and warm beer, jigsaw puzzles, Ealing comedies, City gents with bowler hats, a dutiful and discreet royal family; and hierarchy and deference.

Lodged in memory's crevices, such images played a part in Britain's late-century brooding, the feeling that there had been a falling away from standards of behaviour, education, manners, morals, the way of speaking, law and order and family life. In compiling their catalogue of complaint the British found fault with all their institutions. They arraigned the clergy, the teachers, the judiciary and the police and judged them all guilty, less deserving of respect. The royal family was widely believed to be the mysterious embodiment of the nation and its virtues; but partly because some of its members had fallen into disrepute, the purpose, validity and usefulness of the institution of monarchy itself came into question; and the possibility of a republic was more seriously debated. The reputation of politicians fell into the swill, financiers were found to be less scrupulous and businessmen more avaricious. The brash newspapers seemed to be in the hands of the insolent mob. Criminals appeared to be more brutal, crueller than the sentimentally-remembered old-style villains. As for comedians, they seemed less funny. The British no longer laughed together.

Political leaders and various sages rooted vaguely in the past and proposed the rediscovery of a lost Britain by way of a return to old benchmarks, disciplines and traditions. Some thought that if the Union flag were flown more widely and more frequently and patriotic anthems sung more often, a 'national pride' might somehow be restored, as if a quality so subtle and profound could be applied like paint.

Britain was leaning upon its history and its myths, pausing for breath, looking for direction.

When they gaze around them the British can see a line marking a clear and abrupt disconnection from the past. The statues raised in town and city squares, for example, salute not only warriors and poets but also the men and women who built Britain, who flourished in an age when there was little government and scanty regulation, when the state was employed on light duties and foreign affairs only. There was a frontier to push, a limitless opportunity for energetic and unbridled Titans and much for them to do. Look at the confident poses they strike upon their plinths – they were the heroes of education, public health, transport, medicine, science, engineering and industry. They were the principled reformers and stable-clearers, righters of wrongs, innovators and philanthropists. They ploughed the important furrows, constructed the dramatic bridges and railways, built the drains and hospitals. We know their names: Stephenson, Plimsoll, Davy, Telford, Arrol, Brunel, Lister, Macadam, Shaftesbury, Nightingale. In our age of specialization and refinement we do not erect statues to the improvers of ailerons and computer software. We do not know their names. There will be little labour in future for sculptors of the heroic because there will be very few heroes to honour.

Many of the statues that ornament our towns salute the frock-coated municipal moguls who built the stanchion cities of Manchester, Birmingham, Leeds, Bristol, Glasgow, Cardiff, Newcastle, Liverpool and their sisters. They were leaders of strong city-states which gave us a feeling of continuity, region and national shape. These cities grew up over the centuries around the industries of shipbuilding, shiphandling, coal mining, iron and steel making, textiles, pottery, engineering and fishing. The people who congregated in these places evolved as tribes with their own histories, political traditions and argot.

7

Their skills passed down from father to son. They shared the wealth, excitement, fluctuation and despair of great industries. They founded football and rugby teams which reinforced a sense of their locality and of rivalry with their neighbours. Their cohesion was strengthened by hierarchies of age and of status and, often, by religious belief. This local loyalty was a precious resource, valued above all by the shrewd men who recruited for the regiments of the British Army. Forged into an unmatched fighting spirit, it has ever been envied by foreign armies. Every village and town in the land has its memorial to lads who had been schoolmates and apprentices together, who joined the same regiment and died side by side.

In a very few years, before our bewildered eyes, the once-embedded industries have largely vanished. In the main, they were decidedly masculine, for it was a heroic business, a matter of sinew and muscle, pride and ego, to build ships, forge steel and gouge coal; but that bread-winning manliness has been eroded, and the swagger has gone, with effects we are only just beginning to discover. The trade union barons who led armies of industrial workers were once national figures as well as local heroes, formidable men caricatured by cartoonists, their names invoked to frighten the children of Surrey. Today their successors are little-known functionaries, de-fanged and reduced. The working-class Member of Parliament is a species almost extinct. The age of the proletarian hero has passed, his historic role over. Strikes are fewer because the working class has shrunk. It was not so long ago that millions of British men wore industrial overalls. Now the cloth-cap hangs on history's peg.

Nowhere is the break between past and present delineated more clearly and poignantly than in the obituaries of men and women who served in the world wars. These tributes are compelling and moving, frequently the best and most memorable reading in a daily newspaper. There will never be such obituaries again. They lead us to ponder on the nature of courage, duty and loyalty, and to wonder. They are remarkable tales of adventure, risk, devotion and odyssey, the exploits of ordinary people in extraordinary circumstances. We are all illuminated by them, but the flame is flickering.

I went to France and Holland for the fiftieth anniversaries of the landings in Normandy and the battle for Arnhem. On the dunes and beaches of Normandy, forever Gold, Juno, Sword, Utah and Omaha, and in the streets of Arnhem, old boys gathered and remembered. Lofty, Chalky, Shorty, Jock, Taffy and Paddy – 'Just ordinary blokes, you know' – journeyed to their own youth and joked with each other about their balding heads and whitening moustaches. They stood and reflected at what they did and left their footprints where they had left them once before, in history; and as they walked the medals on their blazers stirred in gentle tintinnabulation. The survivors of those years, both military and civilian, are the living witnesses of great events and have been a resource, the corn in our granary, nurturing our self-respect, reminding us of the phenomenal exertion of the national will that, especially between 1939 and 1945, drew on a reservoir of bravery, ingenuity, leadership, stoicism and grumbling humour. The mobilizing of these qualities against tyranny revitalized the legends of the defiant island, redeemed our failings and underscored the definition of ourselves.

The new generations in Britain are the first who are not shaped by war and the threat of conquest. Nor are they fashioned by the intimate industrial societies. They do not follow their fathers to the pit, the factory, the docks, the steelworks, the mill, the shipyard. They do not qualify for gold watches at the end of long and loyal service. They do not swing around the old newel posts. They do not marry themselves to metal and monstrous machines and steep themselves in grime and share in the hardships, skills, elbow-rubbing and language of those industries. They do not sing the old songs or tell the old jokes or make the old allusions. What was until recently the common experience of life and work for generations has for them already become hearsay, the distant clang of an anvil.

Nor are they moulded by the adventure, opportunity, burden and beliefs of the British Empire. They are not influenced by imperial attitudes. For most of the twentieth century the Empire was as much a part of the natural order of things and of common consciousness as the movement of the tides. To people in their middle age it all seems to have receded extraordinarily rapidly and they have sought to come to terms with the shrunken horizon of the imperial aftermath. To the young, however, it not only belongs to history books but seems to have been an altogether curious adventure and, for some of them, not necessarily a matter of pride. 'Colonies,' a young man said, 'I feel embarrassed by the whole thing.'

War, industry and Empire made and unified Britain and gave it purpose and meaning. The disappearance of these dynamics and an historic confluence of changes have brought us to one of history's grand junctions and to a search for an answer to the question of what it means to be British.

In the Office of a Wall

Down the centuries the British have been enthralled by their insularity and have revelled in their detachment. The moat is our motif, the jagged rocks our strewn caltrops, the cliffs our palisades. The celebration of islandness and particularity permeate our literature and epics and the songs of ourselves. We grew to value and savour the attributes of a fastness and fancied ourselves as lofty as lords, self-contained upon the battlements, the offshore people.

In the seventeenth century the Marquis of Halifax sternly advised his countrymen to 'Look to your Moat . . . We are in an Island, confined to it by God Almighty, not as a Penalty but a Grace, and one of the greatest that can be given to Mankind.'

A history of the First World War, published in the 1920s, observed that 'We in Great Britain, with the sea girdling us, find it difficult to realize that a strip of neutral ground and a row of posts can constitute a frontier.'

The return of our scattered armies from Dunkirk in 1940 was counted a victory because, by regaining the island citadel, they experienced deliverance and renewal.

Drawing deeply on her Churchillian cigar, Margaret Thatcher suggested both fellow feeling and a virtue in islandness when she spoke in 1982 against Argentinian aggression. 'The people of the Falkland Islands,' she said, 'like the people of the United Kingdom, are an island race . . .'

The bones of sailormen form the coral reef of our legends. The pantheon of British heroes is dominated by the stubborn defenders of the Channel, by sea lords, navigators and sea-minded rulers; by Alfred, Henry VII, Henry VIII, Drake, Frobisher, Grenville, Hawkins and Howard; Blake, Rodney, Hood and Howe; Cook and Fisher. And above all, Nelson, who was sometimes thought to be Francis Drake reincarnated. John Keegan, the military historian, has drawn up a list of the fifteen most decisive naval actions in world history: British fleets fought in nine of them and Nelson played a crucial role in three – Copenhagen, the Nile and Trafalgar. Few towns lack a Nelson inn, forty streets in London bear his name and statues of him are posted like sentinels throughout the land. As I discovered, it is hardly possible to travel in Britain without bumping into the man. His flagship, HMS *Victory,* is the most evocative of our relics, a cathedral in oak.

We know our frontiers. They are unambiguous. And it is partly for this reason that to some British people our joining of the European Union seemed the risky lowering of the draw-bridge, a threat to a separate and special condition. For many years suspicious minds saw a Channel tunnel not as an avenue to Europe but as a conduit for enemies, rats and pox. When this marvel was constructed at last, some in Britain felt unable to salute the engineering achievement because they suspected that the French had slid a hand up Britannia's skirt. The French built a fast direct railway line to their end of the tunnel and preened. But the British did not. British trains made a slow, halting, sulky progress towards it, as if dragging their feet. At the time of the tunnel's opening a concert was held in a garden in Kent and an orchestra played 'Rule, Britannia!' and, inevitably, Elgar's 'Pomp and Circumstance', to an audience wearing hats painted with the Union flag. Reiterating the sentiment that the best thing between France and England is the sea, one of the concert-goers said she wished the Channel tunnel could be blown up.

When the British government enraged its European partners in a dispute, a Belgian newspaper wondered if the tunnel should not be stoppered. I imagined a crowd of Englishmen manhandling a mighty red, white and blue tompion and pushing it into the Folkestone end.

In Paris *Le Figaro* declared that Charles de Gaulle had been right: 'England is an island that all the bridges and all the tunnels in the world will never manage to link to the Continent.' De Gaulle never forgot that Churchill said to him just before the Allied invasion of Normandy: 'You may be sure, General, that if we ever have to choose between Europe and the open sea, it is the open sea we would choose.'

More than a few people in Britain approved of what de Gaulle said about bridges and tunnels. John Bull, after all, stands for obstinacy and a suspicion of foreigners. In a book about mountains Alfred Wainwright, the hill walker, wrote – and you have to imagine his northern growl – 'I refuse to insult the noble mountains of Scotland by quoting their altitudes in foreign metres instead of British feet.'

Our fellow Europeans often regarded us with puzzlement: to them we seemed difficult, noisy, suspicious and, quite often, the club bore. A French political institute concluded that Britain belongs to Europe, but has its back turned to the continent. 'English insularity', it said, 'is the motor of its national identity.' At every harbour in Britain signs are erected warning of the horrors of rabies, and some of them have depictions of Baskervillean hounds. The danger of rabies is small but these signs suggest a foreign threat and underline the security of our defensive moat and the comfort of distance.

Backing and Veering

We switched on the radio above the chart table for the shipping forecast. No other country hears such a stirring daily litany. It has a loyal following ashore and thousands listen to it as if it were an incantation. These disciples experience a thrilling resonance in the names of the thirty-one watery estates, recited, almost as blank verse, by authoritative BBC voices.

The names speak of history as well as geography. The syllables of Viking, North Utsire, South Utsire, Forties, Cromarty, Forth and Tyne, Dogger, Fisher and German Bight, Humber,

Thames and Dover, remind the British of their island state. Forecasts of backing and veering in Wight and Portland, in Lundy, Biscay and Finisterre, tell us that we have been shaped, in part, by our capricious and pugnacious weather, its snow-in-summer ability to turn the world upside-down. Storm warnings for the whales' domains of Sole, Fastnet, Shannon and Rockall emphasize that ''tis hard grey weather Breeds hard English men'. Its uncertain nature has made us flexible, phlegmatic, dogged, tough, humorous and appreciative of rare halcyon days; or so we like to believe. Hearing the news of a falling glass in Plymouth and Irish Sea, of gales brewing in the purlieus of Malin and Hebrides, Bailey, Faeroes and Fair Isle, landlubber lovers of the shipping forecast see monstrous waves driven by the remorseless west wind. With the tide of sleep advancing, they drain their cocoa, set aside their C.S. Forester or Patrick O'Brian or Alan Villiers and lie thankful beneath their blankets on the soft quarterdecks of their beds while in their imaginations they strike the topgallants and toe the slippery ratlines in a blow.

The Old Moon Spanner

The schooner's foresails were sabres in the moonlight. The mainsheet creaked and the sea broke and foamed and hissed at the bow. For a while the Australian mate stood in the cockpit and contemplated the sky, his Viking beard tugged by the wind.

'Time for the old moon spanner,' he murmured.

He ducked below for a moment and emerged with his sextant. He did not need to take a sight, but, as he said, modern electronic navigation instruments can fail and he liked to keep up a seaman's skills; you never know. He braced himself in the cockpit, his back against the doghouse, and squinted through the sextant telescope, swinging the index bar along the arc. Shooting the moon, he was at one with Captain Cook. The sextant was invented in 1757, as an improvement on the quadrant, to take lunar sights as a way of fixing longitude. It made navigation more certain, the oceans and the unknown world more comprehensible.

The mate made his observations and went below to busy

himself over the Channel chart with the astronomical tables, tide tables and parallel rule.

'There's nowhere in the world so difficult as the sea around Britain,' he said. 'If you can sail here you can sail anywhere.'

He returned the moon spanner to its box. In the daytime, of course, it becomes the old sun spanner.

A Magic Carpet

In our growing years we accrued the conceits of islanders, notions of our uniqueness and individuality, and combined a swagger with our nautical roll. All the invaders, Celts, Romans, Saxons, Vikings, English, Danes and Normans, who wove themselves into the British cloth and poured their speech into the crucible of the English language, had perforce to risk and suffer the sea. To some historians the sea has appeared as a test, a Darwinian sieve, and they have suggested that the daring nature of our founding ancestors set them apart from the herd, hallmarked them as adventurous.

The counterpoint of our insularity was a growing mercantilist passion. In 1436 the Bishop of Chichester urged us to:

> Cherish merchandise, keep the Admiraltie,
> That we be masters of the Narrow Sea.

The Narrow Sea, or Seas, was the strategic elbow of water formed by the English Channel and the southern reaches of the North Sea; and our command of it was enforced by the Admiral of the Narrow Seas. He ensured that we fished undisturbed by predatory foreigners and that foreign vessels encountering an English warship hauled down their topsails, a naval version of bending the knee.

Although we were moated we looked to the sea as our magic carpet. From our havens we launched ourselves out of our island orbit and into the outer space of oceans. In the centuries of our mastery, the sea was as much an influence on our spirit and imagination as were, to other roaming peoples, the frontier, the pampas, the prairie, the veld, the steppe, the great rivers, the desert, the tundra and the outback. We had an intuitive feeling for sea power and, with the sea our accomplice, created the mightiest empire. Our poets described, not overburdened leaking ships driven by weary and diseased men, but argosies on opal seas; and the poets were preferred. We journeyed as brazenly as robbers for treasure and aggrandizement, and carted our shining swag of ducats and doubloons through seaport streets. We searched for peppercorns and cinnamon which improved our food; brought back tea, coffee and chocolate which improved our sociability; and loaded the holds with chintz, gingham, seersucker, muslin, taffeta and satin which improved our comfort, style and vocabulary. I became, like many others, a distant beneficiary of this trade when, at eleven, I went to the school in Hampshire founded in 1722 by Richard Churcher, who made his fortune as an East India merchant. Our red blazer badge was an East Indiaman under sail; and, to remind us of the sea, the school houses were named Grenville, Drake, Nelson and Rodney.

We British also voyaged for science, for we were scholars as well as corsairs and seaborne magnates. The statue of Drake at Plymouth Hoe has it right: legs set in a confident, buccaneering pose, his left hand close to his sword, his right holding dividers above the globe he circled in the *Golden Hind*. We were pathfinders, eagerly seizing the latest navigational technology, and charted assiduously, labelling the world, giving our British names to distant capes and bays, so much so that it seemed that every last cabin boy had his monicker awarded to some malarial creek or icy inlet. Knowledge was always sought with a beady eye to commerce and strategy; at the same time we were more than mere plunderers, for we grew to believe we had been given a mission to civilize and to govern.

Throughout the years of the defence of the Channel it seemed that even the tides and gales were allies sent by God. Spaniards believed that Drake, whom they dreaded, possessed a magic mirror in which he could observe ships anywhere in the world, that he was a wizard or devil who worked with witches to call up the storms that wrecked the Spanish Armada.

Napoleon Bonaparte massed his invasion barges within sight

of the cliffs of England and promised that a fortnight after landing he would be sitting in London dictating surrender. 'Let us be masters of the Channel for six hours,' he implored, 'and we are masters of the world.' The British cut down their oak forests and sent them to sea to deny him those hours. Their warships were not always as good as those of their French enemies but British seamanship and gunnery and fighting tenacity were invariably superior. The wooden-wall years of tedious and unremitting blockade – Channel-groping the sailors called it – kept Bonaparte chafing and confined.

Like Bonaparte, Hitler imagined himself in London: he planned to seize Nelson's Column, the national sceptre, and haul it to Berlin as a trophy. Those who insisted that Count Zeppelin's airship flights in 1908 and Bleriot's crossing of the Channel in 1909 had made us less of an island were not entirely right: in 1940 the Narrow Sea remained the critical obstacle. The experience of that time, the Battle of Britain, our standing alone on our crenellated cliffs, refurbished our legends and profoundly influenced our view of ourselves for the rest of the century.

The Morning Bugle

A few minutes before six o'clock we heard the BBC's reveille, the daily musical cartoon of Britain with the filing-cabinet title of the 'Radio Four UK Theme'. It alluded to the sea, naval history and imperial glory and the fact that four countries are stitched into one British garment. Beginning softly with the first bars of 'Early One Morning', a folk song suggesting a milkmaid seduced by a squire in a landscape by Constable, it segued jauntily into 'Rule, Britannia!', composed in 1740 as a hymn to our naval knuckle and victories, and was followed by the plaintive 'Londonderry Air', the haunting 'Annie Laurie', a rat-tat-tatting 'Men of Harlech', then 'Scotland the Brave' and 'Greensleeves'.

A shanty returned us to the sea. Work songs like this once gave rhythm to the muscle power of sailors pushing capstan bars and hoisting sails, labour that made oxen of men and hernias a significant hazard: some seamen relieved the discomfort of these by hanging upside down in the rigging and stuffing the protrusions back into their abdomens with their fists.

The sequence concluded with a fanfaronade, 'Rule, Britannia!' with Purcellian knobs on. It was a salute to an antique grandeur and, possibly, a gentle tweaking of our pomposity, of the cocky patriotism of the Britannia cult. Soaring, trumpety and cheery it seemed at odds with the doubt-clouded times; but many of us are easily and mysteriously affected by the patriotic bugle.

In the Mirror of the Sea

As you approach the shores of Britain your eye is often caught by the heliographic flash of sunlight on the windscreens of cars drawn up on promenades and clifftops, beside the edge. Their occupants doze or study the bawdy Sunday newspapers, propping them on the lectern of the steering wheel. From time to time they wipe the misted windows and stare at the sea.

More often than not the windscreen runs with raindrops, the sea is grey and malevolent and the wind whistles testily over sodden sand. We have had good reason to hate the sea's truculence, its thunder and indifference, its sting, its enmity. As *The Seafarer* told us a thousand years ago: 'We often learned that ships are homes of sadness . . . a hunger within tore at the mind of the sea-weary man.' Joseph Conrad instructed us in the terrors of running up-Channel before a gale, the crew, half-blinded by weather, desperately looking for a light on the lee shore, the west wind 'pelting your back with icicles, making your weary eyes water as if in grief and your worn-out carcass quake pitifully'. Poets, musicians and artists told us of the romance of the sea, but it is relatively recently that we came to it for recreation, to splash, swim and sail. 'The Seaside' as an institution, a place of pleasure, dates only from the nineteenth century.

When we contemplate the sea we are drawn to our legends and the spirit of a pelagic people, the notion of our covenant with the waves. But, after a thousand years and more, we also have to confront the sudden shrinking of the significance of the sea in our national life and imagination. As amphibious animals we have struggled ashore. Perhaps we have already forgotten the sea; perhaps we have been waylaid. Our Navy and our merchant and fishing fleets have dwindled. Our dockyards have become museums. The racket of riveters has died and weeds colonize the slipways. Those coastal and riverine civilizations built around ships have seen their traditions and livelihoods shrink and vanish. Our famous tribe of sea captains and navigators has become a small band of survivors. A majestic vocabulary of seagoing is all but a lost language. On the deserted quays of once sea-minded towns, black-painted iron anchors lie embedded in concrete plinths, like widows' keepsakes.

In our brooding upon the sea and the withering of our relationship with it we may feel a sense of diminishment and loss. Yet it remains our source, the repository of memories and myths. The sea may be less a frontier than it was, but it is a frontier nevertheless, much more than a row of posts, and it reinforces our belief in our difference among the nations. It still defines us as a peculiar people, reminds us that through its agency we have known fulfilment and command, that we were once gods of the ocean. In uncertain times this is a comfort not without merit, for it carries with it the prospect of renewal, a hope in the turn of the tide. We may be as susceptible to self-delusion as any other people. The sea, however, is there to dream on, to ignite imagination, to remind us of what we were and help us reflect on what we might become.

2

The Wonderful Rendezvous

I sat on the warm pebble beach at Portsmouth and watched the waves rise and smash down, the retreating water clawing like a croupier at the seething shingle. When I was a child this stretch of the English Channel lay at my door and formed the framework of my growing up. Its changing temper and the traffic of warships and merchant vessels shaped my ideas of England.

The horizon was a boundary I dreamed upon and I waved ships off to Hope and Horn until they slipped over the edge of my world, painting farewell smudges of smoke upon the sky.

I watched the warships make their entrances and departures, their officers and ratings ranked in wind-whipped dark blue lines upon the decks, the marshbird squeal of boatswains' whistles piercing and poignant across the sea.

Great grey castles loomed from the haze at Spithead: aircraft carriers all a-bristle for war, powerful, ponderous and majestic. They squeezed slowly through the narrow gullet of the entrance to Portsmouth harbour as if with only inches to spare; and if you stood on the Round Tower you felt you could lean over the grey

19

parapets and touch them. Their awesome names, *Indomitable*, *Indefatigable*, *Implacable*, *Illustrious* and *Formidable*, were the first magnificent and difficult words I knew; so I like to fancy that the Royal Navy taught me to spell. The names of the warships in which my father served, *Centaur*, *Courageous* and *Revenge*, rolled from his tongue in splendour.

Cruisers crossed the stage in ducal grandeur. Destroyers, long and lean, departed for distant straits. Purposeful frigates came home from Aden, Hong Kong, Bridgetown, Singapore and Simonstown. The sea, never long at peace, was churned by the bustle of minesweepers, minelayers, oilers, fleet auxiliaries, tugs, sloops and terrier torpedo boats. Submarines, sinister and sharky, knifed through the sea. We sat in silence at home, my father's face grave, as we heard the news that the submarine *Affray*, out of Portsmouth, had been lost in the Channel with all seventy-five hands; and in my mind the word 'affray' never lost its sombre resonance.

Against the misty backdrop of the hills of the Isle of Wight, the ruling *Queen Mary* and *Queen Elizabeth* proceeded from Southampton Water in the manner of regal divas, as if perfectly aware of their glamour and of the admiration of the starstruck crowds ashore. Duty done, their tugs had turned away like respectful doffing footmen. We knew that the Clyde-built Queens were the largest and most splendid liners in the world, that every cup and plate was made in English potteries, that every knife and fork was forged in Sheffield, that they were British through and through, down to the last of their ten million rivets. After they had receded from our view the water they displaced struck the shore in a thundering cannonade, to remind us of their might, of their eighty thousand tons. We supposed that they would sail the Atlantic for ever.

From Southampton, too, prompt at four o'clock every Thursday afternoon, lavender-hulled Union Castle ships cruised off to Cape Town. And

> weekly from Southampton
> Great steamers, white and gold

went rolling down to Rio, carrying coffee-merchants, Kipling's armadillo-seekers and white-suited chancers with Errol Flynn moustaches. We imagined the maracas.

More modestly, and more within our budget, red-funnelled ferries, brimming with trippers, went rolling over the bottle-green water to the Isle of Wight. Some were paddle steamers, last of the line. As soon as the ferry gangways were open, fathers streamed into the beery saloons and emerged with trays of bitter, light ale, bottles of Mackeson, lemonade and salty crisps.

On Portsmouth Hard, crowds surged to the ferries and trains and some paused to toss coppers to grinning mudlarks scrambling beneath encrusted jetties. Hard-pressed worker-ferries, their green paint flecked with rust, beetled back and forth to Gosport, punching at the choppy sea in the narrows, the breeze snatching black smoke from their funnels and sucking warm oily air from engine rooms of gleaming brass and copper. The ferries were cloth-cap and dungaree by day, their dark cabins thick with Woodbine clouds; but at night, for the girls who sat in sailors' arms beneath the swarming stars, they were loveboats that lacked only champagne.

In the Portsmouth I knew as a boy the evidence of sea power and the serious purpose of admiralty were everywhere plain. The city and its cohort towns owed their fortunes to the imperatives of seafaring, of war and rumours of war. The tall white monument on the seafront overlooking Spithead recorded the names of tens of thousands of seamen, lost in the world wars, who had no grave ashore. For many years, into the 1960s, the burnt-out Guildhall, the rows of devastated buildings and scorched rubble left by sixty-seven air raids, bore witness to Portsmouth's importance.

Streets met the sea at cobbled quays and at stone stairs worn to concavity by the patter of sailors' feet. At every turn there were boatyards and chandlers, shipsmiths and shipfitters, marine engineers, riggers and sailmakers.

Behind the high fortified dockyard walls, built of stone and red brick, lay a complete naval town, a factory crowded with deep docks, great wharves, gigantic cranes, railways, forges, engineering and metal shops and ropewalks. It was a base for warships in the twelfth century and the first naval dock in Britain was built here in 1540. Many of the buildings dated from the eighteenth century. Armed Navy sentries with white belts and gaiters guarded imposing gates. Every child in Portsmouth must have heard of Jack the Painter, who set fire to the dockyard in 1776, a crime of treason. He was hanged on a sixty-four-foot mast at the dockyard gate, with three hundred and fifty men hauling on the rope. His body was tarred and hung in chains for years at the harbour entrance until two sailors cut him down one evening and installed him in the fireside seat of a pub in Gosport.

On the parade grounds of Victorian barracks men marched to bawled orders, boots and brass-bound rifle butts crashing in dramatic percussion. The entrances to naval establishments were embellished with polished cannon and pyramids of black cannon balls, by figureheads of admirals and sea gods, painted as gaudily as fairground horses, with bright blue eyes and carmine lips, the female figures carved with bosoms bared, in accordance with a sailorly belief that uncovered breasts subdued a stormy sea.

The sense of naval significance was underscored by the pageantry of ships at sea and in harbour, the pomp of the Fleet Review at Spithead, the whoop of sirens, blaring bugles and trill of pipes, the snap of ensigns in the wind, the flutter of paying-off pennants and flags flying tautly at the dockyard signal station. Among the warships weaved a ceaseless traffic of launches and pinnaces, whalers and cutters. Brasswork flashed on admirals' barges. HMS *Victory* was the boss around which all this activity swirled, its yardarms manned, one felt, by the admonitory ghosts of sailors demanding respect for tradition.

Around the port half the population was in uniform and every Wren looked pretty. You knew where a man stood in naval caste and hierarchy – no service more hierarchical – by his braided cuffs and headwear; by his stripes straight or wavy; by his fore-and-aft rig of cap and jacket; by his square-rig of bell-bottom trousers with seven concertina creases, and blue collar, lanyard and black silk scarf; by his chevrons; by the cap tally bearing his ship's name; by sleeve badges proclaiming his skill as an artificer or gunner, diver or signaller.

When summer came the Navy saluted the sun: it valeted away its dark winter cap and donned a white one and at once looked jauntier, in hornpipe mood.

The Navy was the common interest and the big news. The Portsmouth *Evening News*, where I began as a junior reporter, was, to a large extent, a naval chronicle and the Naval Correspondent was a senior hand, his weekly commentary called, of course, Nelson's Column. The staple of reporting was the business of warships, their launchings and refits, their new weapons, accidents, incidents, arrivals and departures. We reported the promotions, parades and ceremonies; and faithfully recorded the number of bottles of rum poured into gigantic naval Christmas puddings, the mixture stirred with an oar wielded by an admiral. We reported the reminiscences of old sailors. One of my first assignments was to interview the gunner who fired the first shot at the Battle of Jutland. We watched the ships come in after many months overseas, described the brimming eyes of wives and girlfriends at the South Railway Jetty and photographed the babies meeting their sailor fathers for the first time. When a naval man died we called at his home for a photograph of him in uniform, to make a proper tribute.

I reported many naval courts martial, stiff-lipped and stiff-necked dramas of uniforms and swords, of marching, foot-stamping and crisp salutes, performed in the language of the sea. Throughout the trial an accused officer's sword lay on the table in front of him; and when he entered the court to hear the verdict he could see at once what had been decided. If he were not guilty the handle of the sword faced him, and there would be a slight exhalation of relief. Guilty, he saw the star-bright point turned towards him in cruel and melodramatic ritual; and his lips tightened.

The Navy endowed Portsmouth with its boisterous energy. Parties of sailors spilled like beans from the incoming trains, shouldered their kitbags and set off to sea, their repartee salting the bustle of the port. The carriages were soon refilled with men bound for home and leave. Sailors bared their biceps, backs and no doubt their buttocks in tattoo parlours. They crowded into cafés and barber shops. They walked girls along the promenade and told them tall tales. Around the dockyard there were surely more bars than one man could visit in a lifetime and when the Navy put on its drinking boots the jack tar pubs, raucous and reeking of beer, were blue with the volcanic smoke of Capstan Full Strength and Player's Navy Cut, to which visiting French matelots added a whiff of Gauloises.

Music halls, ballrooms and cinemas were full of uniforms. So were the packed terraces of Portsmouth football ground, over which there lay an unforgettable tang of beer, tobacco and urine, cut with the camphor of throat sweets called Cough No More, sold by a ragged man with an explosive cough. The Saturday evening football paper carried a cartoon sailor on its front page, his thumbs up when Portsmouth won, down when they lost. At end-of-the-pier shows singers with splendid prows really did belt out 'All the Nice Girls Love a Sailor'. The theatre where girls posed naked in artistic tableaux enjoyed the enthusiastic patronage of the Fleet. In keeping with the law, the girls had to stand as still as statues in a rose garden. Some reporters I knew manufactured a story by putting mice onto the stage so that one of the Aphrodites squealed and quivered; and a sailor, in on the plot, dashed forward gallantly to cover her with his coat and save her from infringing the law. Every schoolboy, I suppose, knew the jokes about sailors and the strumpets in Queen Street and the stories of Pompey Lil, the legendary whore; though whether Pompey Lil was an individual or a generic term I never knew. Portsmouth mothers chased their children out of their kitchens saying, 'What do you think this is, Aggie Weston's?' – a reference to the famous sailors' homes and restaurants founded by the saintly Dame Agnes Weston.

Portsmouth Dockyard was the city's principal employer and the local schools formed academic production lines to supply it with a constant stream of apprentices and managers. Each morning thousands of civilian workmen, accoutred with vacuum flasks and lunch tins, flowed through the dockyard gates on bicycles. Each evening they secured their trousers with cycle clips, tugged down their caps and mounted up. It was as if a sluice were opened. The bell-jingling mass filled the cobbled streets in the homeward rush, unstoppable, acknowledging no law. Hapless traffic policemen held up their hands but were swept aside. The monstrous swarm, grey, black and brown, coughing and cursing, headed north beneath its own dense fog bank of cigarette smoke, up Commercial Road, past the terrace house where Elizabeth Dickens gave birth to Charles in 1812, gradually dividing into tributary swarms which flowed east and west. It was a spectacle Chinese in its scale and one of the awesome sights of Britain.

My part of the Channel, the beaches and fortifications of Portsmouth and its neighbouring shores, was an arena of thrilling events, an imperial coast and the heart of our maritime history. I knew the slope of shingle from which Nelson departed Portsmouth for Trafalgar, picking his way past the bathing machines, then waving his hat to the cheering crowd as he was rowed to *Victory* at anchor in Spithead. 'I had their huzzas before, now I have their hearts,' he said. Three months later his body, pickled in wine, arrived at Spithead aboard the battered *Victory*, *en route* for the Thames. Such history seemed not at all remote.

Off this beach, in 1545, the flagship *Mary Rose*, veteran of three French wars, sank under the horrified gaze of Henry VIII. At Portsmouth in 1755 modest James Cook joined HMS *Eagle* as an able seaman. In 1756, aboard HMS *Monarch* in Portsmouth harbour, Admiral John Byng, who had lost Minorca, was shot by a firing squad as an admiralty scapegoat, the act noted by Voltaire as the way the Royal Navy improved executive performance. Off Portsmouth in 1782, the *Royal George* capsized and nine hundred sailors and their women visitors were drowned. Years later some of the salvaged cannon were incorporated into the base of Nelson's Column. From Spithead in May 1787, eleven ships, crammed with seven hundred convicts, mostly petty thieves from London, set off to found the British colony on the eastern coast of Australia that had been charted by Cook.

From Spithead in December of the same year, Lieutenant William Bligh sailed for Tahiti in the *Bounty*, the floating stage of a peculiarly English drama of arrogance and consummate seamanship, of sex and horticulture. Five years later some of the *Bounty* mutineers were plucked from the South Seas by the long tentacle of the unforgiving Royal Navy, and, as a cannon boomed, three of them were hanged from the yardarm of HMS *Brunswick* in Portsmouth harbour, far from the fragrance of hibiscus.

A visitor observed in 1791 that 'Portsmouth may be called the key of England. This wonderful rendezvous of the Royal Navy is a striking proof of the opulence and industry of Englishmen.' In 1797 Navy crews in Spithead went on strike, an indignant protest against the cheating and bungling management of a neglectful government; and won their case. Not a single mutineer was hanged. In 1854, at the age of thirteen, Jacky Fisher, who was to become the greatest naval administrator, formally entered the Royal Navy aboard *Victory*, then still afloat. In the 1860s, in prudent response to the fear of war, iron and granite sea forts, Nomansland, Spitbank, Horsesand and St Helen's, were built on sandbanks to guard Spithead; and there they sit, irremovable, to brood for ever. In 1897 Queen Victoria's diamond jubilee was saluted by the greatest review of warships ever staged, a thirty-mile parade of steel and iron that was seen by some writers as proof that Britain ruled the seas and would do so until the end of time.

In Portsmouth Dockyard in 1906, at the inspired insistence and demonic driving of Admiral Fisher, the first Dreadnought battleship was built by three thousand men in an astonishing eleven months and at once outdated every battleship in the world. In 1944 this harbour was the springboard for the invasion of Normandy. In 1960, I remember, the last British battleship, HMS *Vanguard*, was towed funereally from the harbour *en route* to the breakers. She ran aground at Portsmouth Point, as if she were a noble animal sensing the knacker's yard, digging in her heels.

For a while I lived in Portchester, at the northern end of Portsmouth harbour. In the third century, long before Portsmouth itself was built, Portchester was developed by the Romans as a port. It fell under the command of the Count of the Saxon Shore who supervised fortifications against invaders from here to the Wash. The castle was our playground. It is one of the best Roman fortresses to be seen anywhere and its high walls and fourteen round towers enfold a space of nine acres and protect the parish church and its graveyard. Richard the Lionheart sailed from Portchester to the Crusades; and Henry V's soldiers departed here for Agincourt where victory over French knights and diarrhoea put substance into the idea of an English nation. I often climbed to the top of Henry I's keep. The Portsmouth skyline lay under my gaze: spindly cranes, the upperworks of warships, the topgallant masts and yards of *Victory*, the Isle of Wight in the distance. To the east, across the mudflats, was the gunnery school, HMS *Excellent*. To the west, in the backwater reaches of the harbour, lay the shrouded forms of redundant ships, sheeted with grey plastic, their cocooned guns never to bark again. To the north rose the slopes of Portsdown Hill, pocked by white quarries, knobbed by Victorian forts and crowned by a tall granite obelisk, raised to Nelson's memory in 1807 by survivors of Trafalgar who each contributed two days' pay. On the other side of the hill spread another world, the true Hampshire of villages of red brick, bluebell woods and stone-speckled fields with scarecrows directing the traffic of gulls and crows. The lanes took me to the strawberry fields of Swanwick and the hangers of the Meon Valley; and the slope of Broadhalfpenny Down where cricket was born.

Like all the villages and towns on Portsmouth's periphery, Portchester had a good complement of retired naval officers, shellbacks who loved to be within sniff of the sea. 'Hello, Commander,' people would say, and the old sea-dogs would look up from tending their roses. Some of them sat on parish councils and others manned the bridge of the magistrates' courts from which they would scold the wretched and tell them to pull themselves together.

During the Napoleonic Wars, thousands of French prisoners were confined in Portchester Castle. While they waited for peace they gambled and made bone-carvings and some of them married into the village or were taken into households as servants. A group of them performed *The Barber of Seville* and earned so much money at the box-office that local theatres complained and had the production brought to an end. Some made and sold exquisite lace, but lace-sellers in the district disliked the competition and persuaded the authorities to stop them.

The village cricket team played on the green within the castle walls. I was once its most junior member. The square-leg boundary on one side was formed by the moat. The dressing room was in one of the towers, by the water-gate, and smelled of damp stone, grass cuttings and linseed oil. The vicar sometimes wore his cricket whites beneath his cassock when he conducted a Saturday wedding and, having blessed the bride, he would make his way out of the vestry, across the churchyard and onto the sunny field to score a half-century or tweak the seam of a ball.

I felt there was something distinctly gladiatorial about walking from the Roman tower, in greaves of white pads, short sword of bat in sweaty hand, throat dry.

'Eye on the ball, lad.'

'Straight bat, mind.'

The light of the setting sun made gold of the powder-grey walls. The fielders crouched and moved in and rubbed their hands and licked their lips and made ready to finish you off, the quicker to get down the road to The Cormorant for a beer. Their shadows stretched long on the grass. In the distance the fast bowler reached the foot of the wall, where centurions once leant on their spears and prisoners had worked at their scrimshaw. Then he turned and charged.

The Plains of Mars

The sea was so central to my existence that when I first visited the middle west of America I was astonished to meet people who had never seen it. My earliest memory is of an open boat crunching into the shingle and my father leaping out and wading through the surf, his shorts and singlet soaked, black hair wet. He hoisted me to his shoulder, passed me over the gunwale and hauled himself aboard. With shouts of 'Hey up!' the crew dug their long oars into the foam and the boat reared over a wave and fell into the trough with a smack and a sensational burst of spray.

On several occasions my father took me out in an amphibious landing craft, a DUKW. He commanded such adventures

because he was a regimental sergeant-major in the Royal
Marines, a military supreme being. The vehicle drove from the
barracks where we lived and lurched down a slipway to splash
thrillingly into the sea.

'This is the stuff,' my father said.

We bucked over the tormented channel to Hayling Island, the
air filled with spume and the smell of fuel, until the beast hauled
itself like a turtle up the beach to gain the sandy road among the
dunes.

In due course, the island became our home. It was only four
miles long, a place of beaches, copses, farms and hamlets and, to
my mind, romantic and far from the city. The sea was close and
encroached upon the land. High tides brought floods. Small
shells and sand and bladderwrack accumulated in roadsides and
gardens. The island was a small resort, not fashionable or well-
known, and did not even have a pier. Access to it was limited.
At the southern end a tubby and pugnacious ferryboat made its
corkscrew passage across the bottleneck strait to Portsmouth,
carrying foot passengers and cyclists. At the northern end a
narrow wooden toll bridge connected the island to the mainland. It was built in the 1820s for horse traffic, and could not
bear the weight of heavy vehicles, so buses were obliged to dis-
gorge most of their passengers and drive across at an Edwardian
eight miles an hour. Boys were always the first to be offloaded
and we walked behind, bowing our heads against gales and rain,
half-expecting, half-hoping probably, to see the bridge crumble
and the green granny-filled Southdown bus swept away like a
Dinky toy, the disaster to be reported in the Portsmouth *Evening
News*, the driver's cap cast up poignantly on the wild strand
where we hunted for flotsam.

In the seigneurial manner of small boys we took possession of
sandy beaches and shingle banks, of piney woods and desert
dunes tufted with coarse razor-sharp grasses which sang in the
wind. We manned dank concrete pillboxes, built to impede a
German invasion, and drove our enemies into the sea, complet-
ing our victories by Saturday teatime.

Our territories were marked by the worn grey rust-streaked
timbers of breakwaters which in summer were our diving boards

and in winter served as castle walls with seaweed banners. We skinny, scab-kneed boys were the first to brave the sea in spring, pale and yelping, and the last to quit in late autumn, reluctant brown-bodied veterans. We learnt to swim at the same time as we learnt to read and seemed to be always in the water, otters all, hair bleached and salty, canvas shoes half-wet and rotting.

Sand gritted our sandwiches and made emery boards of our sheets all summer long. In winter we patrolled the cuttle-boned shoreline, setting frozen red faces against the wind, wading into the sea in punctured squelching boots, plunging our raw fingers into the shallows to pull out wrack-entwined logs and wooden boxes and rope and cork. We pelted tin cans with pebbles, shouting 'Sink the *Bismarck*', and fished out the corpses of gulls for autopsies and funeral rites. A boy we knew discovered a body upon the shore, news we heard with mixed horror and envy.

On the sea wall, in turbulent weather, we raced monstrous grey-bearded waves as they gathered up their strength and towered and exploded in icy spray. We claimed disused oyster beds for our empire and their dried cracked skins of red mud became for us the deserts of Arizona and the plains of Mars. From boats in Chichester Harbour, piloted by Popeye sailormen with stained caps and gnawed pipes, we watched porpoises leap from the green water and sparkle in the sunlight. We reconnoitred creeks and investigated the rotten bones of old boats and conducted low-tide expeditions among whaleback mudflats, returning caked and blackened. We were amphibian, ever damp and smelling of seaweed and the sea, and our childhood shadows had their brief dance in the sun on the long enduring shore.

Russian Cigarettes

I put up at the Sallyport Hotel in the old part of Portsmouth and banged my forehead on the lintel of my room. The hotel is a few steps from the stone bulwarks which overlook Spithead and takes its name from the Sallyport, a gate with steps down to the sea, which was for centuries a point of departure and arrival, a place of mingled emotions. A memorial plaque bears the names of men of the Royal Navy, Royal Marines and the Merchant

Navy who were killed in the Falklands war, many of them waved off from here. The Portuguese princess, Catherine of Braganza, arrived here to marry Charles II, bringing with her, as part of the wedding contract, the deeds to Bombay, a fabulous gift the Portuguese later tried to get back. It is said that from this tenuous connection with Bombay Portsmouth acquired its nickname of Pompey; and since no one knows the origin of it, it is as good an explanation as any.

The hotel is old and brown, a well-thumbed book. The backbone of its spiral staircase is made from a ship's mast, so that the place itself seems half-ship. The floors slope this way and that, as in a cartoon, so that you lurch involuntarily, even before dinner, and think yourself at sea. I wondered if Commander Lionel Crabb had cracked his head, too. He spent the last night of his life in this hotel in April 1956, leaving before dawn to dive beneath one of the Soviet cruisers which had brought Stalin's successors, Khrushchev and Bulganin, to Britain. His objective was to inspect the propellers to discover why the ship was so fast. He surfaced, visited a pub at lunchtime, dived again in the afternoon and never returned. A detective hurried to the Sallyport Hotel, tore out a page of the register and stuffed it into his macintosh. It had been signed, with their real names, by Crabb and his accomplice from the secret service.

At that time the Soviet Navy had opened its warships to the public, and numerous schoolboys, myself among them, were aboard looking curiously at the ships and the thin pale sailors from a closed and forbidding land. The sailors gave us red enamel hammer and sickle badges and also pungent Russian cigarettes, cardboard tubes containing a small plug of tobacco, which, when we sucked them too hard, deposited hot ash in our mouths.

Russian sailors had seen Crabb swimming near their ships. Perhaps his mission had already been betrayed to the KGB. The Soviet leaders protested, embarrassing the British government. After this fiasco, the secret service came under closer political scrutiny. There were stories that Crabb had been killed by Soviet frogmen, or captured; but since he was fifty-six, drinking and smoking heavily, hardly fit for such a James Bond escapade, he no doubt drowned. A headless body washed up months later was thought to be his.

Here Nelson Fell

I had not been to Portsmouth for a quarter of a century. It seemed in some ways a ghost town, a place of echoes, its historic duties discharged, the purpose of its existence fulfilled. It was still our chief naval base, still a place where you could see the Royal Navy about its business, but the city that wore navy blue had been reduced. The giant crane that dominated the skyline for half a century had been dismantled, which seemed to me a form of decapitation. The city rulers had squandered their opportunity in Portsmouth's main square, a large space commanded by the Guildhall and its stone lions. It had had the makings of a splendid plaza, a grand assertion, but the council lacked imagination and filled it with dark glass offices, clerkish, dismal and confusing, a symbol of lost confidence.

I looked around for Tony Verrecchia's café, which had been a landmark, but it had been demolished when the square was rebuilt. It had a gleaming coffee machine, like a warship's boiler, and was furnished with booths of dark wood fitted with oval panes of engraved glass. The coffee was served on tables of Italian marble by Signor Verrecchia's dark-haired daughters. The café was popular with the newspaper reporters whose inky Victorian building was in a side street nearby. It was used as a rendezvous, a place of escape and assignation, a bolt-hole for writing articles in peace with the help of cigarettes and coffee.

I walked to the city museum and was astonished to see one of Signor Verrecchia's booths, complete with a marble table, as an exhibit. I used to write at that table. Now it was heritaged. The table was bare, but I mentally furnished it with authentic props: a coffee cup, an ashtray, a damp macintosh, a sheaf of paper; and myself.

Portsmouth is looking to its past to help provide it with a future. Much of the naval dockyard and its Georgian buildings are incorporated into a museum, a magnificent assembly of naval treasures, including the salvaged fragments of the *Mary Rose*, the rescued and brilliantly-restored HMS *Warrior*, the first ocean-going iron warship, and *Victory* itself, the ark of British naval spirit.

Two thousand five hundred oaks, sixty English acres, were felled to build her in 1759. She has rested in her dry dock since 1922, following an appeal to raise the money to save her from rotting away, and remains in commission, the Royal Navy's senior ship, and flagship of the Second Sea Lord: only Britain has such exotic creatures as sea lords. When I looked at her I was struck once again by that air of menace that all warships exude. The swell of her lines, the bosom of her bow, the tigerish stripes, thick masts and heavy black rigging all spoke of her power as a fortress and aggressor. She looked purposeful, as if she could respond to fantasy and slip the imprisonment of the dry dock and put to sea.

The smell of *Victory* had not changed. I was a small boy when I first climbed the gangplank into the port side, stared at the guns and cannon balls, the heavy tackles and coils of cable, and sniffed the unforgettable smell of hemp, tar and timber, while a large petty officer told me why the orlop deck was painted red – 'So the blood wouldn't show and dishearten the men.' In those days I put myself in the role of powder monkey, a nipper running from the magazine with gunpowder charges. And now, years later, it was still a small step in the imagination to envisage the harshness and stinking intimacy of existence on these crowded and tenebrous gun decks. It was easy, too, to picture the discrete and gentlemanly existence in the gilded and beautifully-fenestrated stern, an elegant tower above the brutish town and a faithful replica of the disparity in society ashore.

Eight hundred and fifty men were aboard *Victory* at Trafalgar. Since warships recruited seasoned seamen where they could, usually from merchantmen, the ship's company included twenty-two Americans, three Frenchmen, seven Scandinavians and several West Indians, Dutchmen and Germans. The complement today is seventeen. Twenty-two civilian guides, all ex-Navy and devoted to the ship, are employed to show it to four hundred thousand visitors every year. Every Trafalgar Day it takes fifty ratings to hoist the flag signals, numbers 253, 269,

863, 261, 471, 958, 220, 370, 4, 21, 19, 24, that spell 'England Expects That Every Man Will Do His Duty'.

Lieutenant-Commander Michael Cheshire, *Victory*'s captain, guided me to a plan of Trafalgar on his cabin bulkhead to demonstrate Nelson's brilliant stroke, the 'Nelson touch', which broke the enemy's line. 'Nelson and *Victory*,' he breathed, 'what a story: blood, guts, sex, intrigue and love.' He was unabashedly misty-eyed about the ship. 'I'm in love with her. This job is the icing on the cake of my career.'

The ship is run day-to-day by the First Lieutenant. When I called on her, Kerry Straughan, the first woman to serve as *Victory*'s First Lieutenant, was in her small cabin on the main deck, working at a computer. It was one of the few modern conveniences on board, for there is no room for lavatories and too great a fire risk for a galley. For the former the gangplank must be walked to the dockside; and in the absence of cooking facilities, dinners served in Nelson's cabin and in the captain's cabin are prepared ashore and brought up the gangplank on heated trolleys. Sometimes these are battled through gales and rain, but the roast beef always gets through. Nelson's cabin is one of the most agreeable and exclusive dining rooms in Britain. The Second Sea Lord entertains here, just as Nelson used to play host to his captains, his 'band of brothers'.

Lieutenant Straughan showed me over the ship, from poop deck to hold, and since she was five feet three inches, about two inches shorter than Nelson, she did not have to move about the decks with a *Victory* stoop. 'It was love at first sight when I was appointed to *Victory*. Every morning I look at her and think: Gosh, that's my ship. My poor husband – he's a lieutenant-commander, so I call him sir – every time I went home I took him new facts. But you can't help becoming deeply involved. She is a living ship and she creaks and leaks. When it rains one of the staff types under an umbrella. I know I shouldn't, but I do feel proprietorial and I enjoy showing the ship off, which is why I like dinners and receptions on board. I sometimes feel that Nelson is still around. I'm not sure I would have liked him ashore – his vanity might have put me off – but I would certainly have liked him at sea, the sailor and admiral, in his element.'

The climactic moment of every tour of *Victory* is the visit to the cockpit, the battle-surgery below the waterline, where Nelson died three hours after being shot by a marksman, the news of triumph in his ears, thoughts of Emma Hamilton in his heart. The story that Nelson said 'Kismet, Hardy' to his friend Captain Hardy, rather than 'Kiss me', was a Victorian fancy invented by those who squirmed at the thought that Nelson asked a kiss from a man.

The public, Lieutenant-Commander Cheshire said, felt an amazing passion for the ship. 'She represents sea power, the beginning of the British Empire and greatness. People often send flowers here, asking us to put them where Nelson died.' He showed me the brass plate on the deck marking the place where the admiral fell. It used to be raised on a plinth an inch or so high and people frequently tripped over it. Indeed, a cartoon in *Punch* in 1895 has a sailor-guide showing a visitor the plaque and saying: 'Here Nelson fell.' – 'I'm not surprised,' says the visitor, 'I nearly tripped over it myself.'

'I had the brass plate refitted so that it lay flush with the deck,' Lieutenant-Commander Cheshire said. 'But the story went around that we had removed it entirely. We were deluged by angry letters. An MP raised the matter in the Commons. It brought home to me again that *Victory* arouses strong feelings. This ship is sacred.'

I went for a drink in the Keppel's Head by the dockyard gate. Two men were discussing their tour of *Victory*.

'The newspapers would have him for breakfast.'

'One arm, one eye – '

'– and a mistress – '

'They would finish him off.'

'Those paparazzi –'

'And their wide-angle lenses.'

Victorians dealt with Nelson's affair by branding Emma a Delilah, an overweight hussy. My *Blackie's Modern Cyclopedia*, of 1899, says 'she acquired an influence over him which was the cause of some of the least creditable incidents in the great admiral's career.'

The power of Nelson to excite the British imagination is truly extraordinary. Churchill loved Alexander Korda's 1941 film with Laurence Olivier as Nelson: it always made him cry. In the Nelsonian age of great naval commanders, a contemporary averred that 'Nelson is the one to love'. It remains true. Campbell McMurray, director of the Royal Naval Museum at Portsmouth, said to me that 'the Navy still worships him. The Nelson tradition of humane leadership and daring, supported by calculated assessment of risk, lives on in a service that thinks of itself as doing a man's job as well as possible in the most difficult circumstances.'

The Nelson library is already immense but books pour out to feed an undiminished appetite: no man's life is more assiduously and minutely charted. A member of the Nelson Society, which is devoted to every last scintilla of its hero's life, told me that before he joined he was embarrassed by his enthusiasm, thinking that he alone suffered. 'Then I found there were many others like me. I came out of the closet. It was quite a relief.' Many women know that their menfolk have incurable Nelsonitis and one told me that her husband's dearest possession was his three-foot model of *Victory*. Trafalgar Day dinners are held in many parts of the world and The Immortal Memory is toasted. Only Shakespeare, Robert Burns and Nelson are honoured with this salutation. Some of the dinners are intimate naval affairs and others are celebrations at which Nelson enthusiasts pick over the details of the admiral's life. One admirer wears his Nelson-era uniform to such occasions.

No Nelson worshipper was more ardent, I thought, than Clive Richards, a businessman I met in London. 'Completely besotted,' he said. 'I read a book about Nelson fifteen years ago and that was it.' Struck by the Nelson cannon ball, he amassed letters, books, pictures, medals, pottery pieces and part of Nelson's dinner service, one of the best private collections of Nelson memorabilia anywhere. No hero was more commemorated than Nelson. His star quality and dramatic death-in-victory coincided with the birth of mass manufacture, and mementoes flooded the market. 'Of course, there were many fakes,' Clive Richards said. 'I've been offered enough tufts of Nelson's hair to make a carpet. It's an obsession, but I do enjoy it. I get a thrill out of using Nelson's wine coasters, for example. The letters he wrote make me feel very close to him. I have a poem he composed for Emma after the battle of Copenhagen; and one of my treasures is the last letter she wrote to him: it arrived aboard *Victory* after his death. I have been captured by Nelson's personality. He was enormously inspiring in a great era of our history. Without him we would have been conquered by Napoleon. He was vain, and perhaps hypocritical, yet he was a very romantic figure, a frail sinner like the rest of us, but also God-fearing. All the excitement and victories were crammed into his last ten years and he died a winner. I visit *Victory* at least once a year and I can almost feel Nelson walking up and down on the deck. My ambition is to live long enough to celebrate the two-hundredth anniversary of Trafalgar.'

Only Sailors Sit on Tables

One of *Victory*'s anchors is mounted on the promenade at Portsmouth, supposedly marking the place where Nelson embarked for Trafalgar, though any Nelson enthusiast will tell you that it is a quarter of a mile too far to the east. Numerous obelisks stand here, mostly memorials to nineteenth-century wars. Wind and spray have all but worn away the inscriptions, the details of expeditions in India, China and Arabia, and the names of the men who died, usually of disease. Not effaced was a large notice saying CITY OF PORTSMOUTH DOGS ON BEACH BYELAWS. YOU ARE NOW ENTERING AN AREA WHERE YOU MAY EXERCISE YOUR DOG. Head of Leisure Services.

I walked along the seafront to the former Royal Marines barracks at the eastern end of the long beach. The farewell bugle had sounded years before. The gates were locked and the wind hustled litter past the empty guardhouse under the clock tower. Weeds grew on the deserted parade ground which once rang to the thunder of my father's voice. We lived in married quarters close to the beach and a short march from the Sergeants' Mess, a place as polished as boots on parade, smelling of wax and tobacco. Its walls were covered with silver trophies and honours boards and sepia photographs of platoons and companies and sports teams. Two brass cannon stood guard in the lobby at the foot of the staircase. A dumb waiter rumbled in its shaft bearing cargoes of food, laughter filled the air and smoke hung in the yellow blocks of light above the snooker tables. My father held court as President of the Mess, lord of the sergeancy. He had a strong feeling for tradition and protocol, saw eye to eye with senior officers who shared his experience and prejudices. He related with relish how keen junior officers who attempted to change the habits and routines of running the barracks were invariably broken on the pitiless reef of tradition, on the stubbornness of the unblinking sergeants.

Under his correction I learnt never to say Marines, but to speak always of Royal Marines. He served in warships when it was the custom for Royal Marines to man one of the gun turrets and in his stories the Royal Marines always outperformed the Royal Navy, were invariably faster and smarter. If he saw me leaning on a table he would scold: 'Stand up straight – only sailors sit on tables.' In our regular walks to see the latest Western at the cinema he taught me the anatomy of the .303 Lee-Enfield rifle, the history of the Royal Marines and the story of their capture of Gibraltar.

His leaving of the Royal Marines after twenty-one years of service was a bereavement. The corps had given his life all its rhythm and meaning. He had perforce to reinvent himself and, since he could not bear not to be in charge, he became a regimental sergeant-major in another form. He took a job as the entertainment manager of a holiday camp.

The people who flocked to such camps were adjusting to civilian life after the war. The link between my father and the pale Londoners and Midlanders who came to the Coronation Camp in Hayling Island was the camaraderie of years in uniform, the shared vocabulary, discomfort, discipline and comedy. It was a holiday of the transition. Men came in their demob suits, women in utility frocks and boys in hand-me-down shorts held up by snake-buckle belts. My father was still the sergeant-major, but he was now the oppressor turned benign dictator, the despot of fun. He created a roll-out-the-barrel, hokey-cokey sort of holiday and in his domain there was entertainment, plentiful food and a river of beer.

Early in the morning his parade ground voice rattled the windows, frightened the seagulls and roused people from their chalet beds. The voice ordered them to breakfast prepared by a man with no cooking experience, an ex-Royal Marine who needed the job. From then on, there was no idle moment: neither my father nor his clients believed they were there to rest. Wearing a whistle on a cord round his neck, he organized cricket matches, football, the tug-of-war, athletics, swimming races, children's sports, the bathing beauty contest, the knobbly-knees competition, the ugly-face contest and the fancy-dress show. He led the weekly walk along country lanes to a pub, striding at the head of a crowd of fifty people, a pied piper in a short-sleeved yellow shirt, warning city children not to eat the deadly night-shade in the bushes lest they return home to Croydon or Birmingham in a box.

He supervised the horse-riding, led the way in the harbour boat rides, shouted out the tombola numbers, made loudspeaker announcements about mislaid false teeth and lost children. He wore foolish hats and never failed to fall in the lake during the water pageant. He directed and compèred the entertainment every evening, introducing the musicians and music-hall per-formers who toured the holiday camp circuit. He called out the raffle results and was first onto the floor when the band struck up a waltz, quickstep or foxtrot, dancing with panache and sur-prising nimbleness, for he had become a fairly round man. He led community singing and, not least, the relentlessly cheerful anthem: 'We are the Coronation campers, we laugh and smile at everything . . .' When I look down the telescope at the adults of my childhood I see their shining eyes and rubicund faces creased in laughter over drinks and brimming ashtrays and I hear them singing 'There'll Always be an England' and 'Roses are Blooming in Picardy' and 'I'll be with you in Apple-blossom Time'.

My father auditioned the talent for the campers' home-made Thursday concert, unerringly seeking out those who could sing, play an instrument, write sketches and act the clown. He produced the show and topped the bill himself with his repertoire of heroic songs.

He loved to sing. He had a strong bass–baritone voice and performed frequently at concerts, dinners and charity events. He sang in hospitals, and on one occasion, in a prison. He modelled his performance on Peter Dawson, the ebullient Australian who came to England in 1903 and sang Kipling and Henry Newbolt, rousing, red–blooded imperial songs about soldiers and naval exploits: 'Drake's Drum', 'Dreaming of England', 'Boots', 'The Old Superb', 'England all the Way', 'Yeomen of England', 'Rolling Down to Rio', 'Boys of the Old Brigade', 'Heart of Oak', 'The Fishermen of England' and 'The Drum Major'. In his recordings a vanished England springs to life. Ballads like 'Up from Somerset' and 'Glorious Devon' – 'Devon's the fount of the bravest blood that braces England's breed' – celebrated the landscape. His best-seller was 'The Floral Dance', written by Kate Moss on a train from Cornwall, where she had seen the Helston Furry Dance. Dawson made his first recording in 1904, onto wax cylinders, singing into a funnel, with an Edison Bell engineer standing at his shoulder, pushing him closer and pulling him away to achieve balance. A master record lasted for only a few copies so Dawson recorded over and over, singing six hours a day for five days, lubricating his throat with pints of beer.

He was a swashbuckler and a gambler: singing in an opera at Covent Garden he once dropped his backstage poker winnings, a shower of coins, onto the stage. Like many other performers he was also a song-pirate. He went to theatres to find new songs and took with him a recording box and a stenographer. He stayed up late to learn the stolen song and next morning recorded it – singer, chorus and musicians forming a scrum around the funnel. As he said, everybody went in for piracy, until the Copyright Act outlawed it. In fifty-one years he recorded three thousand five hundred songs and made his last recording in 1955, aged seventy-three, just as rock and roll was dawning.

My father's Dawsonian repertoire included 'When the Sergeant-Major's on Parade' – 'With Sam Browne belt and buttons bright Behold the Sergeant-Major.' Like Dawson, he was never allowed to leave a stage without singing 'The Floral

Dance'. 'Fiddle, cello, big bass drum' – he threw himself into it and glowed in the applause.

He worked seven days a week throughout the summer, was utterly tireless and, for the most part, regarded the whole business as an uproarious comedy. The holiday camp caper lasted for some years, but the need for such home-grown entertainment faded as tastes changed. My father moved to another way of earning his living in which he could remain a sergeant-major and be in charge and on stage: he ran pubs. Because he set out to create an atmosphere of welcome and merriment, and provided food with the drinks, he was not a typical licensee.

Towards the end of his life I took him on a pilgrimage to Flanders, something he had longed to do. His own father, a miner in south Wales, had marched away from Thurston Road in Pontypridd at the outbreak of war in August 1914. He had a hangover on the morning he left and had cleaned only one of his boots. My father remembered that one shiny boot to the end of his life. He and his brothers watched as their father ate two eggs for breakfast and picked up his kit and left. He was killed shortly afterwards in the retreat from Mons. My father, aged eight, was in a cinema when he learnt of it. The enterprising manager had heard that the telegraph boy had knocked at my grandmother's door. A message was projected onto the screen, a local news item.

My grandfather had no grave and we fell quiet as we drove through the bruised landscape, among the battlefield cemeteries which lie so heavily on the land, searching for the memorial on which his name was inscribed. My father gazed around at the flat fields, the houses and clumps of trees and the wide cloud-piled sky. 'It was here, near here,' he said, almost to himself.

We found the memorial on the road to Ypres, a circle of white columns guarded by leoglyphs. My grandfather's name was half-way up one of the columns. In the silence, I retreated into the shadows. My father looked at the name for some long minutes, standing to attention. In his solitary upright figure I saw the sergeant-major; and also the small boy who had found himself at last at the place of his father's death.

Some years later, at Ypres and Passchendaele, I spoke to the last of the soldiers who fought in these battlefields, men of ninety-nine and a hundred and more. I looked into faded watery eyes that had squinted down rifle-sights in the trenches and had seen their enemies and friends fall in the muddy swamps. Their ears were once filled with fearful noise, their nostrils with the smell of cordite and putrefaction. These old, old men, thin and bony, still had their soldierly bearing and I saw how they stiffened their backs and tilted their chins at the sound of bugles. Their medals shone. In a cemetery one of them pointed to the white gravestones and said he had known this man and that, this corporal and that fusilier, and remarked that remembrance did not necessarily mean mourning. 'I think of my friends as they were then, young men, full of life and laughter.'

Tandoori Spinnaker

From the mainland, the Isle of Wight always beckoned. In fair weather the steeple of St John's church at Ryde could be seen across Spithead. The island seemed apart, mildly exotic with its coloured sands, palms and rhododendrons and deep narrow ravines called chines. Its resorts, Sandown, Shanklin and Ventnor, wound their way up the cliffs, picturesque and old-fashioned; and Ryde had a pier so long that a train ran down it. Holiday posters promised a Madeira-in-the-Channel, a place for sea air and cures; and we used to go for day trips and ice-cream sundaes.

The Romans called the island Vectis, and when writing to the newspapers some residents self-consciously and archly gave themselves the *nom-de-plume* of Vectensian, or Concerned Vectensian or Disgusted Vectensian. Vectensians referred to mainlanders as overners, as Devonians called their summer crowds grockles, the word carrying a tincture of the insiders' suspicion of outsiders. The one fact that every schoolboy knew about the Isle of Wight was that all of the world's people could stand upon it, shoulder to shoulder. In the nightmares of Concerned Vectensian, they did.

And now, years later, I took the ferry which runs down Southampton Water and across the Solent to Cowes. The sky was steely but Cowes Week decorated the sea with its vivid pageant of confusion: the Ben Hur chariot races of jousting yachts, spinning wheels, zizzing winches, cracking jibs, crashing booms, crimson faces, orange oilskins, bullying shouts and cannon fire. Far away from this war at sea there sauntered the distant crinolines of spinnakers. Closer at hand, sailing in company, a couple of old gaff ketches with varnished spars and wine-red sails nodded together like strolling grandfathers talking of the past.

Rounding the dark blue stern of the Royal Yacht *Britannia* the ferry skipper threaded through the swirling flamenco of sail and berthed at the town quay. A sign in a window advertised Massage For The Relief Of Knotted Muscles And Sailing Pains, and I thought I heard the snorting of old foredeckmen at the very idea: before you know it there will be counselling for skippers who come second.

Crowded and steamy restaurants bore salty names like Fastnet and Bowsprit, Ocean Tandoori and English Tandoori Beach Café. By a beer tent on a wharf, a jazz band played 'Muskrat Ramble', as jazz bands invariably do. Excited crews, roaring heartily, burst into pubs and opened their sailing suits with a startling rip of Velcro, falling upon plates of chips and pie. Along the High Street, past the boutiques with their nautical fashions, men in maroon trousers and navy blazers strolled with their wives and yacht molls who wore striped Breton shirts and scarves with motifs of reef knots and bowlines. A blazered man with buggergrip whiskers cast about him with a terrible glare and I felt glad I was not in his crew: he looked a flogger.

Races were being started by the bang of small brass cannon arranged in a twenty-one-gun broadside at the Royal Yacht Squadron's little stone château. On the ramparts, angular ladies gripped their noon gin in scarlet-tipped talons. Race officers in eight-button blazers, piecrusts of white hair beneath their caps, stalked the battlements, raising their binoculars to sweep the horizon for the enemy. They seemed to me to be the same figures I had seen here many years before and I imagined them brought out of store for a week each year to prowl and growl and be part of the pageant.

The Squadron is famously exclusive and at one time the snobbery here could have been strained and bottled as an essence. The stain on its character is its snubbing of Sir Thomas Lipton, the grocery magnate and philanthropist, whose life was a Victorian saga. Born poor in Glasgow, he was twenty-one when he opened the shop that was the seed of his grocery chain and tea empire. The pinnacles of his yachting career were his five failures to win the America's Cup between 1899 and 1930. This was the era of sailor princes and the J-class yachts, of which the loveliest was George V's *Britannia*. Lipton hoped for membership of the Squadron, but the Squadron looked down its nose and, seeing a mere grocer, refused him. Towards the end of his life it elected him, but by then such honour as it was meant little. Cowes did not forget, certainly not old working-class Cowes. Lipton was a local hero. When I first visited the town someone said: 'Don't forget how the Squadron treated Tommy Lipton.'

Sightseers coagulated at the Squadron's stone jetty as a launch approached from the Royal Yacht. A woman daintily disembarked, but not a princess, only a blushing secretary; and the crowd evaporated with a disappointed tut. Cowes likes a prince or princess at the regatta. A royal face brings in money and lends a gossip-column gloss. As a society rendezvous Cowes has seen better days; but then so has that society.

Once, as a junior reporter, I covered the waterfront here and wrote about shipbuilding, boatyards, yachts and seagoing men and women. Cowes was small. The port doctor's telephone number was 5. The chief citizen was Uffa Fox, the boat designer and the Duke of Edinburgh's sailing companion, a pink-cheeked man with a white mane and a squall of a laugh. Whatever he said and did made news and he never failed to provide me with stories, always sending me off with the admonition: 'Now don't you go putting all that in your paper, my boy.' I also wrote speculative paragraphs about the giant Princess flying boat which was parked on a slipway and loomed over the street leading to the ferry across the River Medina. The Princess was a great British failure, a flightless bird. There were always hopes that engines would be designed, powerful enough to lift her one hundred and forty tons; but they never were and she and her two sisters on the mainland remained forlorn behemoths, unkissed princesses.

I lived in digs. My landlady kept a cigarette in her mouth all day, screwing her eyes against the smoke, a permanent ginger tar stain between her lip and nostril. What great smokers people were: a doctor who came to see me had a cigarette on his lip and the ash fell onto my chest as he applied his stethoscope and diagnosed tonsillitis. 'No smoking for you, my boy,' he said fruitily, clearing his throat.

The best events at Cowes were launchings at the J. Samuel White shipyard. An elegant dame in a large hat broke champagne across the bows of the new ship, a frigate or a Channel ferry or a Trinity House vessel. As the chocks fell away it slid into the Medina with a knee-shaking rumble and a roar of drag chains, a billow of brown dust, a gratifying splash and a hip-hooray. I always found it a moving event, though I had to report it in plain prose, quite unlike the purple style of a Victorian reporter who wrote of a launching at Maryport in Scotland: 'On the ship's first kissing her destined bridegroom Neptune, on this her nuptial night, one universal burst of applause rang from the heights of the ship.'

A launching at White's was always followed by a dizzying lunch of champagne and lobster, cigars as large as a policeman's truncheon and rousing speeches about local skills and British shipbuilding traditions. The shipyard closed years ago and ended the supply of Neptune's brides from Cowes.

Life in the island was enlivened, too, by escapes from Parkhurst Prison. Fleet Street men made theatrical dashes across the Solent in speedboats, took up positions in the hotels and made respectable Vectensians cringe as they dictated reports which invariably described the gentle island not as Madeira but as Britain's Alcatraz. Senior detectives in trilbies and belted macintoshes hurried to the scene. Police and prison officers combed forest and farmland and checked the harbours, enjoying the headlines and a break from routine. Superintendents tugged at their pipes and said confidently to the raincoated reporters that the fugitives would not get far; and, generally, they were right. Bedraggled and hungry, the convicts were rounded up after an exhilarating pursuit.

Tennyson's Pipe

In Newport I stopped at a pub that I remembered as a dark place of black pews and firelight serving a muddy and slightly sour local beer drawn from a barrel with a brass tap. Now its walls were covered with Pepsi-Cola stickers and people shouted over rock music and the racket of gaming machines. On a road out of town I saw an inn with a sign saying: If You Want A Juke Box And Plastic Food And Don't Like Real Ale Don't Come In Here. It was becoming harder to find a pub that was just right: on one hand the aggression of noise; on the other, the aggression of virtue. A friend of mine was having a similar difficulty in finding a church to suit his tastes. He wanted a traditional, unadorned Anglican service but found in one church that the organist was replaced by guitarists, in another that the sermon was illustrated by a bearded man with a rucksack, playing a pilgrim, and in another that the vicar, to emphasize a point, batted a beach ball from his pulpit.

I walked from Newport to Carisbrooke, up the hill to the castle. The view from the walls over the downs and crooked lanes was, I supposed, little different from the view Charles I had when he was a prisoner here. He tried twice to escape but each attempt ended farcically. During the first he became stuck in the window bars. In the second he ingeniously used acid to cut through the metal, but the governor heard of the scheme and went to the king's room to remark, with his own drop of acid, 'I am come to take leave of Your Majesty, for I hear you are going away.' In the castle museum I saw the sleeping-cap the king wore during the night before his appointment with the headsman in Whitehall. Looking up, I saw one of the staff. His long hair and Carolean beard gave the momentary impression that the king himself was tending his own relics.

I also saw Lord Tennyson's pipe rack and tobacco jar and the black cloak and broad-brimmed lovat hat he wore while striding about the downs and framing his verses. He cut a melodramatic figure, like a giant bat flapping towards the Needles. He lived at Farringford, a Georgian mansion near Freshwater, from 1853 to his death in 1892, and went there partly to get away

46

from his adoring but pestering fans on the mainland. His presence in Farringford, like Queen Victoria's at Osborne, helped to popularize the island. He liked to read his poems to audiences in his study, having fired himself up with a good pipe and two large glasses of sherry, preferably from his own Waterloo bottles, vintage 1815. He would move himself to tears with the power of his own mesmeric voice and once broke down in sobs while reading his Arthurian epic *Idylls of the King*.

On the highest point of the slope that became known as Tennyson Down his admirers raised an imaginative memorial to him, a tall Celtic cross that can be seen from ships in the Channel. After inspecting it I marched for miles along the Channel coast, what islanders call 'the back of the Wight'. It was once feared by sailing ship crews. Having crossed half the world, and within sight of home, many vessels ended their voyages disintegrating among the mandible rocks and booming surf of this terrible lee shore. The lighthouse at the southernmost point, St Catherine's, is one of the oldest shipping marks in the world, built originally on the orders of an angry pope. A ship loaded with wine from a monastery in France was wrecked at St Catherine's in 1314 and the surviving seamen scrambled ashore, recovered many of the barrels of wine and sold them to the local lord and others. It does not, at this distance, seem too heinous a crime, but the church authorities were furious when they heard of it and threatened the lord with excommunication for buying stolen holy wine. To make amends he was ordered to build a lighthouse and also an oratory in which prayers could be recited for the souls of lost sailors.

A heavy white-capped sea was running through the narrows between Yarmouth and Hurst Point, but the yachts crowded behind the harbour wall at Yarmouth were snug in their pen, halliards jingling like change in a hundred pockets. Only heroes were out at sea, well-reefed, lee rails under; and the pubs were crowded. I remembered a day, bright and hard, the sea like steel slabs, the wind strong, as we flew across the strait to Lymington in a fifteen-foot dinghy, feeling scared and exultant.

I always thought of Yarmouth as intimate and romantic, for when I first knew it there was a mystique about making long voyages under sail, and in this small town escapism and dreams of oceans were married to possibility. The Channel was close at hand and epic voyages started and finished here. Yachts were always being fitted out for ocean adventures and, over beer and plates of bread and dripping, the talk was of ports of call – the Azores, Cape Verde, Galapagos, Papeete, Fiji, Samoa. In the pubs on winter nights you could almost feel the Atlantic trade winds and smell the scent of islands as the conversation turned to teredo worms, williwaws and pirates. The Hiscocks, Eric and Susan, were based in Yarmouth, and I remember a hall with every seat filled when they showed slides of a voyage round the world. They were in a line of small-boat voyagers that stretched back to R.T. McMullen, the pioneer of single-handed cruising. In 1891 he was found at the helm of his yacht in the Channel and it was reckoned he had been dead for twenty-four hours. Shortly after the Hiscocks returned to Yarmouth I went to interview them. Susan was welcoming and talkative, but Eric, feverishly hammering at his typewriter in the saloon, was almost monosyllabic. It was slightly disillusioning to find a god of the sea, who had enjoyed the inspiring freedom of the oceans, fumbling with carbon paper and sweating against a deadline.

Albert's Pin-Up

I made my way back to Cowes by way of Osborne House. Queen Victoria sank here like a galleon in 1901, surrounded by her family, expiring at last in the arms of the Prince of Wales and of her loving and irksome grandson, that pompous Junker, the Kaiser. He measured her for her coffin, a service he was to perform thirteen years later for much of European civilization.

A cast of her beloved husband's hand was placed in the coffin, also his dressing gown, and a photograph of her loyal, quarrelsome companion, John Brown, who used to tell her sharply to stop complaining and whose constant presence led to sniggerers referring to her as Mrs Brown. After lying in state for ten days her body was taken aboard the Royal Yacht *Alberta* which crossed the Solent through a line of warships while dense masses crowded the shore like a black ribbon. In London the prostitutes, too, wore mourning.

Osborne is a family album, crammed with pictures and sentimental oddities like the white marble sculptures of the hands, legs and feet of Victoria's children, objects of parental adoration which today seem grotesque, like dismembered babies. A building in the grounds is stuffed with the doodads and pocket-fluff of imperial travel: a starling shot by the Prince of Wales, a human skull he brought from Germany, fragments picked up after colonial battles, a bullet extracted from the arm of a Sudanese soldier in 1897, the figure of a saint made from bread chewed into plasticity by a convict at Dartmoor, and a key, fashioned from a beef bone, which another Dartmoor prisoner had used to escape.

Prince Albert's study remains as he left it. I imagined him sitting at his desk, bothered and dyspeptic after a row with the Queen, and composing one of the memorandums he wrote to her after their tiffs. 'You have again lost your self-control. I did not say a word which could wound you, and I did not begin the conversation, but you had followed me about and continued it from room to room.' Perhaps he recovered his composure by soaking in his bath. His bathroom is an engine of hygiene, all brass and copper pipes and cocks and valves, commanded by a large painting of a voluptuous nude, so that you picture Albert in his suds, contemplating the lady and stroking his whiskers.

Passing Clouds

Liners were the heart of Southampton and the city has been diminished by their passing. The boat-train from Waterloo was a glamorous institution and Southampton Water and the docks were busy with tugs, ferries, lighters and pilot boats. It seemed that every schoolboy's father worked on the ships or in the port; and Southampton's accent was salted with the sound of Merseyside as people moved to follow the transatlantic trade when it shifted from Liverpool to Southampton. I was just in time to see the end of the epoch of the great liners. When they docked, reporters went aboard to interview film stars and political figures and were treated to lunch; and I thought as I boarded the *Queen Mary*, to be brushed by the soft butterfly wing of Hollywood, that this was the life.

At that time I wrote pieces for *Hampshire* magazine in Southampton and in an Italian restaurant one day Denis Stevens, the editor, introduced me to John Arlott, his star contributor. We ate there several times and Arlott gave me wine lessons, refilling the glasses and telling the stories of the regions the wine came from; and describing, as he had many times before, his own introduction to wine in Sicily in 1949.

We sat for hours under the fragrant smoke of his Passing Clouds cigarettes and he related his comic, melancholic and serpentine anecdotes of cricket and wine, of broadcasting and his years as a Southampton detective. He was proud of his Hampshire roots, and knew more about the county's history and landscape than any man alive. He cooked his stories like casseroles, very slowly, with long digressions, and he would pause at critical moments in the narrative to pour more wine, the sound of the pouring forming an interlude. He was a good cricket commentator because he was a good storyteller. His large face creased into laughter as he raised his glass and teased out the last line.

I met him, years later, when he was on holiday in the Isles of Scilly. 'Come to dinner,' he said. I went to my hotel to buy wine to take with me but the selection was meagre. I chose a claret and the landlord said, 'You're in luck, there's been a run on this and it's the last bottle.'

Arlott's burly figure filled the doorway of his cottage. I gave him the wine and his face lit up. 'How lovely,' he said, stretching out the vowels like dough. 'I shall open it at once.' As he applied the corkscrew I saw that the sideboard was covered with ranked bottles of the same wine.

The Heritage Man

'It's him.'
'Never.'
'Yes it is, it's him.'

'You're right, it is him. Mum, look, it's him.'

'Who?'

'Him.'

Heads turned as Lord Montagu strode through Palace House at Beaulieu. He knew it was good for business for him to be seen taking a turn around the goldfish bowl. The British, on the whole, like their lords and enjoy observing how they live. Seeing an aristocrat and his family eating cucumber sandwiches with the crusts cut off is at least as entertaining as watching a chimpanzees' tea party at the zoo.

Lord Montagu recalled that soon after he opened his home to the public he was indeed having tea in a private room, marked Private, when someone appeared at his window and beckoned to a friend, saying, 'Come and look at this, they're actually having tea.' Lord Montagu learnt long ago that in a stately home the words Private and No Entry are not at all a deterrent, but a magnet. 'The British', he said, 'are probably the most gratuitously inquisitive people in the world.'

Nevertheless, our unembarrassed liking for the keyhole has helped Lord Montagu and most of his brother peers to keep their mansions and estates in good order, to the benefit of the economy and the appearance of the countryside.

He tapped in a code to open the door of his private apartment. We sat down to a lunch of gulls' eggs, fish and summer pudding, and he poured a Beaulieu estate wine. Visiting the homes of aristocrats, he remarked, was not at all a post-war phenomenon. Most of the great houses of England had been open since the eighteenth and nineteenth centuries. In 1778 Lord Lyttleton complained that sightseers were chasing him from his apartment 'or strolling about the environs keeping me prisoner in it – the lord of the place can never call it his'. The Marlboroughs were annoyed that crowds descended on Blenheim Palace even before it was completed. A traveller, refused entry to Lord Guilford's house, grumbled: 'Very rude . . . unlike an old courtly earl!' Many large houses, however, had open days and servants earned shillings showing visitors their splendours. The Earl of Leicester allowed noblemen and foreigners to tour his home in Norfolk most days of the week, but hoi polloi on Tuesdays only.

The British have always regarded it as something more than a privilege, something veering towards a right, to inspect the homes of the nobility, to survey the family silver, four-poster beds, portraits and photographs and satisfy their curiosity about the lavatories. An Englishman's home may be his castle, but an English lord's castle is his home only up to a point: he is expected to share it; and even if he does not care to, taxes and debts usually oblige him to do so.

The enlightened aristocrat sees himself as the keeper of his inheritance, rather than its owner. That is how the people see him, too. Far more than its continental counterpart the British aristocracy has made itself approachable. It has certainly had its contingent of reactionary old buffers, but its adaptability has enabled it to survive social turmoil. It has thus prospered while European aristocratic families have sunk under the weight of their foolishness and mistaken ideas of their own importance. The British aristocracy has also been fortunate as well as pragmatic, for it has not had to endure the wars and revolutionary cataclysms of Europe.

The British know all about the ancestry of their dukes and earls, that today's peers are the descendants of chain-mailed gangsters, egregious parvenus, grasping plotters, kings' bastards and barmy barons. Yet they have a place in the British pattern and it can be argued that had they not had a function as a caste they would have withered away long ago.

As custodians of the grand houses they are links in a chain of continuity. They work at the heart of the heritage industry, that amalgam of showmanship, nostalgia and history which they have done much to promote and which helps to preserve them. The hereditary element in the House of Lords may be absurd, utterly indefensible in a democracy, but many hereditary peers say that their experience of stewardship, a sense of duty and tradition, and perhaps their independence, make a valuable contribution. Their position is eccentric, but also innately British. The question of reform of the House of Lords may turn on common sense rather than logic, on whether the abolition of the hereditary element would actually lead to improvement.

Lord Montagu said that the peerage had earned respect by

moving with the times and remaining relevant. Having spent his life making an enterprise of his own inheritance he is a champion of the stately home and its professional management. 'Heritage is an overworked word,' he said. 'It covers wildlife to Churchill's papers. It means anything from the past which is British or epitomizes our national character and history. As a boy I loved history – I was reading it when everyone else was reading *Just William* – so it was lucky for me that I was born into a place like this. In Britain we don't have sunny beaches or great food, but we do have history and we can sell it!'

The linchpin in Lord Montagu's own history was his ancestor, Thomas Wriothesley, one of the sharp Tudor nouveaux riches who bought estates and established a dynasty during the Dissolution of the Monasteries when the land of England was up for grabs and a third of it changed hands. He bought the abbey at Beaulieu and its estate for just over thirteen hundred pounds. Another ancestor, Ralph Montagu, acquired the fortune he needed to qualify for a dukedom by marrying the wealthy Duchess of Albemarle. Since she was mad and had vowed to marry nothing less than a monarch, he won her by disguising himself as the Emperor of China. His son had a showman streak, too, and in 1749 drew a large paying crowd to a London theatre by promising, among other stunts, to climb inside a wine bottle and sing a song. It slowly dawned on the audience, as they faced an empty stage, that they had been conned. They therefore rioted.

Lord Montagu's father was a pioneer motorist, founder-editor of *Car Illustrated* whose covers showed automobiles as winged chariots. He was one of the first to be prosecuted for exceeding the twelve miles per hour speed limit. He also introduced Edward VII to motoring. One day, taking the King for a drive in a Daimler, he found Lymington toll bridge closed and said to the bridge-keeper that he and the King wished to cross. The man was not to be pushed around. 'I know them kings,' he said. 'Two of 'em slipped by me this morning. You pay your tanner first, and then wait until this donkey cart has gone through.'

Lord Montagu inherited Beaulieu when he was three and took responsibility for it when he was twenty-five, in 1951. A thirteenth-century estate that has survived more or less intact, it includes the abbey ruins, the Beaulieu River, shoots, farms, houses, commercial woodlands and the village of Buckler's Hard; in all more than nine thousand acres stretching down to the Solent shore, one ninety-sixth of the county of Hampshire.

Its new master was rich and poor at the same time. On the estate's annual income of less than fifteen hundred pounds he could not afford the coal bill for Palace House and his sister cycled to work to save the bus fare. He could have sold but 'I decided to fight. I didn't want the house to become a hotel, with the estate broken up. I didn't want it to be like one of those pathetically empty French châteaux.' He opened Beaulieu to the public and was pictured in the newspapers scrubbing floors. 'The aim was, literally, to keep the roof over our heads.'

Most historic houses are in private hands. Among the owners of less well-known houses there is an abiding dread of being the one who lets the family down, breaks the continuity, sells the house and sees the contents scattered. Many are financially pressed and find that, as government grants towards maintenance have declined, they have to sell off the heirloom silver to pay for a new roof.

Lord Montagu started the Montagu Motor Museum as a sideshow with five veteran cars, including his father's 1903 de Dion-Bouton. It grew into a great collection and archive and became the National Motor Museum in 1970. He has made Beaulieu one of the country's leading tourist entertainments. The stately home business, which he pioneered, grew to be recognized by the government as a national asset. 'We had such small beginnings and I look back on it all with amazement. I was an amateur who became a professional. I have used Disney techniques to help keep my English roots alive. Without such methods many of our great houses would have become roofless ruins. My life has been in historic buildings and museums. I was chairman of English Heritage for more than eight years. The Historic Houses Association, of which I was president for five years, became a powerful lobby. We used to run courses here for stately home owners, teaching them how to manage. We have taught the National Trust and the government how to do it. We have shown the government that the cheapest way to preserve houses that are national treasures is to ensure that their owners keep them. In this way we have helped prevent the country becoming a concrete jungle. Many British big houses, mine included, are in better condition now than before the First World War, thanks to money from tourism and grants. A century ago an owner would look out from his drawing room and say: "I own all I survey." Now he says: "I manage all I survey." We are lifetime curators. It isn't a question of wealth: the whole point is to manage a successful estate with efficient farms and woodlands.

'I was lucky to take over the business in my twenties, when I had a lot of energy. Some sons do not come in until they are in their forties and there can be tremendous problems because some fathers die having told their boys nothing. I've seen to it that my son Ralph has been involved since he was a child.

'I've actually enjoyed the crowds. We've even learnt how to tame those French schoolchildren who invade in masses: the secret is to give them a lot to do. The heart of it all is that stately homes are not museums but remain family homes. People like to feel that they might see me playing croquet or having tea. From a silver service, of course.'

Heart of Oak

As I said, Nelson is everywhere. His favourite ship, HMS *Agamemnon*, of sixty-four guns, was built on the Beaulieu River at Buckler's Hard. The eighteenth-century village survives, a broad gravel street between terraces of bright red brick. Henry Adams, master shipbuilder, drew *Agamemnon*'s never-bettered lines and Nelson exulted in commanding the fastest ship in the Navy, reaching eleven knots on a broad reach. She fought at Calvi, Copenhagen and Trafalgar. After 1790 Adams passed the management of the shipyard to his sons but could not resist interfering. Increasingly cantankerous, he built a crow's-nest on his house, climbed into it on a rope ladder and watched the shipyard through a telescope. When he saw something he disliked he rang a bell and ran up signal flags spelling the identity of the guilty workman, summoning him to the crow's-nest for a tongue-lashing. He died in the year of Trafalgar, aged ninety-one.

Her Showgirl Leg

In Bournemouth I asked the receptionist at a small hotel if she had a room. Yes. Could I have a look at it? No. I went across the road to another hotel. Was there a room? Yes, but only for a minimum of two nights.

I have served my time in British hotels of a certain kind. I know the stained candlewick bedspread on a low bed, the mauve nylon sheets, the bedside lamp just out of reach with a burn mark on the shade, the mirror hung for a dwarf, the picture of the child with a tear on his face, the carpet seen only in hotels, the cold bathroom with the mean tablet of soap, the thin towels, the shower with the dribbling plastic head, either scalding or chill, the breakfast room where, once you have settled yourself at a table, you are invariably moved to another, where you cannot get scrambled eggs because they are not doing them today, and where marmalade is a smear on a piece of plastic like a specimen for the microscope.

Still, in Bournemouth that evening, the third hotel I tried was warm and welcoming. I followed the sound of laughter and went into the bar. It was full of elderly men and women, mostly from the north of England, the women with bubbly hairdos, floral frocks and ample figures. The men buying drinks at the bar said proudly: 'You can't stop our Freda when she gets going.' 'If Doris goes on to the shorts we'll be here till morning.'

A pianist played Edwardian music-hall tunes, Ivor Novello, Rodgers and Hart, songs of the 1930s and 1940s. Everyone joined in singing 'If You Were the Only Girl in the World', 'Some Enchanted Evening', 'South of the Border' and 'Show Me the Way to go Home'.

The older people knew the words by heart, but the younger ones were groping for them after a line or two. This was a dying culture, the last of the sing-songs around the piano, for songs are no longer written with lyrics to be sung. In all the hilarity a woman hitched up her skirt to dance and thrust her showgirl leg onto the piano and everyone said Whoo! and the men grinned from ear to ear.

In the morning, rosy and in rude health, they ate breakfasts of grapefruit segments, eggs, bacon, sausage and fried bread, and some of them tackled huge glistening kippers as big as wicket-keepers' gloves. They wriggled into their wind-cheaters and headed out into the rain, promising themselves that the weather would improve and that they would see the distant Needles when the clouds lifted.

Don't Forget the Diver

Graceful dark-eyed girls sauntered in the heart of Winchester. Students from France and Italy, on their summer sojourn, they sat in pubs and sipped half-pints of beer, or strolled the shadowed grass of the cathedral precincts. Young Englishmen, sitting under an oak, made chirping noises at these elegant gazelles and called out 'Senoreeta' in squeaky Mexican accents.

I was woken in my hotel room next day as if by thunder. Cars in the street outside juddered on their springs, the drivers shaking their shoulders, rock music at full volume. This is how young Britain goes to work, strapped inside a drum, concussed and screaming.

The bones of the Saxon kings of Wessex and the early kings of England have, however, rattled to ruder disturbances over the years. They are stored in painted mortuary chests in the cathedral which commands the city, the Hampshire downs and all of Wessex. In Winchester the Middle Ages seem not too distant and the city's stone walls and old red brick and cobbles form an easy bridge from ancient times to our own. This was the old Wessex capital, the place where the idea of England was forged. Alfred the Great prevented the destruction of Wessex by ninth-century Scandinavian invaders and ordered the compilation of texts which became *The Anglo-Saxon Chronicle*, a foundation stone of English language and literature. His spirit lives on in his bronze statue atop granite blocks in the heart of the city and an inscription commemorates the 'Founder of the Kingdom and the Nation'. We like to think of him as noble, though he must have been ruthless and thuggish as well. Sword upraised, hand on shield, he urges us on.

The cathedral is a custodian of imperial memory. Brasses and marble tablets tell of conquest and victory. They trace the footprints of the British across Africa, Asia and North America, as they scooped up islands, countries, continents and peoples; and fought and died in deserts and paludine wastes. While you can read brutality between the lines of some of the inscriptions, they nevertheless make you wonder at the scale of what the British did, at the impulse and confidence that propelled their acquisitive journeyings. Some of the tablets are flag-and-drum enough to look like pages from the yarns of G.A. Henty, whose adventurous life as a Victorian soldier and journalist gave him material for two or three books a year. A plaque honours a captain who died exploring the Congo,′ another an officer wounded while 'nobly planting the British standard' at the siege of Chandra, another the Rifle Brigade men who died in the Afghan campaign. There is a tribute to a colonel 'shot by a fanatic' at Peshawar in 1899. Another memorial honours an officer killed 'while leading his men with the devotion of an English gentleman' against tribesmen in west Africa, a campaign Henty himself reported as a war correspondent. These memorials are like those I have seen in British graveyards and churches in the Khyber Pass and Meerut, in Calcutta, Kampala, Isandhlwana; and in Madras, where inscriptions record the soldiers, lords and ladies 'who fell martyr to an ungenial climate' and a clergyman 'destined to labour in a peculiar vineyard, that of the conversion of the natives of India'.

A jet-black effigy in Winchester commemorates General Sir Redvers Buller, VC, one of many memorials in England to a man in name, deed and appearance the quintessential Victorian warrior. With such a name he could hardly be anything else. He is actually buried near his home in Devon. He was bulldog-jowled, heavily-moustached, bibulous and hot-tempered. He once threw a man through a glass door because he was irked by the way the fellow hung about watching him play billiards. Buller's conduct of the fighting in the Boer War was strongly criticized and he was relieved of command. The disaster of

Spion Kop hung about him. But he had his defenders: he was a jolly and inspiring man, popular with soldiers. A month before her death he told Queen Victoria he had not thought the Boer War would drag on. His cenotaph in Winchester is inscribed China, Red River, Ashanti, Zululand, Egypt, South Africa – a Victorian soldier's grand tour. He is weighted with medals, hand upon sword, and you fear he might give an irritable harrumph if, like the billiards-watcher, you hang around too long.

Nearby lies the effigy of Sir Arnaud de Gaveston, died 1302, loyal servant of Edward I. Like his master, he was a father with a son who went to the bad: Piers Gaveston was a crony and lover of the wretched Edward II. Sir Arnaud's effigy grasps a sword; and in his mailed mitts, I noticed, someone had placed a tribute of four scarlet carnations.

A small statue honours the Edwardian superman William Walker. Without his dogged exploits the cathedral might have fallen down. He saved it with his bare hands. At the beginning of the century surveyors observed that the cathedral's foundation of New Forest beech logs, which had borne its weight for eight hundred years, was sinking, and the east end was starting to collapse. Stones tumbled from the roof and the walls bulged. Between 1906 and 1912 Walker, a deep-sea diver, an heroic figure with a walrus moustache, dived day after day into the muddy water beneath the cathedral. He pulled out the logs and replaced them with sacks of concrete. He laboured on his own for six hours a day, twenty feet down. In the black swamp water he could not see his hand in front of his face and worked by touch, carrying the sacks one by one to build this foundation. In 1912 he was in the congregation at a service of thanksgiving for the cathedral's safety. The statue shows a man in diving dress, but the head is not Walker's. By mistake, the sculptor modelled the face of the consultant engineer. It lacks even the moustache.

I walked from the cathedral to the thirteenth-century Great Hall, presided over by a massive statue of Queen Victoria, her face wearing her usual expression of disapproval. A German had written in the visitors' book: 'Victoria seems to be everywhere.' And so she is, placed like a mighty paperweight all over the world.

The Great Hall, grand and lofty, is the only survivor of Winchester's castle buildings, destroyed on Cromwell's order in the Civil War. For more than five centuries it was a place of trials. Sir Walter Raleigh was condemned to death in this hall in 1603, though later reprieved; and Judge Jeffreys conducted one of his Bloody Assizes here. Its notable ornament, hanging on a wall, is the oak table known as King Arthur's Round Table which was built between 1250 and 1280. It is eighteen feet in diameter, weighs more than a ton and is scarred by musket balls fired during the Cromwellian siege. At Henry VIII's command the table was painted in the distinctive Tudor livery of green and white, with the storied names of twenty-four Arthurian knights inscribed on the rim.

I first sat in the Great Hall in the days when it was the setting of the Hampshire Assizes. On the press bench, engrossed in the theatre of justice, the jostle of clerks and counsel, whispering detectives and flitting ushers, I had an education in law and human nature. The witness box and jury seats, the dock and knee-numbing press bench, the barristers' seats among Pisas of books and documents, were surprisingly close to the judge, who sat on a canopied bench beneath the Round Table. It all made for a fearsome intimacy, especially when His Lordship was irritable.

During the adjournments reporters, policemen and lawyers gathered to smoke and gossip. A whisper came down the corridors: 'Jury's coming back.' Cigarettes went underheel. The court filled, the prisoner was brought up by grim-faced prison officers. The jury foreman gave the verdict and eyes turned to the prisoner. The judge, hunched in his fur-trimmed red robes, his face flinty, delivered his warning to other rogues and wretches. The sentence fell from his lips in words of ice. There was a gasp and the prisoner descended to the cells. Outside, the old reporters and policemen lit each other's cigarettes and talked about favourite cases. Since they did away with hanging, they said, murder trials had lost their edge.

The Great Hall is no longer a court, but the judge's bench is kept as a relic, with a notice requesting that you do not sit on it. For sentiment's sake, however, I sat on the red cushion and wondered how many people had been sent from this bench to jail, to the gallows and to Australia. The seat was a comfortless pew and I thought it might have put judges into a peevish mood.

I walked towards Twyford Down, on the southern outskirts of Winchester. Once a beauty spot, it is the site of a famous lost battle. Local people fought for seven years to stop the government driving a motorway canyon through the Down, an officially-protected area of outstanding natural beauty, but the government won and bulldozers cut an irredeemable gash in the chalk. Many local people swore they would never drive through it, though others saw it as a *tour de force* of transport engineering. The fight against it was a battle royal because Winchester is an ancient city in the southern English heartland. Although contingents of beards and sandals joined the opposition, it was essentially a middle-class revolt, a protest dressed by Jaeger. Barbara Bryant, for example, one of the leaders of the campaign, was a Tory councillor. 'Some of us were part of the Tory establishment and we shook that establishment and made a nuisance of ourselves. Many people were left disillusioned by defeat, disenchanted with our democratic system, but something good came from the fight: the intensity of our opposition had so bruised the government and exposed the undemocratic nature of road planning that the way was opened to a more sensible process. One lesson I learnt was that you have to get in early, before the decisions are made. By the time the public inquiry comes it is too late, a momentum has built up against protest. I also learnt how powerless Westminster politicians are, how supremely strong the executive is.'

I sat in the sunshine by the cathedral, beside the tombstone of a soldier who died in 1764 and whose epitaph runs:

> Here sleeps in peace a Hampshire Grenadier,
> Who caught his death by drinking cold small Beer,
> Soldiers be wise from his untimely fall
> And when ye're hot drink Strong or none at all.

I had bought a copy of the *Hampshire Chronicle*, founded 1772. It bears a royal coat of arms on its masthead, like *The Times*, which was founded thirteen years later. It remains a weighty broadsheet, reliable and slightly old-fashioned, reflecting the variety of local life and demonstrating that the inhabitants of local newspaperland are too busy to worry too much. My *Hampshire Chronicle* reported the week's activities in one small town: the Historical and Literary Society's coach excursion to Churchill's home at Chartwell, the Wine Circle's barbecue and tasting session, with a record number of bottles consumed, the Flower Club's practical session and garden visit, the Lunch Club's picnic, the Over Sixties' Club's coach trip to Eastbourne, the British Legion meeting, the Sight Seeing by Train Group's excursion to Didcot, the Christian Men's Group's summer walk; and much else. In other villages camera clubs roamed, amateur dramatics companies performed, walkers walked, men and women gathered to learn cheese-making, a village poetry reading raised more than sixty pounds for children in Uganda, horticultural shows settled the contests between growers of shallots, beetroot and peas, and a dog show gave prizes for the Handsomest Dog, the Dog Most Like its Owner and the Dog with the Waggiest Tail, whose name was Pericles. Collections from the bottle bank in a certain village, I noted, would henceforth be twice a week, rather than once, because people were enjoying so much wine.

This sense of the familiarity and security of home was reinforced by a reader's account of his holiday in Africa. 'After a lengthy delay as local bureaucracy and corruption were attended to', he and his fellow tourists arrived at their hotel and 'concern for the baggage grew as locals swarmed over the coach'. Mud huts in nearby villages, he said, could not fail to shock the holidaymaker more used to sanitized regions of Europe. The holiday took a turn for the worse as a military coup began and there was 'panic as soldiers appeared demanding bottles of brandy, threatening staff with machine guns'. But relief was at hand when 'an English aircraft could be seen over the airport and the mind ran ahead, visualising the sanctuary of air-conditioned calm'.

The sports sections of local newspapers do not concern themselves with 'England's Shame'. Out of the *Chronicle's* pages emerged sturdy men in wife-washed whites hitting sixes on the village green, while rock cakes and salmon sandwiches and tea were set out in the shade of elms and lindens. Men in their fifties were scoring centuries.

The pages that chronicled the pleasures of blessed ordinariness, reflecting busy and charitable lives, also noted the irritations: burglaries, vandalism, window-smashing, arson and swindling, the thefts of golf clubs. I saw that Winchester Fire Brigade had been called out to prevent flooding in a house after a waterbed was punctured during a domestic dispute. But the *Hampshire Chronicle* also dips into its archives to show what is obvious, that our age is not uniquely oppressed by crime. One of my forerunners on the press bench at the Hampshire Assizes, two hundred years ago, reported that two men were sentenced to be hanged, and then gibbeted in chains at Portsmouth, for murdering their overseer. 'They fell upon him with iron shovels, with which they gave him such wounds that his brains fell out. He lived eighteen hours. This seems to decide the long-contested point between physiologists, whether the seat of life is in the heart or the brain? and evidently shows it to be in the former.'

I folded the paper and went for tea. I had bought one of those little books of local reminiscences that are so popular, the sort that have faded photographs of Victorian butcher shops, Edwardian grocers with straw hats, primary schools with pinafored girls, pubs with beer at twopence a pint, ostlers and grooms. I sipped my tea and with pleasurable expectation opened my copy of *The Lost Cinemas of Winchester*.

3

The Where and When

The sign at the Devon boundary had a galleon motif and the legend 'Keep Devon Shipshape'. It suggested the Devon Sea, the smashing of the Armada and the Spanish Main. It was a nod to the Devon adventurers John Hawkins, Richard Grenville, and Francis Drake — especially Drake, whose voice, formed on the rich red loam, Queen Elizabeth could listen to for hours. She sat enraptured by his roguish stories when he returned from his circumnavigation, the *Golden Hind* heavy with looted Spanish treasure. This venture paid its investors at 4,700 per cent and gave Elizabeth a jackpot to pay for the war against Spain and to invest in trade in the East.

The land gave off a smell of damp soil with a zest of manure. Two dead foxes lay at the roadside, their gingery brushes rippling in the slipstream of rushing vehicles, as I pulled off for tea at a service area. I found a seat beside a jungly clump of green fronds. These caravanserais are classless oases — no first class lounge or roped-off enclosure — and, like the new glass shopping arcades, proclaim prosperity and the elastic-waisted tracksuit comfort the

British have come to expect. They are warm, carpeted, beige and pastel with notices announcing that their lavatories are cleaned regularly. Decorated with flowers and large pictures of food, equipped with idle-hour electronic games, shops, easy-listening music and restaurants, these palm courts of the highway have made museums of the few greasy roadside cafés that remain.

Four men, white-haired and sprightly, wearing cardigans over Viyella shirts, brought their trays to the table next to mine. One of them leant on a thick walking stick decorated with badges from places he had visited, like the rear window of a car in the 1960s. His ferrule had tapped the avenues of Europe. They all sat down to a replica of a schoolboys' tuck shop feed: dark fruit cake, doughnuts oozing jam with every bite and cherry-nippled pastries. They were contented badgers out to tea.

Perched on stools nearby, middle-aged men sank their faces into squashy breasts of cheeseburger, nuzzling like hungry babies. A sign over a glossy poster of eggs, baked beans, sausages and fried bread said 'Fill Up Here'. People were obeying. They were eating all-day breakfasts, steak and kidney pie, coiled Cumberland sausage, fried chicken, pizzas, sticky pastries squirting yellow nectar, Eccles cakes and two-handed buns as big as horse droppings. They chewed outsize chocolate biscuits and scribbled their chips in pools of ketchup. They dithered over the array of colas and the choice of coffee: Kenyan, Colombian, Brazilian and Javan.

Snow lay on the tors of Dartmoor as I headed for the Tamar. I suppose that I first heard of Cornwall at primary school where we learnt traditional songs by rote: 'The Ash Grove', 'Barbara Allen', 'The Lincolnshire Poacher', 'The Dashing White Sergeant', 'The Yeomen of England' and many others. 'The Song of the Western Men' was similarly dinned into my memory. I smelt milk and ink and heard thirty voices squeaking:

> A good sword and a trusty hand,
> A merry heart and true,
> King James's men shall understand
> What Cornishmen can do.
> And have they fixed the where and when?

And shall Trelawny die?
Here's twenty thousand Cornishmen
Will know the reason why!

We did not know who Trelawny was. I later learnt that Bishop Jonathan Trelawny, the chief symbol of Cornish defiance, was held in the Tower of London for protesting against James II's Declaration of Indulgence which granted toleration to Catholics in 1686. There was no 'where and when', no Cornish march across the Tamar, for the bishop was released and became an enthusiastic supporter of William of Orange.

There had, however, been two famous Cornish crossings of the Tamar intended to show the English what's what. In 1497, angered by oppressive taxes, fifteen thousand men marched on London and were beaten at Blackheath. The heads of the two leaders, Michael Joseph and Thomas Flamank, were spiked on London Bridge, the capital's trophy room. Cornishmen marched again in 1549 to protest against laws which abolished the Latin Mass and replaced it with a service in English, a language many of them did not speak. They were slaughtered at Exeter and, again, their leader's head ended up on a pike at London Bridge.

The rousing 'Good sword and a trusty hand' made the Cornwall of my imagination a place of indignant defiance, romantic as well as remote. Posters advertising the Cornish Riviera Express promised a mysterious and exotic country and crossing the Tamar conveyed a sense of entry into a different place. The dipping cat's paw of Land's End always beckoned and the names of villages seemed to come from legends: Zelah and Zennor, Goonbell and Gweek, Polyphant and Praa, Bojewyan and Bokiddick.

On the way over the moors to Redruth I came upon a 'wind farm', tall masts with flailing semaphore arms, environmentally 'correct' and erected by the righteous; but in practice noisy, alien and infuriatingly ugly. Falmouth was lashed by rain. All the guest houses offered bathrooms En Suite, and just as well: we British are not as robust as we were and few of us will now endure the grim walk to the distant dank chamber and the fear of finding it occupied. En Suite is one of the great changes in Britain in the past few years. We have embraced lavatories and bathrooms. We have moved on at last from the time when an Oxford professor said to undergraduates who asked for better washing facilities: 'Baths? Why do you want baths? The term only lasts eight weeks.'

The landlady said that times were bad and there were fewer visitors. 'We really feel the recession in Cornwall and a lot of people have to tighten their belts. Go up to Redruth you'll see why it's called Beirut – so much of it has been closed and boarded up.'

She recommended a bistro near the quay and I walked down through the storm. I had the place to myself. The proprietor cooked fresh fish and played music from the 1960s and 1970s, from the time before pop music ran out of tunes and vanished into the swamps. When I emerged the rain had stopped, the sky was clearing and the velvet harbour water gleamed with the reflections of the lights of the ships in the anchorage of Carrick Roads.

I called at a pub on the waterfront for a final binder of whisky. It was an informal museum, decorated with a ship's wheel, cork lifebelts, a hefty block and tackle and well-used brass. Sepia photographs of barques and brigs crowded the walls. They used to call at Falmouth to await the orders of their owners, the directions to set off on voyages to the earth's corners. There was a picture of Captain Kurt Carlsen, the stoical Dane who was the hero of a drama that gripped the country. He stayed with his ship, the *Flying Enterprise*, for a month before it sank off The Lizard in 1952. A crowd of seamen, pints in their hands, were arguing good-naturedly beneath a beam inscribed with an elegy for old-time seafaring: 'Many a ship's crew have sung their song here. History hangs on the walls. So much has been seen, said and sung.'

A gale blew next morning and the palms in the guest house gardens shook furiously. I went up to Redruth and Camborne. They are run-down in any case, but in this witches' weather they looked desolate. Unemployment is high and many people here know hardship.

For some years in the second part of the nineteenth century Cornwall supplied half of the world's tin and two-thirds of its copper. Cliffs are still stained red from tin and streaked green from copper. Cornishmen were masters of mining and engineering technology. Two of their heroes are Richard Trevithick, pioneer of the steam locomotive, born in Camborne, and Humphry Davy, chemist and inventor of the miners' lamp, born in Penzance. Cornish miners took their expertise across the world, particularly to America and Australia, and they bridle at the outsiders' idea of Cornish insularity. By the beginning of the twentieth century, however, Cornwall's domination of the tin trade was at an end and one of the first industrialized societies in Britain became the first to be deindustrialized. The South Crofty mine, near Redruth, is the last tin mine in Cornwall and for many Cornishmen an emotive link with the past. It nearly closed when the government withdrew backing in the early 1990s but was saved when local people, their passion allied to nostalgia, bought shares and helped to keep it alive.

I had a good soaking walking around the foot of Cornwall that day. For all the palm trees and postcard picturesqueness, and the popular idea of whitewashed cottages and cream teas, the peninsula's landscape is soft and lush in only a few corners. Rather, it is dramatic, a weathered kingdom of granite and old red sandstone, wild and rubbled, notched and pleated. Villages are tough and tight, sheltered in crevices, and in many places a meagre soil stretches over the bones of the land like dried skin on an ancient skeleton. It is an antique land, laced with deep, high-hedged medieval lanes, pitted with relics and studded with ruins, its history signposted by burial chambers, megaliths, Celtic crosses, engine houses and austere Methodist chapels, the raised hands of mine buildings and the fingers of their chimneys always an evocative silhouette. As everyone in Cornwall knows, exuberant and disobedient youths and maids who danced on the Sabbath were turned into standing stones by the Almighty.

It would be easy enough to describe Cornwall as a story with a beginning and an end. The frayed rope of the Cornish language broke with the death of Dolly Pentreath, the last native speaker, in Mousehole in 1777, and, while some work to revive the language, the only Cornish word that everyone in Cornwall knows is Kernow, the old name. The decline of industrial virility left a persisting sense of loss, a hurt pride, a yearning for an age when Cornishmen and their knowledge counted for something. For that reason many people take pride in the ghostly mine ruins, seeing them as honest scars, and they do not share the views of some outsiders that they are litter on the landscape.

Although the language and industry that made a Cornish identity have largely gone, Cornwall denies that its story has finished. 'The end of Cornwall has often been trumpeted,' Philip Payton, the director of the Institute of Cornish Studies, said to me, 'but Cornwall reinvents itself, creates a different Cornwall. Distinctiveness endures, but a different kind of distinctiveness.'

Over the years, travellers to Cornwall and people who have fallen in love with it and settled here have often ascribed to it the qualities of magic and mystery. Timeless, they say, whatever that may mean. Some writers have peopled their Cornwall with superstitious folk and had them groping in Celtic mists and soldiering with King Arthur. Many have referred to it as 'the most un-English of English counties' – and it is true that it has little in common with Essex or Bedfordshire. Daphne du Maurier, who adored Cornwall and made it her home, saw it as a golden province, 'the tail of England, aloof and rather splendidly detached from the activity across the Tamar hailed as progress.' She wrote of 'the Cornish character, smouldering beneath the surface, ever ready to ignite'.

Romance, the metaphysical and notions of destiny play their part but are hardly a sustaining diet for people who believe they have a difference to express. Something else must account for the fact that thousands of Cornish people display Kernow stickers in their cars and some proclaim 'I am not an Emmet'. An emmet is an ant, the name the Cornish give to outsiders, particularly swarming holidaymakers who for many years have sought to put their quart into a pint pot.

Many cars, too, sport the flag of St Piran, a white cross on a black background. St Piran was one of the hazier Celtic saints, possibly one of those ragged Welsh ascetics who spread the word along rocky western coasts. He may have lived in the sixth century. Whether or not he existed, Cornish tin miners long ago adopted him as their patron and observed his feast day, the fifth of March, and this is now regarded by many Cornish people as their national day. St Piran's banner, not often seen a few years ago, now flies at the county hall in Bodmin, on bank buildings, hotels and fishing boats. The *Western Morning News* I read over my breakfast in St Ives gave its support to a call by the Grand Bard of Cornwall for more people to fly the flag. 'It stirs many Cornish souls,' the editorial said. 'A notable aspect of the growth of Cornish consciousness has been the use and recognition of the cross of St Piran.'

The flag is carried by thousands of Cornishmen to county rugby matches. Rugby generates intense loyalty and people talk animatedly not just of rugby but of Cornish rugby. Male voice choirs and brass bands which flourished in the industrial era are also regarded as Cornish institutions. Festivals celebrate the Celtic past, the evidence of which is everywhere, especially in the names of churches. Two thousand people attend classes in the Cornish language, which is used in bardic ceremonies, and about fifty can speak it with some fluency; though a genuine revival of spoken Cornish seems as likely as the reconnection of a severed head.

Some assertions of Cornishness can appear cranky to outsiders. A resident of Ponsanooth, summoned for failing to complete a census form in 1992, pleaded not guilty on the ground that this would require him to say he was English. 'Our people are not descended from the Angles and Saxons so . . . we are most certainly not English.' In the 1970s I attended a sitting of the stannary parliament in Lostwithiel, an attempt by Cornish enthusiasts to revive the ancient rights and privileges of tin miners. A diplomat from the Cuban Embassy arrived to observe this blow for independence by the oppressed Cornish. Eccentric as they seem, such events are perhaps the surface ripple on a larger pool of Cornish feeling awaiting more realistic and satisfying forms of expression.

Judging by parentage and birthplace, about half the people of Cornwall count as natives. The accents of many hotel and guest house proprietors are northern; but most of the people who have come to settle, who were enchanted by Cornwall on holiday, or have fled from the rat race, are from the south-east of England. Some claim a Cornish forebear, others describe themselves as 'adopted Cornish'.

Not long ago Cornwall county council stated in its official guide that, culturally speaking, the Tamar is a national boundary. Cornish people often feel themselves at the bottom left-hand corner, and the Tamar remains the decisive frontier, symbolic and psychological. It marks not only the division between Devon and Cornwall but, to some minds, the frontier with England. A man I talked to, as we looked out at the yellow beaches of St Ives, said Cornishness should not be difficult to understand. 'We feel different', he said, 'because we are different.' But that was as far as it went with him. To say he was Cornish was enough.

Cornishness has something to do with distance and isolation. Partly it lies in the belief that Cornwall has suffered economically; or, as it was put to me, 'We are disadvantaged. Who are we who are disadvantaged? We are the Cornish.' Cornish people are irritated by their inclusion in a shapeless 'West Country', the eastern border of which is hazily drawn, and are sensitive about being in the grip of a monster they know as Devonwall, in which Plymouth and Exeter exercise control. Nor do they like being combined with part of Devon in a European parliamentary constituency. They feel the lack of a Cornish university and a movement is growing to secure one. They resent having local television beamed from Plymouth across the Tamar, as if they were 'the people over there'. Significantly, the BBC's Radio Cornwall is the most popular local radio station in Britain. It has become an expression and reflection of Cornishness; and also a creator of it, a Cornish institution.

Mercy that Does not Quail

In Penzance the amateur operatic society was performing *The Pirates of Penzance*. The Long John Silver pirate with his bandanna, eye-patch and parrot is a commercial motif in Cornwall and the Cornish independent radio station has just such a logo and is called 'Pirate FM'. Brutality was long ago brushed by romance and I saw a Pirates Hotel, a Wreckers Bar as well as the usual Smugglers Arms. We are not yet ready for a Cocaine Runners Arms.

At Newlyn, Cornwall's largest fishing port, there were mugs for sale inscribed 'British Fishermen Are Great'. More than thirty fishing boats lay alongside the quays and flew the Canadian flag to show solidarity with Canada in its quarrel with Spain over fishing rights. For both Cornish and Canadian fishermen, Spanish trawlers are a common enemy. Some boats flew the flag of St Piran stitched to the Canadian maple leaf. A fisherman grumbled, 'The Spaniards are backed by their government – but our so-called government doesn't stick up for us.'

There's a jut of the chin at Newlyn, a stubbornness illustrated by the plaque on the quay commemorating the voyage a fishing boat made from Newlyn to Westminster in 1939. It carried a petition to Parliament to save old houses in Newlyn from the demolition plans of Penzance council. The petition succeeded and Newlyn kept its history intact.

The same pugnacity was displayed in the little local newspaper I bought. An article began arrestingly 'Bugger objectivity . . .' It went on to describe a former inhabitant of the district as 'an inept, inconsiderate, unintelligent and greedy bastard . . . shifty, crooked, amoral, dishonest, breathtakingly greedy, not too bright but cunning.'

I walked down to the lifeboat station at Sennen, a mile from the cliffs of Land's End. The lifeboat sat on its slipway ready to go in an instant. The coxswain and his crew, alerted by pagers and rockets, are usually on their way within fifteen minutes of being called. To my eye the boat was the toughest craft that ever went to sea, an acknowledgement of the sea's power, with heavy rails and thick steel doors, its hull made with kevlar and carbon fibre. If capsized it would right itself in five seconds. It was called *The Four Boys*, in memory of four schoolboys drowned near Land's End, and a memorial fund raised a hundred thousand pounds towards the lifeboat's cost of six hundred and fifty thousand. The Royal National Lifeboat Institution spends fifty-five million pounds a year to run the oldest national life-saving service in the world. It is one of the largest charities, and determinedly independent, wanting not a penny from the government. Three-fifths of its money comes from legacies.

Winston Churchill held up lifeboatmen as exemplars of British qualities. 'The lifeboat drives on with a mercy that does not quail in the presence of death. . . a testimony that valour and virtue have not perished in the British race.' This is true. It is a voluntary service and, although more than four hundred life-boatmen have perished, places in a lifeboat crew are coveted. Ever since Grace Darling helped her father save nine lives from a wreck in a storm off Northumberland in 1838 our lifeboat service has represented our better, humane selves.

Churchill placed the lifeboat in a stern British code of discipline and gallantry at sea which includes the tradition that in the event of shipwreck women and children go first into the life-boats and the captain is the last to leave. In 1854 four hundred and fifty-four officers and men of the sinking troopship HMS *Birkenhead* stood in unflinching ranks, and drowned, while the women and children were saved in the boats. The doomed pursers of the *Titanic* shook hands with their shipmates and said: 'Goodbye, old man' – and the captain is said to have shouted heroically in the final moments: 'Be British!' These examples make us feel we have a monopoly on the tradition of selflessness at sea and we feel superior when we read of foreign passenger ships foundering and the officers and men leading the race to the lifeboats.

At the end of the day I came out of the rain and into a pub. It was all that a Cornish pub should be, hard by the harbour, snug and warm, with a beamed black ceiling and dark walls made interesting by framed drawings of local faces. The lights were dim and people were playing dominoes. Two men came in and one ordered a pint of beer for his companion and, for himself, two Diet Cokes in a pint glass, with ice. Another man standing at the bar cocked an eyebrow at this. The man with the cola felt obliged to explain.

'Dodgy pancreas.'

'You used to sink 'em, though,' said his companion, taking a long pull at his pint.

'Dodgy pancreas now.'

'You used to sink 'em with the best of 'em,' said his companion, draining his glass, savouring the beer.

By the Ninth Green

Next day I walked along a sandy path to St Enodoc's church. The morning was bright but a gale blew from the Atlantic, over the Doom Bar and the estuary of the Camel River. Spray smoked from the ragged ridges of the waves and seas lunged against the distant rocks. A sign on the path warned that I was crossing a golf course and that balls were hit from the right. To be felled by a golf ball while walking to church would test the faith of any pilgrim.

St Enodoc's grows from its hollow in the down, within sight and sound of the sea, its thirteenth-century spire cocked to one side like an ear. It takes its name from another of those wandering Welsh saints. In the walled churchyard lie many sailors from ships wrecked along this coast, some drowned when their vessels disintegrated in the surf on the Doom Bar within a few yards of the haven. The church bell comes from an Italian ship driven ashore in 1875. A simple white memorial stands over the resting place of A Seaman of the Great War.

The church is a refuge, its thick walls shutting out the roar of gales. In the parish magazine there was an appeal for money so that candles and oil lights could be replaced by electricity. For more than a century St Enodoc's lay buried beneath an immense towan, a drift of sand, the steeple sticking out like a bent finger. A clergyman visited once a year to perform a service so that the building should not be considered abandoned, descending into it from the dune through a hatch in the roof. I imagined him abseiling in his cassock. The church was dug from its sand mountain in the 1860s.

Sir John Betjeman loved this part of Cornwall. He frequently expressed his nostalgia for his bucket-and-spade holidays – 'Blessed be St Enodoc, blessed be the wave' – and often wrestled here with matters of hope and faith. He died at Trebetherick, not far away, and is buried in St Enodoc's churchyard, his place of sanctuary, hard by the lych-gate and the tamarisk-feathered wall, beneath a slate stone facing the Atlantic. I bought a little guide book from the rack by the Norman font and when I opened it at home some days later it gave off the evocative cave odour of the damp church and brought to mind the stained-glass windows, small and tough against storms, the painted rood-screen, the smell of the bible open on the lectern at The Sermon on the Mount; and, most of all, the silence.

Merrie England

In the Somerset village of Batcombe, a pretty place of grey stone cottages among mazy lanes, Derek and Claire Blezard told me about a certain evening. They arrived home at dusk. As they approached their front door they saw a dark shape hanging on it. It was a dead badger.

They knew that some of the local people hated them. Glue had been squirted into the locks of their car and firework rockets had been launched from a hillside onto the roof of their home below. Insulting graffiti had been daubed on their walls. But the badger seemed primitive, a pagan curse.

Claire Blezard bought The Three Horseshoes in Batcombe when it was run down and making no money. She and Derek saw an opportunity and turned it into a pub-restaurant, serving candlelit dinners and family lunches. They welcomed children and built a playground. Making a virtue of Batcombe's remoteness, they put its latitude and longitude in their advertisements. They also changed the name from The Three Horseshoes to The Batcombe Inn, a risky thing to do because people often resent such changes. Some of the villagers promptly started a petition and gathered one hundred and fifty signatures protesting against the new name. Some said they would boycott the pub, and they did. The village was divided. 'Many folk in Batcombe are on our side,' Derek said, 'but I can't deny that others feel we have robbed them of something. The fact is, though, that the traditional English village pub, the spit-and-sawdust local with an old boy in a cloth-cap by the fire, is dying out. You can't make a living out of it. Thousands of pubs have closed because they've failed to keep up with changing tastes. Customers are more choosy these days and you have to offer a lot more. In any case, our bank manager wants to see us make a profit.'

It is a metropolitan myth that village life is idyllic. The attacks on the Blezards and the tensions in Batcombe led the vicar to appeal in the parish magazine for reconciliation. 'It hurts me to be aware of divisions. We have to be able to live in harmony . . . the unpleasantness with The Batcombe Inn has gone on too long.'

I asked one of the villagers about the row. 'It's the only pub in the village and people don't like the fact that it is no longer theirs, the village pub they knew, a place for a pint and a natter. Some remember when it had straw on the floor. Now they don't feel at ease and don't feel welcome. The pool table was taken out, you see, and people were upset about it. The people who nailed up the dead badger were venting their anger.' Derek Blezard said he had heard that one of his opponents, a woman, had been delighted by the badger incident and had said, 'Serve them jolly well right.'

The Blezards were more than newcomers. They brought to Batcombe the revolution that swept pubs throughout Britain in the 1990s. The traditional pub was redesigned to aim at a particular section of the market. The outcome of the changes is that some are quiet, and others have disco music, some ban children, some have nappy-changing rooms, some are temples of traditional beer, some are giant eating and drinking halls, some have open fires and dominoes, some are like continental cafés. In a break with British tradition, a number of pubs began to serve drinkable wine. One of the benefits of the revolution is that it is putting an end to the dreary, dirty, foodless pub, unwelcoming, with middens for lavatories and curmudgeons for landlords. A brewer told me that the days have passed when the British were grateful for anything.

But brewers can seem high-handed. I visited a pub in Surrey where they had decided to create a restaurant and sweep away the public bar where gamekeepers, farm workers and water bailiffs met for pints in their working clothes and boots – with their dogs. The villagers fought back and told the brewers that this would not do. The brewers retreated and redrew the design so that a man and his dog could continue to meet friends after work.

Pubs that have adapted to changing demands are prospering but hundreds of inns, especially in the countryside, have closed. The old pub on the green, the place where the cricket club and darts team and church bellringers meet, belongs to a fading tradition. It is a tradition worth defending where it is genuine, but as I was told by a villager at Batcombe, 'Many of the people who romanticize village life and the village green are incomers, escapers from cities, who do not understand that the country-side is at work. They like the idea of the village with its church and pub but they complain that the tractors are noisy. They complain when they get stuck behind herds of cows being driven down country lanes. They complain about hunting. They complain about the mud and the manure that sticks to their cars . . . and they drink at home.'

Bristol Fashion

A lovely aroma of seasoned timber rose from the riverside yard in Bristol. In the pale light of a winter afternoon I watched ship-wrights and carpenters at work on a replica of a fifteenth-century ship, the *Matthew*, fashioning oak, larch and pine. There was something moving in their endeavour, a faithfulness, the way they worked among the planks and spars, using techniques that were already old in medieval times.

The caravel they were shaping was not intended for a shel-tered museum life, but for adventure, for risk: it was being built to bend before storms in a crossing of the north Atlantic. Its construction was a work of imagination as well as of craftsman-ship, a leap across the centuries. Five hundred years ago, when the original *Matthew* was built, Bristol was prospering on the wool trade with Ireland and the Baltic and the local merchants had money to invest. In 1497 they weighed the dangers, con-sidered the profits, and put up the money to send John Cabot, a well-dressed Venetian navigator, on a voyage across the Atlantic in the hundred-ton *Matthew* with a Bristol crew of eighteen.

Cabot knew the world was a sphere and sailed in the belief that he would find China and the wealth of the east; but he landed in Newfoundland. He claimed it for King Henry VII and returned to the acclamation of Bristol's crowds, telling them how, on his voyage home, he had crossed the shallow waters of the Grand Banks, the immense breeding ground of cod, and his men scooped up the fish simply by lowering baskets into the sea. Cabot's voyage was the beginning of the Newfoundland fishery which attracted thousands of British fishermen well into the nineteenth century. Annealed by this distant-waters experience, such men were a vital pool of manpower for the Royal Navy. The dried and salt cod they brought home from the Grand Banks were a staple of the British winter diet for many years, so dry and salty that they needed rivers of beer to wash them down.

Bristolians were hoping that the recreated *Matthew* would be a symbol of renewal, a salute to the venturing tradition that made the city rich. The city certainly needed a leg-up. It was not that it had fallen on hard times, but it had run into economic difficulties and its situation was riskier than many people imagined. This was a surprise, for the name of Bristol has always suggested an ample, well-endowed city with generous vowels and a large collar-size.

After making its first fortunes from wool, Bristol grew wealthy on the East India trade, on privateering, tobacco and slavery, sherry, chocolate, paper and corn. The Bristol Commercial Rooms were opened in 1811 primarily for the conduct of the corn trade and the first president was John Macadam, the road builder. Business agreements were struck on the four stubby bronze pillars outside, known as nails; hence you paid on the nail. When I first knew the Rooms they were famous for their lunches, but now I found that they were closing because of the decline of the institution of lunch. Membership had dwindled because modern businessmen sip mineral water and eat salad and no longer address themselves to steak-and-kidney pudding, chops, spotted dick, treacle tart and claret. The Rooms were a temple of such benedictions.

Bristol is independent, with its own cultural resources, and has no need to look towards London. It is something of a capital itself, of the south-west region, even if that irritates other cities. It makes much of its living from financial services, education, electronics: more brains, less brawn. It has a prosperous look, with mellow Georgian streets and squares, Victorian terraces and dock buildings and warehouses that could garage an airship. It is a water city, with the river in the heart of the town. Within the natural boundary made by the limestone gorge of the River Avon lie Clifton's spacious streets and its grand down, perfect for flying kites.

For all its good looks, Bristol, like many British cities, was damaged from the late 1950s by hideous development, third-rate architecture and complacent leadership, so that some of its advantages were squandered. Among the self-inflicted wounds are nasty and discordant tower blocks in the heart of the city and brutalist façades which seem designed specifically to undermine the spirit. The city crassly permitted the insertion of an ugly office block among the seventeenth-century houses in King Street. Powerful business corporations, who do not care much what cities look like, have not had much opposition. Some of the housing estates are corroded by high unemployment, drugs and illiteracy.

I said to George Ferguson, an architect in Bristol, that although we now shudder at the tower blocks, the planners and councillors who permitted them were no doubt well-meaning. Yes, he said, but in the 1960s we were all gullible and adhered to the belief that European and American ideas of architecture could be transferred to this country, which is on a different scale. In Britain four-fifths of the people live in houses and a fifth in flats, but in Europe it is the reverse; and in America, with certain exceptions, people do not live in the hearts of cities. People followed fashion, he went on, and were seduced by photographs of soaring new-age towers. The buildings seemed to solve economic problems and were relatively cheap. There was a stampede for them at a time when the car lobby was more persuasive than the conservationists. Planners and developers lacked a sense of reality, believing that a city could be designed around the car, when they should have been finding ways of making the car fit into the city.

He said the awful towers should be knocked down as part of any renewal and there should be a demolition 'hit list', an unpopularity poll in which the public name their most-hated buildings. Liking or disliking buildings is not the privilege of architects, he added. People are more aware of style in architecture today, more questioning; and the Prince of Wales's speech about 'monstrous carbuncles' of buildings had had, overall, a good effect. Design is getting better and there are improvements on the badly-designed housing estates which have wrecked parts of suburban Britain. Bristol, meanwhile, is in the process of renewing its centre. It wants commerce back in the heart where it belongs. Too much has been sucked out by a vast shopping mall built on the edge of the city. Such out-of-town malls are as fashionable and seductive as the tower blocks of the 1960s and 1970s, and in many cases even more destructive.

'People must be guided back into the city to work,' George Ferguson said, 'where they can be part of a lively place, where the fun is. You can't have that out in the desert.'

He came to Bristol as a university student in 1965 and fell in love with it. 'It is a good, elegant place. I like being part of something that is rough as well as beautiful because that is reality. I am strongly conscious of the deprivation in parts of the city, the bad housing and poverty. As an architect I want to make things better. I was irritated by the lousy developments of the 1960s and 1970s, the office blocks and the roads smashing through. The authorities were going to allow a hotel to be built in the Avon gorge, but that, fortunately, was stopped by the government. Bristol had to be saved from itself. Planning *laissez-faire* does not serve people.'

So I asked him if cities needed enlightened despots. 'No,' he said, 'inspired guidance and a lot of public participation.'

The cafés and pubs around the University were crowded with students. Gaunt and shaggy young men sat in doorways, blankets around their shoulders, holding out their hands; and more than a few people slipped them a coin. 'Bristolians are good-hearted,' I was told. 'Beggars and travellers like the south-west because people are fairly kind to them and it is warmer here than in the north.'

The University's tower, which is sometimes thought by strangers to be a cathedral, was built by the Wills tobacco family. J.B. Priestley noted during his *English Journey* in the 1930s that 'the smoke from a million Gold Flakes solidifies into a new Gothic Tower'. He toured the Wills cigarette factory and was impressed. Mass production here left him with an impression 'not of miserable slavery, not even of grim soulless industry. But perhaps the kindly influence of Nicotina herself was at work.' The factory closed in 1990, with the loss of five thousand jobs.

Nightingales

It was a short walk from the yard where the *Matthew* was being built to St Mary Redcliffe, the parish church already four centuries old when John Cabot sailed. Queen Elizabeth, who visited Bristol for a week in 1574, admired its beauty. A municipal road scheme in the 1960s left the church in its present wretched setting, a crime for which no one was pilloried and pelted; but Bristolians are working to restore its lost dignity.

In the church I thought myself alone in the gathering gloom until I heard beautiful voices raised in song. I saw two girls in the pews singing their hearts out, their voices clear and soaring. It was enchanting and haunting, a gift. They sang for about fifteen minutes and when they stopped the sound seemed to hang in the air, as if the church itself were savouring it. They signed the visitors' book and left. I went to look at it and saw that they were from Hungary, nightingales on their travels.

An Ice-cream Hour

When Queen Elizabeth I visited Gloucestershire the itinerary was planned by her vice-chamberlain, who wrote to mayors along the route. A court harbinger and his staff went ahead to make arrangements for accommodation and feeding, for the slaughter of deer, oxen and sheep and the gathering of oysters and fruit. The Queen travelled in a convoy of scores of wagons and hundreds of baggage horses accompanied by platoons of guards, managers, courtiers and minions. On hot dry days the dust plume must have been visible for many miles. The visit to Gloucestershire, as with all of Elizabeth's progresses in England, made an unforgettable impact on the people. There was, on one hand, the sheer scale of the enterprise and its costly magnificence; there was, on the other, the Queen's own enthusiasm, her rapport with the crowds which streamed to see her, her understanding of esteem and the mystique of majesty. She showed herself, took pains, looked lively and attentive through long entertainments and speeches, put nervous officials at their ease, radiated enjoyment and won hearts in the cause of the unity and stability of her country.

More than four hundred years later, when it was proposed that Queen Elizabeth II should visit Gloucestershire, the key figure in the arrangements was the Lord-Lieutenant of the county. A Lord-Lieutenant forms a link between Buckingham Palace and his county. He ensures that when the Queen visits his territory she has a balanced programme, that over the years she sees the spectrum of culture, industry and education, that the royal magic is judiciously sprinkled. A Lord-Lieutenant is usually a genial official, often with a military background, so that he understands protocol and uniforms. He keeps himself trim in spite of a busy lunching programme and learnt long ago that, when wearing spurs, it is easier to walk upstairs than down.

On this occasion the Lord-Lieutenant telephoned the managing director of the Birds Eye Wall's ice-cream factory at Gloucester. 'The Queen would like to visit you. Would that be convenient?' The proposed date soon became The Day, the fast-approaching destination. Will she need a bathroom, who will ensure the royal standard does not fly upside down, what will be done about parking, invitations, security, carpets, teacups, photographs, flowers and umbrellas? The Queen is someone to put on a clean white shirt for. Hair-cutters, nail-buffers, frock-sellers, gardeners, painters and cleaners must play their parts. A royal visit is a catalyst that heats up the trouser-press, clears the clutter, mends the gutter. It is the state visit of a mother-in-law. Behind the dry announcement in the Court Circular 'Her Majesty this afternoon visited . . .' lie weeks of planning and an earnest determination to eliminate banana skins.

The shape of the tour was agreed at a meeting between the managing director, the Lord-Lieutenant, the Queen's assistant private secretary, a royal bodyguard and a local police officer. The visit would be exactly one hour. The Queen and the Duke of Edinburgh wished to meet as many of the factory's staff as possible, the people who produced the ice-cream, lollies and chocolate gâteaux. A cross-section of staff, chosen by age, gender and race, was selected to have tea with the Queen and the Duke. The tour route was walked and timed. 'Every footstep,' said the managing director. A final programme was accepted by the Lord-Lieutenant and approved by Buckingham Palace. Small points of detail emerged. No, the Queen would not need to withdraw. No, it was not her custom to sample the product. Yes, she would sign the visitors' book. Yes, she would plant a tree: please make sure the soil is dry and sifted.

The next step was a dress rehearsal, the Queen acted by the managing director's wife, complete with hat and handbag, accompanied by a major-general roped in to play the Duke. Under the company's strict hygiene rules – no watches, no nose studs, nail-biters to wear gloves – white coats and hats were obligatory. New coats were ordered for the royal party and an ironing board for a final pressing. One of the staff said, 'We've been told not to speak unless spoken to, but I will definitely give the Queen and the Duke a smile.' Another said, 'I don't care one way or the other: the Queen doesn't mean much to me.'

The manufacturing services manager walked me around the royal route, including the shining chocolate gâteaux production lines. 'I see this visit as a project: the Queen is a package and we are processing it. The rubber matting in the doorway will have to be covered because high heels get trapped in it. We'll switch off those wall phones. The Queen will be presented with a posy by my granddaughters, who have been practising their curtsies for weeks. I'll make sure the royal standard flies the right way up and that there's artificial grass for the Queen to walk on when she plants the tree. I'm not worried about the timetable. We've been told the Queen has been doing this for so long that she has a mental clock and knows exactly where she is on a route.'

An ugly old fence was replaced and the factory, already spotless, was being given an extra holystoning. More security staff were taken on. Numbered tickets were issued to guests. Children from the neighbouring infants' school were invited. The production manager was chosen as the Queen's principal guide. He was master of such facts as that a year's production of chocolate gâteaux would stretch from Gloucester to Cairo. Another rehearsal was held. A Territorial Army cadet practised opening the door of the royal car with his left hand, while saluting with his right. More white coats for the security men were ordered. A royal standard arrived from Buckingham Palace. A spade was delivered for the tree-planting and was polished. A red chestnut tree arrived from a nursery. The company's best bone china tea service was selected and more catering staff recruited. Umbrellas were ordered in case of rain. A royal driver toured the route. Because snow was forecast for the day, a snowplough was ordered to be on standby. Men put on their best suits. A woman put on her second-best dress: 'My best one's too skimpy to meet the Queen in.'

As the Queen and Duke arrived the royal standard was broken out and flew right side up. The schoolchildren hurrahed and waved flags. Sunlight shone on the Lord-Lieutenant's sword. His wife wore a hat with a brim that could have sheltered two. The Queen and Duke put on their white coats and set off. The people were met and the tea was drunk. The Queen planted the tree with the sifted soil and she and the Duke talked animatedly to the crowd before departing. The schoolchildren waved until the plum-coloured royal car was out of sight.

People gathered to talk. Didn't it go well? The Queen said this and the Duke said that. Weren't they friendly? Really nice! So natural!

'They must have talked to three hundred people,' said the managing director. 'Nothing went wrong.' The production manager said: 'She gave the impression she really wanted to be here. She was fascinated by the way we assemble the chocolate gâteaux.' The personnel manager summed up: 'She left us all with a warm glow.'

It was an unexceptional royal visit and did not make the national newspapers or television. It was simply the royal river, rolling on as it always has, through crisis, doubt and discontent; the Queen dutiful, worn, enduring, inscrutable, the steward of tradition, the constant, through change unchanging.

Coffee with the Abbot

Depending on the quarry from which they are taken, the stones of Cotswold villages have biscuity shades, from shortbread to digestive. In the slanted light of late afternoon, they exude the glow of certain opals. I remembered, as I passed by Prinknash Abbey, the enjoyable lunch I had been given by the hospitable monks there some years before. In those days the thirty-seven monks still occupied the old abbey house, a manor, partly four-teenth-century, which had been a Royalist headquarters in the Civil War. Holding their joy in reserve, they were awaiting completion of their new abbey, the foundation-stone of which had been laid more than thirty years earlier. The guestmaster took me around the nearly-completed building and showed me the monks' cells, which had tiled floors, wash-basins and razor points. 'Some American monks would say we were roughing it a bit without individual bathrooms,' he said. 'The belief that monks live a hard life in cold cells is mistaken. If people think we have straw on our beds they are just being romantic. We do not have Slumberlands, but there is no point in going to absurd lengths of frugality. Discipline in our life stems not from the physical conditions but from the daily routine and the effort we have to make to live together in harmony. We are men of dif-fering temperament and background in a small community and we have to live with one another's idiosyncrasies. If we allowed the annoying things to get on our nerves, life would be impos-sible. It is sometimes difficult to suppress feelings, but that is part of the discipline, and so is the pattern of life which occasionally conflicts with the way we would like to live. We are united, however, in the common purpose, to live the lives of Prinknash monks.'

I was invited, at lunch, to sit next to the Abbot. I had imag-ined that I would be able to interview him, but I soon saw that the monks did not talk during the meal. The refectory, however, was not silent. A duty monk stood and read from a book over the gentle clatter of cutlery. A space on the refectory wall, where once a painting had hung, reminded the monks of their blessed stroke of fortune: they had sent the picture, by the sixteenth-century Venetian artist Jacopo Bassano, to auction in London, expecting it to fetch a few thousand pounds for their new abbey. Instead, it was sold for more than a quarter of a million pounds, nearly half the cost of the building. I had my talk after lunch. The Abbot and a number of monks took me to a small room for coffee. One or two of the monks lit cigarettes and inhaled with expressions of bliss. The coffee was poured from a veteran cracked pot into little cups with crenellated rims and fissures through which the coffee welled like tears. My memory of the talk we had is of the happiness and merriment of amiable men. The reading in the refectory, incidentally, was from Robert Southey's *Life of Nelson*: that man again.

4

Kingdoms May Go

I walked to the source of the Thames in Gloucestershire, following a footpath beside meadows and ploughed fields and walls
of Cotswold stone. On the way I picked a sweet apple from a
tree.

If they were cemented together, all the volumes of rapturous
verse about the noble and silver Thames would be enough to
dam the river at Greenwich; but at the river's source there is little
to sharpen a pencil for. The spring bubbles up only after heavy
rain and all I saw was a scatter of pebbles in a parched hollow
beneath a tall old ash.

Compared with awesome rivers like the Nile and the Ganges,
the Thames is a mere stream, but its splendour is measured in
other ways. It is, after all, the senior river: there is no Father
Severn or Father Trent. Poets' tributes to Father Thames
acknowledge the significance of the river and the city to which
it gave birth. London was for centuries the largest city in the
world, the supreme centre of maritime trade and the core of the
greatest empire. It grew in the first place because its river faced

Europe and was readily accessible from the continent. In Roman times it bloomed into the strongest and richest settlement in Britain and became unchallengeably powerful. Its position in the south-east corner of the British oblong, its distance from the other countries and regions of Britain, its pre-eminence and glamour, its metropolitan might and hauteur, have ever been a factor in the British story. As Philip Howard, a shrewd biographer of the Thames, has written, London still has 'an unbalancing gravitational pull on the people and resources of the rest of the country, consequently being partly responsible for the notorious regional and class divisions of Britain'.

I left the source and went to Lechlade where the Thames gains maturity and personality, and where Oxfordshire, Wiltshire, Gloucestershire and Berkshire meet. Here the river is much more like a painter's English scene. A stone bridge is in the heart of it and there are pensive anglers beneath green umbrellas, willows reaching down to brush the clear water and cattle cropping the meadows. The flatlands of Wiltshire lie to the south, a blur of distant spinneys and poplar groves. In the small Georgian town, antique shops sell Victorian thimbles, pre-war motoring manuals, cigarette cards of 1930s cricketers and old school desks, ink-stained and doodled, with white china inkwells, evoking the miseries of algebra on sleepy summer afternoons.

The Cygnet Ring

I braised beside the Thames under the weight of noon, imagined beer and wished for a palanquin. A flotilla of six long varnished skiffs came into my view, in slow motion it seemed, rounding the trees on the riverbank bend. They formed a brilliant Tudor spectacle, a colour plate from a child's book, as if princes and their indolent friends were about their summer pleasures on the generous river. I strained my ears for the sound of a lute.

A gaudy heraldic pennant fluttered from the stern of each boat. The watermen at the oars wore shirts of red, white and blue, with caps to match, and the curved blades of the oars, painted in the same colours, dipped like brushes into the brown water, leaving sparkling hoops eddying in the skiffs' wakes. At their approach a dozen foraging ducks ceased their nibbling and darted towards the trailing strands of willow, tutting at the inconvenience. Herons in their slate-blue uniforms stood in the manner of impassive doormen, as if they would refuse entry to the rushes to creatures not properly dressed.

The watermen rowed into a lock to ascend the river and shipped their oars with a clatter. They were doughty and strong-armed, likely lads in their fifties and sixties, a few of them older than that, their cheeks florid from exertion and exposure to the sun. Convivial was the word, a chortle of watermen, and they laughed a lot and enjoyed their raillery. Some of them reached up for pints of bitter handed down in dimpled glass mugs from an accompanying launch. They raised their drinks in their fists and called out 'Aye, aye!' and 'Cheers!' and winked at spectators and each other.

Water rats of a sort, messing about most agreeably in boats, they were engaged in the improbable ritual of the annual swan voyage. For a whole week in this hot July they were rowing upriver from Sunbury to Abingdon in search of swans and cygnets; for they were the swan-uppers of England.

Swan-upping is a pageant of skiffs and swansdown, of flags and feathered caps, an exotic and eccentric spectacle conducted largely for its own sake and for the enjoyable perpetuation of a tradition at least seven centuries old. It is a caper conducted with dignity, as summery as strawberries; and, since the original purpose of it has vanished, it is, strictly speaking, as pointless as it is charming. But that is not to say it does not have some value.

'A bit of England,' one of the swan-uppers said to me.

'Old England,' his companion put in.

He meant Olde.

'It's yer 'eritage, innit?' another said earnestly. 'It belongs to the Thames. And you know what the Thames is?'

I waited for his answer. I had no wish to spoil his moment.

'The artery of England.'

He let the phrase hang there, for effect.

Having chanced upon a tribal rite, foreign tourists looked on, bemused and doubtful. *Les Anglais* . . . you could never be sure about them. Children waved and asked their fathers what the men were doing and the fathers, not at all sure – for who knows anything about swan-upping? – said: 'Watch and you'll see.'

When the lock had filled, the far gates opened onto a new stretch of the river, more willows and water birds, and the oarsmen bent in the slow rhythm of cellists. In the stern of three of the skiffs there sat enthroned the chief swan officers, panjandrums in the braided blazers of their profession, river-kings, magisterial, straight-backed and alert, eyeing the rushy riverbanks ahead. The accompanying launches, a cricket-pitch length astern, sported swan-shaped vases full of pink and white blossoms on their foredecks.

Quite soon, a large family party of swans and downy grey cygnets was sighted. The cry went from skiff to skiff – 'All up!' The first word in this jargon of the ancient mystery was elongated into a kind of howl.

'A-a-a-ll up!'

The rowers hauled at the oars and the skiffs sped quickly to their quarry. The trick was to get the boats to overlap each other, forming a fence around the swans to prevent their escape. As the boats jostled by the bank there was splashing, a rattle of oars and shouts of 'We've got 'em' and 'Watch out, George' and 'Over a bit' and 'Go on, grab the bugger.'

The cygnets were two or three months old and too young to fly. They were deftly spooned into the skiffs where they lay still, squeaking softly, puzzled, their legs tied. The parent swans were scooped up by strong brown hands, a muscular arm under the belly. The legs were quickly secured with twine, an action that locked the wing joints and prevented the wings flapping, rendering the birds docile.

'You have to show the swan who's in charge,' one of the men said, 'and contain those wings quick or you'll get a black eye or a broken finger.'

The swans sat with expressions of affronted dignity. The rowers inspected their beaks to identify them. This was the heart of it all, for swan-upping is entirely a matter of identification. In the Middle Ages swans were a source of food and ownership of them, like the possession of deer, was a mark of wealth, property and prestige. In 1274 a goose cost five pence and a swan cost three shillings, seven times as much. The penalties for stealing or killing them were severe; and as late as the mid-nineteenth century a man was transported for seven years for taking a swan.

For their regal appearance as well as their value the Crown claimed swans as royal birds, much as the sturgeon was deemed a royal fish. Swans were roasted for banquets and their feathers were used to stuff palace mattresses and chairs. The Crown granted the right to own a 'game' of swans as a privilege; and on the Thames today the only legal owners are the monarch and two London livery companies, the Vintners and the Dyers, whose exercise of the privilege was well established by the fifteenth century. The Vintners have a pair of swans as supporters of their coat of arms.

Swan-upping began as an annual round-up and census in which the swanherds of the king and the livery companies travelled the river and marked the new crop of cygnets on the beak so that their ownership could be easily determined. Marks were once elaborate, but a century ago they were simplified at the request of Queen Alexandra who thought that ornate beak-nicking might be cruel.

Cygnets claimed by the Vintners' Company are marked by two small nicks, the cygnita, cut quickly with a scalpel, one on each side of the beak. The name of the London pub called The Swan With Two Necks is a corruption of The Swan With Two Nicks. The Dyers mark their cygnets with a single nick on the right side, while the Queen's have no nick at all. Thus the cygnets of unmarked parents remain unmarked. If there is a mixed marriage, that is if the cob, the male, belongs to one owner and the pen, the female, to another, the cygnets are shared.

Once the swans and cygnets were secured in the skiffs the watermen called out the identity of them.

'Queen's pen.'

'Vintners' cob.'

'Two for the Queen.'

'One for the Dyers.'

After a few minutes the swans were launched back in the

water and swam off, as if muttering 'Really!' and 'The impertinence!' – for they are haughty and cantankerous birds and seem to know that they are celebrities of the river, flattered by poets and with roles in many a legend. The cygnets hurried after them like feathered pedalos.

Swan-uppers are boat builders, launch operators and ferrymen who have spent their lives on the Thames. They count it an honour to be invited into the brotherhood of swan-uppers; and the upping makes a blissful week out. Many are keen rowers and by custom are Freemen of the Watermen and Lightermen's Company. As such they are the descendants of the once-mighty tribe of Thames ferrymen which flourished when the river was London's main highway, when it lacked bridges and echoed to the shout of 'Oars!' from numerous landing stairs and piers. There were forty thousand of these rumbustious and ribald men in Elizabethan times and, until 1751, when Westminster Bridge was built, there was only one bridge over the Thames, and they had the river to themselves.

The three senior swan-upping officials are paid an honorarium. The Queen's Swan Marker, appointed by the Royal Household, wears a scarlet blazer with brass buttons, and a cap. The Dyers' man wears a blue blazer. The Vintners' Swan Marker has a bottle-green blazer with rings on the cuffs and swan badges on the lapels, a long swan feather pinned rakishly to his peaked cap.

'Swan-upping, you see, is like Trooping the Colour,' said Bill Colley, the Vintners' Marker. 'The original purpose has gone, but people like to see it and we like to do it. It does have its uses, though. It was the swan-uppers who first sounded the warning when the swan population fell rapidly. The problem was lead: swans were eating small fishing weights which poisoned them, ruined their digestive systems, leaving them to starve to death. They were in danger of becoming extinct on the Thames. Because of the publicity the fishermen started turning to other metals for weights, so we see much less poisoning these days. As the Swan Marker I'm on call round the clock to help sick and injured swans. People who see one in distress will tell the police who call me to remove hooks and other fishing tackle from beaks and feet.' He said he wished fishermen were a lot more careful with their gear.

The menace of lead poisoning led to a study of Thames swans by the Institute of Field Ornithology at Oxford. These days two ornithologists travel with the swan-uppers and each swan is checked, ringed and weighed.

The oarsmen entered another lock and while they waited for the chamber to fill some of them sipped glasses of milk into which they had poured a measure of rum. 'Old swan-upping drink,' one explained.

Out on the river again they rowed hard and constructed a thirst and an appetite. They tied up at the steps of a pub and disembarked with jokes and chuckles. A sumptuous lunch was set on tables in the back bar and pints of bitter were waiting and the staff were smiling. I had lunch on the terrace under a parasol with others of the accompanying party. When I went in to the bar the plates were being cleared away and the swan-uppers broke into song: 'Who were you with Last Night?' and 'Hello, Hello, who's your Lady Friend?' At last, on the cry of 'A-a-a-ll up!' they drained their glasses and left the pub in jolly mood. Into the skiffs they clambered and off they rowed in search of more swans. A cob, a pen and four cygnets were soon sighted and in the excitement of cornering them one of the swan-uppers fell into the river with a grand splash and was hauled aboard a launch and wrapped in a rug as one of the Swan Markers raised his eyes to the sky.

Late in the afternoon the flotilla entered Romney Lock at Windsor. The skiffs were arranged, gunwale to gunwale, like fish in a box, for another ritual. As the lock filled and the skiffs rose, the crews put on their blazers and straightened their caps. The Queen's Swan Marker, as master of ceremonies, took out a fancy wooden rack holding twenty sparkling glasses and filled each one with whisky, a decent measure. Taking care not to rock the boats, the swan-uppers stood, raised their elbows and toasted the Queen.

By my observation, the whisky gave them that vital little spurt of energy to carry them into Windsor, the end of that day's leg. The skiffs were hoisted from the river and stored in a boathouse and the watermen set off to a hotel to discuss, long into the evening, the upping of the swans, for after the swans are upped the beers are downed.

Next day, members of the Vintners' Company went out in a launch to watch, continuing the tradition of a corporate festive jaunt on the river. The Vintners used to eat swan at their annual swan feast in February, but for many years now no swan has been slaughtered for eating and the main course is goose. At the feast the Swan Master presents the roast bird to the Master of the Vintners' Company and says: 'For the delectation of your guests.' And the Master replies: 'Let them be served, Mr Swan.'

The Vintners' Company is one of the twelve 'great' livery companies of the City of London, others being classed as 'minor'. Many companies were established in medieval times. They were trade guilds, known as misteries, from the Italian word for a trade, and were organized partly to compete with the foreign merchants who found London so profitable. Many had their origins in religious brotherhoods founded to give their members proper burials and to say prayers for their souls. The companies' grand halls, medieval robes and banquets, their customs, pageants, masters, wardens and beadles, are survivors of an age when these companies commanded the commerce of London. They elected the aldermen, the City's ruling élite, who in turn chose the Lord Mayor; and they did their best to keep foreigners out. Rivalry between companies was often fierce, sometimes deadly, and caused riots in the streets. After particularly vicious fighting between the Fishmongers and the Skinners the ringleaders were hanged.

The Vintners' Company has maintained its base on the banks of the Thames for more than six hundred years. It is at the place where wine was first landed in Roman times. After the collapse of Rome, the drinking of wine, important in Christian ritual, spread with Christianity and many vines were planted in monasteries. The wine trade between England and France burgeoned after the Norman Conquest; and Henry II's marriage to Eleanor of Aquitaine in 1152 gave England access to the wines of Bordeaux and Gascony, the beginning of the passionate affair with claret. London wine merchants grew in power, and, significantly, London's representative at the signing of Magna Carta in 1215 was a Vintner. English merchant shipping was built on the export of wool and the import of wine and the ships were measured by the number of tuns of wine they could carry, a tun being a cask of two hundred and fifty gallons. Wine fleets sailed for France twice a year, and as well as cloth they carried grain because Bordeaux so devoted itself to slaking the English thirst that it stopped planting corn in order to grow more vines.

In the fourteenth century the Vintners' Company won a monopoly of the Bordeaux trade. It controlled the price of wine, known as the assize, which was fixed at the assize court. Like other guilds it had an interest in setting and monitoring the quality of goods, workmanship, prices, wages and working conditions; and it set the standards by which apprentices were trained. It established a wine police whose officers searched taverns and checked that wine was wholesome, that it was not watered, was served in approved standard measures, that old wine was not sold in new bottles and that taverns closed when church bells rang at nine o'clock. Innkeepers who overcharged were fined and jailed. A history of the company records that in 1364 a taverner who sold unsound wine had it poured over his head and was expelled from the Vintners for five years. The company often quarrelled with the Crown, which wanted an ever-larger share of the profits.

As their power waned, the livery companies endowed schools, scholarships and almshouses. They were thus in the position of demonstrating that they did good works when their political enemies in the 1880s demanded their abolition on the grounds that they were parasites and eaters of lavish dinners. A Royal Commission exonerated them. Today the one hundred livery companies dispense more than twenty million pounds a year to charities, and still eat sumptuous dinners.

Few liverymen today have much direct connection with the trades that spawned the companies: there are not many bowyers, armourers and horners. The Vintners' Company, however, retains strong links with the wine trade and sponsors wine education and apprenticeships. It also enforces European Union wine laws, in much the same way that it policed the trade in the fourteenth century; and it supports charities which help individuals ruined by drink.

'The Company pays its taxes and does good works,' said Brigadier Gregory Read, the Clerk of the Vintners' Company. 'It is a vehicle of tradition and has an inherent gentlemanliness. Many of the male employees are former servicemen, so that within the Company you have the public school and the army translated to a different milieu. I rather admire the Englishness of it, its hierarchical nature. It is not necessary but that is how it is. The Company is also very English in its concern for regalia, ritual and heritage and it takes pride in doing things properly. Indeed, we talk a lot about performing ceremonies in the correct fashion and maintaining traditions. In our processions men go ahead to clear the way with brooms; and people hold nosegays. I know it sounds bizarre, but it re-creates something that was real.

'Ritual is necessary in the English psyche. The members of the Court of the Vintners' Company adore the ceremonial side and the sense of belonging. The swan-upping is part of the English thing, isn't it? For us it is an excuse for an outing, a junket. It has no practical merit or value these days, though there is now the scientific purpose of checking the swan population. But do you really need a group of chaps in blazers and hats to spend a week doing it? Best not to ask the question. Just enjoy it.'

The Keys of England

The black cobbles by the Bloody Tower gleamed in the dim yellow light of a lamp. It was almost ten o'clock, January and very cold, a thin mist drifting over the river. Drawing a shivering huddle of us into the spirit of the place, a Yeoman Warder, crowned by a black Tudor bonnet and warm in his long scarlet coat, spoke of the ghosts we might see; and if any place is haunted this should be. Behind us, the river lapped softly beneath Traitors' Gate. In the sepulchral ambience of this gate, shivers have causes other than cold. Up these steps and into the gloom of the English kremlin stumbled the guilty and unfortunate on their way to imprisonment, torture and the axe. The passage of time has not made it merely picturesque. Its horrors are part of the attraction. 'Hideous and barbaric,' Nikolai Karamzin, a Russian traveller, wrote of it in 1790. 'Who', he wondered, 'will love the English after reading its history?'

'What you will see here tonight', said the Yeoman Warder in a strong London voice, 'is a military ceremony that has been going on for more than seven hundred years. It is not a spectacle for your benefit. It would take place even if the public were not here.'

A guardsman, ramrod-straight, stood across the road in bearskin and scarlet tunic, the bulbous caps of his boots highly polished. He shouldered his rifle, marched off, turned after a few yards and marched back, stamping his feet, to resume his place by the gate. The Chief Yeoman Warder appeared in the gloomy archway of the Bloody Tower, carrying a lantern and keys. A squad of four guardsmen formed and marched with him towards the Middle and Byward Towers on our left. The measured trat-trat-trat faded and was swallowed in the darkness. Silence. The Chief Yeoman Warder was locking the outer gates.

Just before the clock struck ten, he and his escort returned, trat-trat-trat. The sentry by the Bloody Tower sprang to life, like a clockwork soldier wound up and suddenly released. His chin jutted. He levelled his rifle at the approaching party, the short bayonet glinting. The guardsmen halted with a drumroll of nailed boots.

'Halt!' shouted the sentry. 'Who comes there?'

'The keys,' answered the Chief Yeoman Warder, with all the confidence of a man on important business.

'Whose keys?' demanded the sentry dramatically. His tone implied that, Chief Yeoman Warder or not, he would not allow passage to any old keys.

'Queen Elizabeth's keys,' responded the Chief Yeoman Warder, in a voice of unshakeable authority.

The sentry paused for a sliver of a moment.

'Pass keys,' he said, stepping back and withdrawing his rifle. 'And all's well.'

The keys party marched stiffly into the gateway. The Chief

Yeoman Warder passed the keys to the waiting Governor of the Tower. Guardsmen raised their rifles in a slapped salute and called out: 'God bless Queen Elizabeth.'

The soldiers marched away, trat-trat-trat; and Traitors' Gate and the Bloody Tower were left to their ghosts.

It was touching, this dignified devotion to ritual for its own sake. The Ceremony of the Keys has taken place every night, even during air raids. An accountant might argue that a function of this kind could be carried out more cheaply and efficiently by a security man with a dog, but the ceremony is a symbol of continuity amid pell-mell change, a thread running from the past to the future, something our ancestors knew and that our descendants will know.

My Liege

A small crowd gathered on Tower Hill, twenty-four people standing with their collars up against the bitter wind blowing up from the Thames, hands thrust into their pockets, the cold pinching their cheeks. They stood in a semi-circle around a green stepladder bearing a notice saying West London Mission of the Methodist Church. On it sat a white-haired man with a large noble head and a strong face with blue eyes. He wore a thick navy blue jacket over a black cassock and his knees were covered by a rug. His hands were unprotected. Since mine were cold, even in my pockets, his must have been frozen. He wore a hearing aid in his right ear and spoke in a clear, cultured voice without any quaver. 'I am over ninety,' he said, in response to a question from the crowd, 'and so I remember the First World War . . .'

This was Lord Soper, a living monument, the picture of a stoic. It was his regular Wednesday lunchtime debating session, and he was gently and persistently setting out his views as he had been doing in this place for more than forty years. The crowd bowled questions at him, about politics, war, Northern Ireland, pacifism, the existence of God. One man kept addressing him as 'My liege'. He put his interlocutors on a straight-and-narrow path where the meaning of words was concerned, an insistence on precision that was the essence of it all. 'It is extremely hard to practise Christianity,' he said in answer to a question, 'and I continue to be a pilgrim.' After forty minutes or so he was lifted from the ladder and placed by his helpers into his wheelchair and a slight flicker of pain crossed his face as they did so.

Servant of the House

Newspaper work took me from time to time to the press gallery, bars and restaurants of the Houses of Parliament; but it was my father-in-law, in the years after his retirement, and often over the stiff gin and tonic which he liked to take at six o'clock precisely, who gave me the most valuable insights into the establishment and its inhabitants.

Sir Barnett Cocks served Parliament for forty-three years, retiring as Clerk of the House, the senior parliamentary servant and the master of its procedure and ritual. He loved the institution deeply. His sardonic sense of humour enabled him to survive it. He knew the appeal it had for the ambitious politicians he saw over the years and he called it 'the old enchantress'.

His view of Members of Parliament was not at all sentimental. He noted in his earliest days that 'better-off Members did not carry money: once elected, they expected that the average man would stake them, either because he was a government official or because he would probably be seeking a favour'. He remembered that when he accompanied some parliamentary delegations overseas, certain MPs usually found themselves without money in their pockets when the drinks bill arrived. One day, carrying a new briefcase, a birthday present, he was approached by an MP who asked, 'I say, where are they handing those out?' Arriving at a parliamentary function he found MPs crowded around the buffet. One of them emerged from the scrum with a heaped plate and his mouth full, saying, 'Get in quick, the smoked salmon is going fast.' He liked to recount how, during an overseas visit, MPs complained about a flunkey who appeared to bar their way to the food and drinks, not realizing that it was the country's president, there to greet them.

When he started his career in Parliament he was instructed by gentlemen who had kept Gladstone and Disraeli in constitutional order. The Clerks' offices still received a Stationery Office issue of quill pens; and inkwells were replenished from half-gallon jars of red and black ink by messengers who slopped it on the carpets. Blotting paper was graded, the best going to cabinet ministers who did not really need it. As in most public buildings there were few lavatories and, for the convenience of the Clerks, a grand white chamber pot was provided, the bottom of which was stamped with the royal cipher VR in House of Commons green. One senior Clerk would retire behind a screen to use it, continuing to instruct juniors on points of parliamentary procedure. In those days there were no women in the Clerks' offices, not even a 'typewriter', as secretaries were called. Open fires in the offices burned eighty tons of coal a week, and, in the absence of vacuum cleaners, the dust and grime lay thick. Leather-bound books in the Commons Library disintegrated in that polluted atmosphere, not that MPs read the books much. The library armchairs were used mostly for sleeping and the librarian grumbled that MPs borrowed his scissors to cut their toenails.

Clerks had little to do with ministers. 'It was a matter of sighting but not speaking. I was Clerk to the Committee of Privileges for seven years and later principal witness before the committee for twelve years. After a lengthy sitting of the committee during the first seven years Winston Churchill said good night to me on one occasion. Clement Attlee, as chairman and Prime Minister, never exchanged so much of a personal observation as that. Harold Macmillan, as Prime Minister, once complained to me, in my capacity as Clerk of the House, that I had permitted a parliamentary question which, he thought, should not have been allowed. He backed down when I suggested that if he did not like the rules of the House he should take steps to change them.'

Sir Barnett Cocks was the thirty-eighth holder of the post of Clerk of the House in an unbroken line going back to 1363. As such he was keeper of the memory of the House of Commons. On most occasions the word of the Clerk was absolute on matters of law, privilege and usage of Parliament. The notes,

records and recollections were handed from one Clerkly generation to the next. One day the Speaker of the House told him
that the Prime Minister had remembered a certain procedural
episode, adding that he had perfect recall. My father-in-law
said he had no recollection of it and suggested to the Speaker
that the Prime Minister should look it up in *Hansard*. 'He was
unable to find the passage because it did not exist, a salutary
lesson.'

My father-in-law, who had an Edwardian boyhood in North
Devon, took a severe view of any idea that there had been a
golden age either before the First World War or after it. He
wrote in a notebook of recollections that he remembered, above
all, the 'choking, inhibiting snobbery which crushed all
originality and regulated all daily life. It was shameful to be
without money but disgraceful to have anything to do with
earning money in trade or industry. It was honourable to be of
independent means, discreditable to be in trade and no disgrace
for a gentleman to disregard a tradesman's bills. Men were found
out by their accents. Schools which played soccer rather than
rugby were looked down on. For the educated and uneducated
alike Britain offered little opportunity for material advance. The
"golden age" before 1914 was a time of heavy and heartless
unemployment, when those who did nothing were assumed to
be wilfully idle.' His father, an Appledore shipyard owner, was a
magistrate. He imposed half-crown fines on Appledore men
found drunk and, knowing they were penniless, discreetly paid
the fines himself.

The Devon of my father-in-law's youth was 'a territory of
divisions into social classes. It was axiomatic that church-goers
were broadly honest and appropriately cap-touching while
chapel-goers were churlish and unreliable. Within the Bideford
Tennis Club there were anxious discussions: if a curate were eli-
gible for membership, should a bank clerk also be admitted? The
dropping of aitches was almost punishable among the cliques of
retired Army and Navy officers of the Royal North Devon Golf
Club. But the village lads who went caddying there were ruined
for life by the foul language they learned from the beautifully-
spoken officers and gentlemen.'

When he went to Oxford University he applied for admission to Worcester College because, he said, in a mischevious recollection, the food was well spoken-of and no great intellectual pressures were foreshadowed. 'The Provost and Fellows were gentle characters of little attainment. The throwing of plates in Hall was an art form; undergraduates hurled them towards the ceiling and raced across tables to catch them. On special occasions of celebration lavatory seats were treated as substitutes for the discus. At a supper once, when undergraduates introduced geese into the dining hall, missiles were thrown at them and the Provost could only request, "No champagne glasses, please." Drunkennness was quite acceptable to those in authority but speaking to town girls, however innocently, was not.'

He taught briefly at a school in Berkshire and the headmaster remarked to him that another master had a first-class honours degree and was an Oxford athletics blue; adding, in a regretful tone, that the man's father was only a jeweller. When he went to the House of Commons he found that school and regimental neckties were important, although 'regimental ties were less favoured because they could be worn by quite humble men. Old Etonians would make regular visits to their hosiers for their black and blue neckwear. My counterparts in the House of Lords in my early days must have been appointed on the ground that they knew somebody of importance. Merit did not enter into it: the name, the tie, even catch-phrases and how to pronounce them, were all-important. It was wholly unacceptable to stumble over the pronunciation of Belvoir or Cesarewitch or to have coat cuffs which did not unbutton.'

Sixty-eight Fahrenheit

In the warrens of the Houses of Parliament I was once invited to peer through a periscope. It gave a view of the Commons chamber, of the Members of Parliament slumped on the green benches in attitudes of languor. The engineers who look through the periscope can tell the difference between boredom and drowsiness, and while they can do nothing about the former they take steps to alleviate the latter. A little-known detail of the working of democracy is that before Prime Minister's Question Time the temperature in the Commons is lowered by two degrees because, within a few minutes, all those hot, dark-suited bodies raise the temperature in the chamber to sixty-eight degrees Fahrenheit; and long experience has shown that this is the heat at which MPs function most efficiently. The engineers in their green control room are the punkah-wallahs of Parliament, moving hot air out of the chamber, admitting cool air, fanning the brow of democracy. They are alert to political moods. A crucial debate, a sudden crowding of the sealed chamber, can literally change the atmosphere. Through the periscope they have the feel of the House, the emotional condition.

The engineering staff have many responsibilities, including the light on top of Big Ben which indicates that the Commons is sitting, the water softeners which ensure that glasses in the numerous bars are not smeared, the whistle which shrills when Parliament disperses and the steam engine, more than a century old, which is the emergency power for Parliament's sewage ejector. On ceremonial days the resident engineer wears morning dress.

Roll-up

Into their blue van George, Colm and Annette loaded a large vacuum drum of vegetable soup, flasks of tea, a large packet of tobacco, cigarette papers and a plastic sack of sandwiches. It was nine o'clock. Colm drove the van from King's Cross to Victoria and parked by the Roman Catholic cathedral. George and Annette walked around the area, looking in the doorways of shops and offices for people who had set up camp and were huddled in coats, sleeping bags and blankets on this cold winter night.

The first rule, George said, is that people who are asleep are not disturbed. If they are awake you offer them a roll-up, a cigarette. Most people sleeping rough enjoy a smoke, he said, and a smoke can lead to a chat.

George was cheery and brisk, kindly, middle-aged. He knew a lot about these homeless people. At one time he had been on the road himself, so he was understanding and also practical. He knew some of the doorway dwellers because they were regulars and he hunkered down and talked to them softly and sympathetically and asked if they wished for anything.

He came back to the van. 'A roll-up and a soup,' he said. 'Soup and a sandwich, just another roll-up and a tea.' Annette came back from her patrol with similar requests.

George walked up and down Victoria Street, checking all the doorways. He gave a beaker of tea and a cigarette to a young man wrapped in a blanket on the pavement. I asked George why the man sat in that exposed place when he would have been better off around the corner, out of the knife of the wind. George said that the place where he was sitting was more public, a better pitch for begging.

The presence of the van, and George's net-casting, drew half a dozen men who walked unsteadily and stood clutching cans of lager, swaying gently. Some drank soup and tea and smoked cigarettes and exchanged banter with George. One grabbed a tea and hurried off without a word. George was pleased that a well-spoken woman, wrapped in a sleeping bag, who had for weeks refused anything, had finally said yes, she would like a tea.

We drove to the Thames Embankment, to the pavement behind the Savoy Hotel. A dozen people were swaddled in blankets. One of them was a girl of about sixteen with a pleasantly impish face. She tossed her head and said she wanted nothing to eat or drink. She rummaged in the mess of bags and blankets around her and produced a toothbrush and said that as it was bedtime she would clean her teeth. She was talkative and revealed why she was feeling pleased: she had been interviewed by a Swedish television company making a programme about life on the streets of London.

A middle-aged woman in a sleeping bag accepted tea, sandwiches and a roll-up. 'Oh that's lovely, thank you.' It was not so bad here, she said, better than some places. She complained that when she slept in certain doorways security men would knock on the door at four or five in the morning, to wake her up, to annoy her. I need my sleep, the same as anyone else, she said. One of the dangers of sleeping rough was that young men, fresh out of the pubs, would set upon you and kick you. What people don't understand, she added, quite angrily, is that this place, this doorway, is my home and my privacy should be respected. 'I'm not dirty. I look after myself and shower at the homeless centres. I'm cleaner than most of the people who abuse me.'

Colm, who drove the van, had a long chat with her. He was training to be an accountant and drove the van on the soup run because, he said, he wanted to do something constructive. He, George and Annette work for the Simon Community which runs a house at King's Cross, a rough-and-ready place with a common room full of chairs, a kitchen and sixteen beds for people coming in off the streets. It is a front-line place, first aid, a shelter for people who sleep rough as a way of life and who need an occasional break from the harshness of it. It offers, not a permanent home, but a respite for a maximum of seven nights, with food, warmth, tobacco, some medical care, clothing if necessary; and conversation. Those who come in are called guests and they are invited in by trust workers who go out in pairs, always a man and a woman. The rules are strict. No one gets a bed by knocking at the door and while guests are often brought in drunk they are not permitted to keep drink or drugs inside the house. If they break this rule, or are violent, they are thrown out.

Edmond, a Cambridge theology graduate of twenty-four, said he planned to work at the house for about a year. 'I get twenty-five pounds a week and sleep on a mattress on the floor. The work is fatiguing and there is not much sleep. You run the risk of becoming lousy and we have to delouse ourselves. We know that tuberculosis is on the increase among street people. Some of the people who come in here are very dirty, frankly, and smell terrible. We encourage cleanliness, provide soap and shampoo and wash the chair covers every day, but it isn't our job to tell people they should be clean. If furniture is soiled we throw it out. The doctor comes twice a week. Some of the people who come here are infested with lice, some are epileptic, others need treatment for dermatitis, alcoholics need vitamins and some guests need anti-depressants. A life on the streets is hard and people who sleep rough age quickly. At forty they can look sixty.'

He showed me the stores of donated food, bedding and clothing. 'Practical things, like jeans, long johns, hats and gloves are important, but you need clothing that is fairly fashionable. Just because you are homeless and on the streets doesn't mean that you are not interested in fashion. The test is: would you wear it yourself?

'We work on the principle of treating people as they are, with respect, providing them with a chance to deal with their problems, without setting out to rehabilitate them. People are homeless and sleep rough for many and complicated reasons. The work we do is often harrowing. You have to be tough. Because of our policies you have to be ready to turn people away and that isn't easy. I see a lot of sad sights and I cope with it by talking things over with other workers. On the other hand, the work can be rewarding. Being at the sharp end like this gives me the chance to put something back into society. You start talking to people and you gradually break through and win their trust and you realize they have not had a proper conversation for years.'

Mrs Thatcher Never Came

In the tentative early light two young foxes emerged from the cover of trees on the edge of the playing field, raised their noses and looked about. Seeing that the coast was clear they scampered into the long-jump pit and chased each other's tails, tumbling, rolling, cuffing and nipping. They streaked across the running track, wheeled and rushed into the sand to tumble some more. A wash of primrose light advanced across the ashy sky and put a gleam on their coats. They ceased their game and looked around, panting gently through their grins, and, as a bird sang, they stole away. The foxes of Dulwich prosper on picnic crusts and pizza rinds. They ransack the litter bins and forage in gardens and get into kitchens through the cat-flap. I have often seen them at night and heard vixens screeching in the street. I encounter them in the park in the early morning. They step from rhododendron patches to survey their estate in a squireish manner and look me up and down.

The journalist's adjective for Dulwich is leafy. It is a middle-class suburb of south London; of London but not really in it. If it were in America it would be called Pleasantville. It has a good art gallery, some fine Georgian buildings and a toll gate which is an irritation but is tolerated as picturesque. The appearance and shape of the district are due chiefly to the almost Oklahoman land rush of late Victorian and Edwardian times. The tree-lined avenues and streets, mostly too narrow for the motor age, are a picture of bourgeois, almost Belgian, content-ment: popular housing at its most pleasing and comfortable, red brick and a little stucco, white porches, paths, stout front doors with leaded and stained-glass windows, hallways of black and white chessboard tiles, ample rooms, French doors leading into gardens with shrubs and trees. There is plenty of work here for plumbers, painters, builders, gardeners and artisans of all kinds. I offered an electrician tea and he looked uncomfortable and said: 'I'd love some, but have you any proper tea? Every time I do a job in Dulwich I get offered that Lapsang Souchong or that Earl Grey, when what I'm dying for is a real cup of tea.'

The principal industries of Dulwich are education and child-rearing. Young mothers go out into their gardens to smoke. Many cars are fitted with a child seat or two and some sport yellow stickers proclaiming Baby On Board, as if they were badges of fecundity. Many display the finger-wagging stickers of middle class concerns: Say No to Foxhunting, Greenpeace, Save the Whale, Ban the Ivory Trade, Ban Seal Hunting, Toad Watch, Say No to Fur – a far cry from the previous generation's We Have Been to Bude and We Have Seen the Lions of Longleat.

Dulwich College is the senior school of the suburb. Its two most famous students were P.G. Wodehouse and Raymond Chandler. Wodehouse left his typewriter, desk and pipes to the College and they may be seen in the library. In America, where he lived most of his life, a pipe would possibly be too provocative an artefact to be put on display where children could see it. Chandler was born in Chicago but came to London with his mother in 1895 when she divorced his alcoholic father. He was an outstanding Classics scholar at the College, and always felt that his classical education lent precision to the writing of his Philip Marlowe stories, many of them composed in a haze of alcohol.

After the foxes have finished their morning patrols in Dulwich Park, the early runners and dog-walkers appear. These are followed by the men who stop their cars beneath the horse chestnuts, maples and oaks and read the newspapers, perhaps having told their families that they must fly or they will be late for work. At lunchtime people arrive in their cars to eat sandwiches and listen to the news and *The Archers*. Younger men fill their cars with pop music. In the afternoons a number of men drive into the park, put their car seats into the recline position and sleep with their mouths wide open. Others, though, work on ledgers or portable computers, or enjoy a smoke and watch the squirrels. The car is the only place where they can be deliciously alone. Geese meet on the grass and on the pond in large congregations. People row boats on the lake and play bowls, tennis, cricket, rounders and football. They fly kites, throw frisbees and go roller-skating. Horses are ridden on a sandy track. Some are police mounts, ever ready to break up a London mob; and the smell of the manure is as evocative as any madeleine, though no one scoops it up for the roses any more. Nor have I seen anyone gathering and playing conkers. Middle-aged joggers flap by like penguins. In summer, young men and women sprawl on the grass and open the doors of their cars, the better to hear the thunder of pop from their radios.

I saw two cars crash gently in the park and their middle-aged occupants remonstrate with each other in a middle-class way, waving their fingers.

'You have no intelligence,' she said, seething.

'You have no manners,' he said, glaring.

After her political assassination by her colleagues, Margaret Thatcher chose Dulwich as her retirement home and bought a large and secure house, modern and quite without charm. It seemed that the suburb might become Dulwich-les-deux-Églises, blessed by the brooding patronage of the queen-in-exile. In the event, she never lived in the house. She decided Dulwich was not for her, and she was quite right. It was too much on the edge of things and not in the thick of them. It was, to be candid, rather dull for a woman of her energy and proclivities. People in Dulwich usually sleep more than four hours a night. The tortuous drive into central London would have irritated her. She would have had to negotiate dreary streets, littered and congested, many of them flanked by peeling blocks of flats, the mistakes of 1960s public housing. Her chauffeur might have had to drive her frequently past the Elephant and Castle Centre, a giant shopping mall painted in a mauve-pink, like a harlot's lipstick or a bishop's soutane. No, it would not have done at all.

So Dulwich, which has never had a truly famous resident, missed having one. It did though, have a truly notorious inhabitant. William Joyce, Lord Haw Haw, lived here in the 1920s and 1930s and used to set up a soap box on a street corner to make his fascist speeches. Although he was an American citizen, born in New York, he was convicted at the Old Bailey of treason on the evidence of his application for a British passport. This was made from his home in Dulwich. Thus quiet, leafy Dulwich played its part in sending that preposterous man to the gallows.

Ackee Soup

It is a short walk from Dulwich down the hill into Brixton. Turn a corner and you plunge into the hot dazzle and clamour of the market. Your nose is suddenly pricked by peppers and spices, your ears buzz with the dissonant din of rap, and calypso and steel-band throb. The meat is piled in bloody mountainous stacks, beef, whole lambs and goats, great hunks and joints and quarters, gizzards, oxtails, immense heaps of chicken, mounds of liver, the astonishing cornucopia manned by busy butchers and salesmen in colourful caps, haranguing and cajoling. The smell of meat and fowl mingles with the sea tang of shining slithery fish, snapper, tilapia, coley, catfish and prawns. Caught up in the ebullient throng, the babble and badinage and the clashing music, you are pushed to and fro in the amiable scrums of buxom matrons at the stalls selling yellow yams, saltfish, saffron, sweet yuca, Ghana puna, ogi, fufa, okra, rice, hot peppers, plantains, papaya, alligator pepper, dried banga fish and succulent mangoes. Amidst all the pungent smells are softer scents of herbs, sandalwood, carnations, coconut and the perfume of women. Sassy girls in short skirts, their outsize earrings clashing like cymbals, clack in and out of shops which sell African carvings, Caribbean tapes, Nigerian videos, packets of crimson and yellow spices, skin-lighteners, and mosquito nets for the trip back home to St Kitts and Grenada. Melodies ring in your ears and the piquancy stays in your nose. Down the road a sign in a chemist's shop says 'Any Needle-Change Client Abusing Staff Will Not Be Served'; and a notice on a car repair workshop advises 'Please Do Not Park Here As A Dent Often Offends'.

A Colonial Boy

Donald Hinds had his first history lesson in a little school high in the hills of Jamaica. It was about the English wars with the French in medieval times and the burning of Joan of Arc. It is difficult now, he said, for people to understand what colonialism meant, what it was to be a part of the British Empire, to grow up in Jamaica as a colonial subject. 'This was during the war. We felt so British, there is no other way of putting it. We were the first British colony to raise money to buy a bomber for Britain. I wanted to do my bit in the war and was by no means alone in that. We boys looked forward to fighting for Britain and felt slightly cheated when the war ended.'

His ambition was to be a teacher and writer, but he never thought of settling permanently in Britain. His stepfather went to London in 1947 to work in the post-war rebuilding. That was the year before the arrival at Tilbury of the *Empire Windrush*, with nearly five hundred immigrants, mostly Jamaican, an event which marked the start of modern black settlement in Britain. His mother went in 1951. In those days British firms advertised jobs in Jamaican newspapers. The *South London Press*, carrying columns of employment vacancies, was on sale in Kingston.

Some landlords in Brixton put up signs saying 'No Blacks. No Irish.' But Brixton nevertheless became a centre of West Indian settlement. It had a large number of boarding houses and migrants were directed to its employment exchange. It had a lively market, entertainment and black companionship and was within easy reach of central London.

Donald sailed for London in 1955, aged twenty-one, and

immediately got a job on the buses, the fifth black conductor at Brixton garage. In the mid–1950s, he said, that was a rather prestigious job to have. He knew West Indians in Brixton who were living more than twenty to a room, half on day shift, half on night. 'But I didn't want to share. I had my own room, just me and my typewriter. Life was good. I spent nine and a half years on the buses. That was too long and I should have been more ruthless with myself. But my West Indian conservatism was at work: I wanted to pay my rent, buy my clothes and go to college; and the job was secure.'

On the buses many white people were friendly and enjoyed a conversation. Some were insulting. 'A woman asked me what the fare was and when I told her she took the money from her purse and put it onto the seat beside her. She put on a white glove and handed the money to me. When fares were increased some passengers grumbled and said, "You blacks." I remember a white man apologizing for being rude and saying, "I am sorry – I am white, you are black, but I am apologizing to you." A woman looked at me and said that I reminded her of someone; and she thought for a moment and said, "Yes, you remind me of the golly on Robertson's strawberry jam." I knew at that moment what it was to be speechless. For years I could not buy Robertson's strawberry jam. I could not look that golly in the face. I can laugh now. It wasn't hatred on her part. There was a lot of ignorance. A black woman showed her backside to her fellow workers to prove she did not have a tail. In the 1950s people did not know each other, but Britain had had an empire for three hundred years, so how could we be so unknown? Relationships between white women and black men never went down well: they caused hackles to rise. When I was working on a particular bus route I used to see a lady working in a shop by the bus stop and we used to wave and smile to each other. Then, out of the blue, when I was off-duty, I saw her on a bus and I sat next to her and we started talking. Seeing this, a white lad came over and pushed up her skirt. His meaning was quite clear. It was a terrible insult to her and she screamed.'

The 1950s were not exactly an age of innocence, he said, but attitudes were different. 'People of my generation have a different view. I lived in Brixton for the first fifteen years and never came across anything really nasty. The word was out that West Indians did not get into trouble, that they were well-behaved family people. Policemen popped into the bus station for cups of tea and there was a different attitude in the police. But things began to change after the rioting at Notting Hill in 1958 and everyone was on edge. We started to get the backlash of the American civil rights campaigning, too. Noisy parties and clubs were closed down in police raids. Now when you see a report of a crime on television and they show an identikit picture of a wanted man, you breathe a sigh of relief when he isn't black.'

Most immigrants, he thought, had the idea that they would work for a few years and then go home. At twenty-one he saw himself studying for a degree and then going back to Jamaica to teach. But he stayed, worked, wrote, left the buses to write a book, did some broadcasting for the BBC. He married a nurse who became a social worker, had three daughters, earned his MA. He achieved his ambition, went into teaching and eventually became head of history at a comprehensive school.

'The story of my wife and myself is an ordinary one. We came here, nothing was given, but there was an opportunity to move along and get things done and bring up our children, not asking for more or less than others. You have to take part in the country you live in and I was never going to shut myself off. I like Britain and my ties to it are so strong that I could never sever them. I don't think of it as my adopted country, rather I think that Britain has adopted me. My daughters don't want us to go back and even though I hanker after Christmases in Jamaica, Christmas in my shirtsleeves, I don't want to be separated from my grandsons. I have never regretted coming to Britain. I have not been disillusioned. I wanted to write and to teach and I have done both moderately well.

'It is an agreeable country but there will always be strains, just as there are everywhere. I live in Eltham and a black youth was murdered there recently and you cannot set aside or forget that kind of thing. There are certainly tensions between kids and the police. The innocence that existed when I first came here has gone. Still, I'm optimistic. The British are good at compromising and some of that has rubbed off on us, the former colonials. If you observe life through your children's eyes you can see that they have a confidence that my generation did not have.

'My generation is fading now. I am a Jamaican who has lived all his life abroad and I feel British. My children are not Jamaican. This is their home. I notice that black British boys now play football rather than cricket and they no longer see things our way. "Dad is watching cricket," they say, "so boring." I was brought up in the British Empire, on Shakespeare, Walter Scott, the Brontës, Dickens, Wordsworth and Byron. The Empire is dead but an essence of it remains. My mother saw very little of Britain but we have seen a lot of it. One of the reasons we like going to Wales is that the mountains and valleys remind us of Jamaica.'

The Honour of a Name

It is only a small leap in the imagination to stand at the tomb of William Bligh by the Thames at Lambeth and hear Fletcher Christian's anguished exclamation: 'That, Captain Bligh, that is the thing. I am in hell, I am in hell.'

In the light of a South Sea dawn Christian stands distraught upon HMS *Bounty*'s quarterdeck, a cutlass in his sweating hand, for he was notoriously sweaty as well as bandy. Bligh is in his nightshirt, hands tied behind his back, the trembling Christian threatening: 'Hold your tongue, Sir, or you are dead this instant!'

It is extraordinary how this moment has crystallized and endured. From it have sprung more than a thousand books, five films and countless scholarly studies. Bligh relics and Bountyana go for high prices at auction. And, more than two centuries on, the descendants of Bligh and Christian are still touched by the drama on the quarterdeck, and still offer partisan views of what happened. Maurice Bligh, the great-great-great-grandson of William Bligh, has devoted half his life, more than a quarter of a century, to a study of his ancestor, amassing material for a book he hopes will change the popular belief that Bligh was a bully. It is a full-time job, as if *Bounty* sails through his living room in Kent.

'I am a man with a mission,' he announced. 'I am out to exonerate a maligned officer who has suffered the smears and lies of his enemies.'

Ewan Christian, a director of a London hotel company, and a descendant of Fletcher Christian's uncle, told me that he took Christian's side. 'I like the fact that in the *Bounty* films Bligh comes out badly and Christian comes out well. There was something the matter with Bligh. Fletcher Christian broke the rules but Bligh was a bloody man.'

'How can he say that?' demanded Maurice Bligh impatiently. 'How blind can you be? Christian cast nineteen men adrift in the ocean, knowing he could be sending them to their deaths.'

When *Bounty* sailed for Tahiti, to collect breadfruit seedlings, Bligh was thirty-three, Christian, his protégé, was twenty-three, and had twice sailed under Bligh's command on transatlantic voyages. *Bounty* stayed twenty-three weeks in Tahiti and her men believed they had entered paradise, flowery, warm, abundant and sensuous, an island of bare-breasted girls with hibiscus in their long black hair. Bligh, as befitted a commander, was a pillar of rectitude and one can only guess at the torments. But every other man had a girlfriend and Christian's lover was a chief's daughter. Christian had himself tattooed, and he fell further in Bligh's estimation: he was an officer and had gone native. Three weeks after *Bounty* sailed from Tahiti, Christian's mind exploded. He talked crazily of building a raft to escape. Someone suggested seizing the ship.

The quarterdeck showdown has been construed as justice-loving Everyman rebelling against vile tyranny. Bligh's defenders, however, think Christian and his followers betrayed their mates for sex and sunshine. Maurice Bligh believes that Christian may have been at the opium in the ship's medical chest.

Bligh and eighteen loyalists were crammed into a twenty-three-foot boat without charts and with meagre provisions. Their voyage of nearly four thousand miles across the Pacific to a Dutch base in Timor was an epic. Bligh reached England in March 1790 and got his retaliation in first. His book blamed the mutiny on conspiracy and sex. 'I can only conjecture that the mutineers flattered themselves with the hope of a more happy life among the Tahitians than they could enjoy in England . . . the women are handsome, mild and cheerful.'

While he became a celebrity, the Christian family were shamed and Fletcher was disowned, the black sheep. But accounts of Bligh's harshness seeped out and Fletcher's lawyer brother Edward interviewed *Bounty* seamen and used their testimony to paint Bligh as the bully who drove Christian to mutiny. In 1831 Sir John Barrow, Secretary of the Admiralty, published a semi-official account which, while admiring Bligh's seamanship, noted his 'unruly temper and tyrannical conduct'. The popular view of the conflict was established by the 1936 film starring Charles Laughton as a glowering Bligh and Clark Gable as a noble Christian. It was based on the fictionalized *Bounty* story by Charles Nordhoff and James Norman Hall, both South Seas romantics who married Tahitians and fitted Fletcher Christian into their own dreams of paradise.

Retribution and determination were the sub-themes of the mutiny, and were no less extraordinary than the main event. The Royal Navy made it clear there was no hiding place, even at the earth's ends, and sent HMS *Pandora* to bring the *Bounty* crew to book. Fourteen were rounded up in Tahiti. Four drowned when the *Pandora* sank on a reef in Australia but the survivors reached Timor, another remarkable open boat voyage. Bligh, meanwhile, returned to his unfinished business in Tahiti, to gather the breadfruit plants to feed plantation slaves in the West Indies. I have seen the tree in St Vincent, grown from his first seedling. The scheme was a failure: the slaves did not like the breadfruit.

In his search for material, Maurice Bligh has travelled the Pacific, in *Bounty*'s wake, and visited Pitcairn where nine mutineers settled and where Fletcher Christian was murdered by his Tahitian followers. I asked him if his crusade were an obsession. 'No, a passion for truth. Bligh needs someone to stand up for him. He was incontestably a great man and it is a pity he is not honoured much more in his own country. We are still divided, the Blighs and Christians. We are not at each other's throats, but it's time the Christian family faced the facts.'

'Fletcher broke the law,' said Ewan Christian, 'but was right to do so. I don't see how the Blighs can say anything other than that William Bligh was cruel.'

Maurice Bligh is no doubt right. His ancestor was a great seaman, irascible but certainly no brute, and resorted to the lash much less often than other captains. As for Christian, he had been softened by the scent of hibiscus in long black hair. He was not up to his job. But the story insists that Bligh was an ogre with marlinspikes for fingers and a cat-o'-nine-tails for a tongue. Without a brutal Bligh the tale is shorn of the dramatic conflict which makes it magnetic and enduring. But we prefer the drama as it is. Bligh's doughty descendant paces the quarterdeck of the *Bounty*, locked into a doomed struggle with romance and myth.

A Polar Bear's Picnic

Crossing Tower Bridge, I was often approached by tourists proffering cameras and asking me to take their photographs. My portraits of smiling couples, families and old buddies with their arms around each other's shoulders, posed against the Victorian Gothic towers of that slightly preposterous structure, are in albums all over the world. Even on the coldest and wettest days tourists swarm to this place, and I have framed them holding their hats in a gale and grinning through the snow. I have often stood in the crowd as the eleven-hundred-ton bascules open to let a vessel through and have heard tourists cry: 'Isn't that great!' and also heard world-weary eighteen-year-olds say: 'Is that all there is?'

Like Sydney Bridge, Charles Bridge and the Golden Gate, Tower Bridge is the unmistakable landmark of its city. It is the frontispiece of London and as such is the goal that travellers resolve to reach, the touchstone.

I sometimes hear people grumble about the ant-armies of tourists, but what do they expect and what do they think a thousand-year-old city is for? It is true that coachloads of French teenagers are a test of anyone's magnanimity and you understand why their wise parents have them transported to Britain, but I enjoy the bus tourists and their enthusiasm for the city, their faces in the polychromatic and amorphous swirl on the streets, the Oriental crocodiles following the upraised flags of their guides. We grumble about London's litter, dirt, crowded transport, nauseating smells; but the tourists point their fingers and exclaim and look up and remind you that your commonplace, your half-forgotten, your taken-for-granted, is the jewel they have longed to see, have worked and saved for.

When I see them staring at the river I remember that I first looked over the parapet of Tower Bridge when the Pool of London was busy with ships and lighters. The wharves bustled. We all knew then that London was The Smoke, with terrible sulphurous fogs, the notorious pea-soupers which killed hundreds of people and had once concealed Jack the Ripper. With his Clean Air Bill, Gerald Nabarro set out on the seemingly hopeless task of stopping everyone in London lighting a coal fire. He eventually won and since then London has had clear skies even on a winter's day; which shows that one man can make a difference.

Stand on Tower Bridge today and you have to imagine the activity of the Pool, the ships, the cranes turning, the warehouses full of cargoes and the canyons between them smelling of spices. And you have to imagine harder to see the thick forests of the masts of sailing ships afloat on a Thames that was a dead-dog sewer, its stench so bad that in the mid-nineteenth century sheets of disinfectant were hung in the House of Commons to provide relief; and, nevertheless, MPs fled one day with handkerchiefs over their faces. It was not until the 1960s and 1970s that sewage processing, drainage and pollution control cleaned the Thames and made it hospitable again to birds and fish, and even saw the return of the salmon.

The river now is almost empty of ships and Tower Bridge opens for spritsail barges and occasional cruise ships. Captured for ever in the Pool, as if locked in amber, is HMS *Belfast*, the largest cruiser ever built for the Royal Navy and veteran of action off Norway, Normandy and Korea. She would have gone for scrap but ex-Navy men raised the money to keep her as a floating museum. In the river, her bow facing upstream, she looks confined, out of her true element.

The Tower of London, on *Belfast*'s starboard quarter, is the oldest occupied fortress in the world, built by William the Conqueror, and extended by his successors, to make London tremble and obey. It was the strongest of the hundreds of castles built throughout England, Wales, Scotland and Ireland to sustain the conquest of unruly and resentful peoples by a small French-speaking élite. The Norman castles were displays of brutal armed force, reminding the people that they were conquered, second class and without freedom. The fierce and exotic creatures in the Tower's menagerie were adjuncts of the power of kings: lions, leopards, elephants, bears. In 1252 a collar and chain were purchased for a polar bear to enable it to walk from the Tower to the river to fish for salmon.

It is a pity that the bridge is out of scale with the Tower and subtracts from its aspect of awesomeness; and it is a shame, too, that planners permitted construction of the remarkably ugly modern hotel nearby. Indeed, the Tower is half-surrounded by a lynch-mob of hideous building. From transpontine restaurants in the old warehouses on the south bank there is a good view of the surging river, the Tower and its jumbled background. You can see Wapping, too, where, at Execution Dock, pirates like the Glaswegian Captain William Kidd were hanged and left dangling until three tides had covered them. This is something to reflect on when considering supercilious waiters and insensitive architects. Disraeli, in a light-hearted comment on the architect Charles Barry, said in the Commons: 'No profession has succeeded in this country till it has furnished "an example". For instance, you (executed) Admiral Byng and the Navy increased in efficiency till we won Trafalgar. We decapitated Archbishop Laud and thenceforth secured the responsibility of the bishops. The principle we have never applied to architects; and when a member of that profession has utterly failed, it really becomes the government to consider the case, and they may rest assured that if once they contemplated the possibility of hanging an architect they would put a stop to such blunders in future.'

Fortunately, London has many more magnificent spectacles and pleasures than it has mistakes and monstrosities, which is why the admiring tourists come. Labyrinthine, cluttered, compelling, weary, ancient, haphazard, sprawling, grand, stylish, rich, fast, London is everything, its resources and culture inexhaustible. Some hate its immensity, others find its size and anonymity liberating. Like all cities it is a try-your-strength machine, drawing people to perform on its stage. It has no caliph, no chief citizen as New York and Chicago and Berlin have. It is a jumble of petty republics. It is hard to say that there is any London identity or distinguishing characteristic, particularly since the epoch of shipping and dock labour faded, the insular East End lost its common cause and cockneydom shrivelled. There are, however, wellings of pride in the old beast, in its history and attributes.

Of course, no Londoner can ever know all of London. Like a sultan with a large harem, he knows some parts intimately and others barely or perfunctorily. Londoners do not usually move from familiar territory. They tend to be north people or south people, for the Thames is a divide, as it always was. Londoners tell me there is a difference in the voices, the hint of a whine north of the river, a more pronounced glottal stop in the south.

Taxi drivers often have firm views about north and south of the Thames.

'Dulwich, please.'

'The Outer Hebrides, you mean.'

'Come on, you'll get a fare from Dulwich back to London.'

'That is a myth put about by people who live in Dulwich.'

A driver beamed when he was congratulated for finding a swift, traffic-beating route from north of the Thames to Dulwich. 'You were lucky to get me,' he said. 'A lot of cabbies lose their bearings once they get over the water.'

5

The Possibility of Wizards

As I set out from Chiswick, at the start of the road to the west, I caught a glimpse of a sign.

'Last Pub Before Wales'.

A few hours later, atoning for metropolitan sluggishness, I was on foot, panting gently, paying my respects to the dragon among towering slabs, boulders and drystone walls. I crossed a stream and headed upwards. Strewn here and there on the path, the stripped bones of sheep and crows awaited any passing poet with lamentation on his mind. I gained the top of a ridge and looked out. Clouds were mobbing in ruffianly force. Far below me a pool gleamed, a spoonful of mercury in the dark rock, and I heard a shepherd's whistle and a buzzard's call.

The central fact of Wales is that it is mostly upland, tough and ancient, and it seems not too fanciful to me that there is something in the Welsh spirit that matches the hard rock. In its craggy carapace Wales looks a fortress. A scowling sky augments an appearance of intractability. Centuries ago, English travellers gathered up their courage as the mountains filled their gaze and they forded the rivers.

'It is not easy of access,' Gerald of Wales wrote of the Welsh mountain country during his travels on horseback in the twelfth century. 'The Britons who were left alive took refuge in these parts when the Saxons first occupied the island, and they have never been completely subdued since, either by the English or the Normans.'

It remains true. Wales is a land defined on three sides by the sea and on the fourth by stubbornness.

Ferry ports serve Ireland but apart from these Wales is not a staging-post. You do not transit Wales. It is a goal in itself, a destination. Because it has always maintained an apartness, and seems to conceal a secret, there is at the river crossings a thrilling sense of the drawbridge, of discovery, of passing into an enclave, another country.

I went to Cardiff and had lunch with a Welsh friend. He thought for a moment and distilled in a few words the essence of Wales, of fifteen centuries of experience, of a whole library of histories.

'We're still here.'

Survival is the heart of things in Wales. The slogan *Cymru am byth*, Wales for ever, is commonly painted on walls and rocks as a prayer of hope; but 'We're still here' asserts and celebrates the more satisfying fact of enduring.

Wales might so easily have emerged in modern times with a legacy of old books and grey stones, of bones to be gnawed by scholarly rummagers, a story with a beginning, a middle and a long dying. But down the centuries an idea of Wales was carried like a candle in a labyrinth, shielded by a cupped hand. It endured without any separate political structure at the heart of an imperium and centralized state; and its language has lived alongside pre-eminent and omnivorous English and has yet flourished.

The story is an extraordinary saga of resuscitations, peppered with the comic and bizarre, so that you wonder at the power of belief, the potency of myth and the possibility of wizards.

The historian Gwyn A. Williams remarked that the Welsh have lived in a permanent state of emergency since the fourth century. I picture Wales as an old-time cinema hero, hanging by his nails at the end of each episode, the crocodiles snapping at his ankles, and next week miraculously climbing free.

The endurance of the Welsh difference suggests a relevance for England and for Britain as a whole. The Englishman always struck the Welshman as a self-assured fellow who never fretted about who and what he was because he was certain of it. He hardly knew the words of his national anthem and, indeed, often fled when it was played in cinemas. He could not tell if his flag was flying upside-down and had no need to celebrate the feast day of his patron saint, even if he knew the date of it. The English applied themselves to the abundant pleasures of being English and enjoyed the lion's share of being British. They swaggered carefree about the stage, knew their prestigious place upon it and eschewed introspection. No wonder many Welshmen hoped that, if reincarnated, they would return as Englishmen, freed of the torment of Welshness.

At the end of the twentieth century the English are confronted by a question that grows ever larger in their minds. They must decide what it means to be English, and British, too. They have to say who they are. The Welsh know all about this. They are old hands in the matter of identity, educated in the school of precariousness and raised to wear the scratchy shirts of ambiguity and uncertainty.

As with any country, some of the story in Wales, and the rules of the game, are derived from geology and climate and the lucky twists of history. But for the rest of it Wales owes its modern form essentially to unrottable belief. It has been created by poets and patriots, yes, but also by hard-headed men. There has been some assistance from amiable liars, fabulists and forgers. And also from the poppy. Modern Wales, as we shall see, owes something to fantasies born in an opiate haze.

Welsh Crabs

I was invited to a school in Wales to present the prizes. At lunch beforehand the headmaster gave me a copy of the programme. I saw that the letters MA ornamented my name.

'I'm afraid', I said, 'that I am not an MA.'

'Don't give it a thought,' he said genially. 'In Wales we are all MAs.'

English minds might see in this the evidence of Welsh clannishness; and suspicion will be reinforced by the description a Welshman gave me of his encounter with a policeman in London. Stopped for a minor traffic offence, he gave his name and address. The constable put away his notebook. 'Look,' he said softly, in accents fashioned west of Chepstow, 'I'm here in London to book Englishmen: now clear off back to Wales.' A friend recounted that when he was a student he had a summer job driving an ice-cream van and was summoned to a court in rural Wales for sounding its bells on a Sunday. He defended himself in Welsh and, although the court was impressed by his eloquence, he lost his case. 'We have to fine you, I'm afraid,' the chairman of the magistrates said regretfully. 'Will a pound be all right?'

I do not think the Welsh especially clannish, though they may seem so when observed from across the border. When the Saxons invaded Britain they called the Celts the Welsh, meaning foreigners. In their own language the Welsh called themselves the *Cymry*, meaning fellow men. Travellers noted seven centuries ago that the Welsh were devoted to neighbourhood and genealogy. These characteristics persist. I think that most Welsh people regard themselves as distinct. My observation, based on visitors' books in hotels, museums and churches, is that many more people today than, say, twenty years ago, describe themselves as Welsh.

That is one thing, but to define Welshness is quite another. Wales is not monolithic and Welshness is not a constant or uniform phenomenon. It ranges from passionate to vestigial, from full playing membership to arm's-length association, and varies from place to place, from group to group, from individual to individual, from week to week, from day to day. A man may wake up on a Saturday feeling more Welsh than he did on Friday. Welshness, for some, is a steady secretion from a gland unknown to science, for others a dizzying pint of wine. Many are sure that the foundation of Welshness rests on the Welsh language, but others believe it is a rugby field and a Labour majority. One day, perhaps enthralled by the landscape, a man may say with the poet that it is sweet to be a Welshman. The next day Welshness may seem like grit in the eye or as irksome as any chore.

Many arguments turn on the question of Welshness, on what Wales is, was and should be. It is a controversial place and, since it is in one sense a family, these arguments are sometimes charged with Welsh acrimony. Eight hundred years ago, observing this disputatious disposition, Gerald of Wales remarked, 'Were they inseparable they would be insuperable.' But that applies to many peoples. Like any society, once the veneer and stereotypes have been penetrated, Wales is a dish of subtleties. There are, for example, twenty-two principal valleys of south Wales and each sees itself as having a character slightly different from, and better than, its neighbour. There is some resentment of the attention given over the years to the big and famous Rhondda. 'No need to go to the Rhondda,' people say. 'They're all big-heads up there anyway. If you want to see the real south Wales come to the valley where I grew up.' As in many countries there is in Wales a difference between north and south, east and west. The south mined coal and the north quarried slate. In this century the south has become mostly English-speaking and the north has remained largely Welsh-speaking. It was not so long ago that a southern girl announcing her betrothal to a man from the north could expect dismay to spread over her parents' faces, as if she had chosen a cave dweller. The south enjoys the story of an army officer who applied for the post of chief constable in north Wales, citing as a qualification his experience among the wild tribes of the north-west frontier of India. To southerners the north Walians are gogs – from *gogledd*, the Welsh word for north. A modern epithet is Tibetans. Southerners are *hwntws*, meaning the people beyond. A notorious nineteenth-century murderer was Yr Hwntw Mawr, the Big Southerner. The north sees southerners as roistering drinkers, volatile and profligate – 'don't bank up that fire, you're not in south Wales now'. The north has a dry, leg-pulling wit, the south a quicksilver repartee. The north plays soccer, the south rugby. A Welsh international rugby player from the north is as rare as the unicorn. North and south have different accents and each thinks the other speaks slightly funny Welsh and slightly funny English. A popular television comedy series was based on wry observation of the north–south differences. The national eisteddfod, the gathering of poets, musicians and singers and the greatest Welsh cultural institution, is consciously bipolar, travelling to the north one year and to the south the next, a needle threading Wales together in a perpetual act of union. Better roads and sexual attraction have softened the differences: north and south meet and marry more frequently. And radio, television and the growth of political and academic institutions have brought about a stronger sense of unity and common interest. Differences remain the pepper and ginger in Welsh life; and Wales is an entity both in spite of them and because of them.

The English influence is powerful, but in spite of the centuries of union England does not define Wales. A survey in rural Wales some years ago revealed that three-quarters of the people believed there was a Welsh way of life different from an English way, sixty per cent of Welsh people would be upset to be called English, forty per cent were happy to welcome the English in Wales and nearly forty per cent said the English acted as if they owned the place.

In more than one sense England does not know where Wales is. 'We are more boring to the English than they are to us, which is saying a great deal,' wrote the poet Harri Webb. Many Welsh people have learnt that it is not necessary to choose between two cultures, for it is perfectly possible, enviable and profitable, to live in both of them. To be Welsh is often to lead a double life. An Oxford professor pursued the spiritual life of a High Church Anglican while he lived in Oxford, but at home in rural Wales he worshipped and played the organ in his chapel. Caradog Prichard earned his living as a sub-editor on *The Daily Telegraph* and few of his colleagues knew that in his other life in Wales he was a poetry star.

England and Wales have pressed on each other's bunions for hundreds of years. The word Welsh can still be invested with a pejorative note. There is more to 'Welsh windbag' or 'Welsh womanizer' than mere alliteration. 'Out of the way, you Welsh bastard,' came the ripe Midlands voice from a car when I was slow in crossing a road. The Welsh have a saying, 'To go to an Englishman to learn manners', as if that is the last thing you would do. A man behaving badly may be referred to as *bachgen o Loegr* – a boy from England.

In the Welsh relationship with England, suspicions still seep from the peat of the Middle Ages. After Edward I's conquest in the thirteenth century Englishmen insisted that the Welsh should be thoroughly screwed down. Safe behind the walls of their new fortified towns, but afraid for their security, they demanded discriminatory laws against the Welsh, coldly discouraged intermarriage, kept Welshmen out of top jobs and made them aliens in their own land. Wales chafed. Apart from the harsh laws, the country was treated as a milch-cow by greedy English lords. For comfort the people turned to prophecies that a warrior would come and pick up the sword of freedom. In the first year of the fifteenth century it seemed that the moment had arrived. Owain Glyndwr, a leader of genius, emerged as the spearhead of a revolt that was energized by grievances over the extortion of English conquerors, by humiliation and by a belief in the prophecies that the Welsh would be restored.

Glyndwr's armies rapidly won control of much of Wales. English authority retreated. For a few years the dream seemed to have been realized. But English forces returned to crush the rebellion a dozen years after it flared. Glyndwr went into hiding in Herefordshire and was not heard of again. But his legend and inspiration did not die.

English power now reasserted itself with even greater severity. Laws forbidding the Welsh to hold property or office were reinforced. The English deliberately accentuated the differences between themselves and the Welsh, just as they did between themselves and the Irish. But English hysteria faded as Wales ceased to be a military threat and the countries settled into their cohabitation. Shakespeare had his fun with Wales – 'Heaven defend me from that Welsh fairy! lest he transform me to a piece of cheese' – but he generally gave it a good press, perhaps, as some say, because his grandmother was Welsh. His Henry V proudly professed Welshness and his Fluellen gave Pistol a leek-whipping and a lesson in manners – 'let a Welsh correction teach you a good English condition'.

Welshness has not been English'd out, but the Welsh live with the problem that besets all minorities: they must confront the indifference and perhaps the contempt of a larger neighbour and assert their own individuality without being so strident, obsessive or narrow about it that they are swamped in the folds of their own flag or choke on their own rhetoric.

Some Welsh people feel that to be Welsh is to be, to a greater or lesser extent, part of a cause; and Wales has survived because its people have employed the skills that all small nations must have if they are to flourish: subtlety, nagging persistence, cunning and deviousness. Goronwy Rees, who was a principal of the University of Wales College at Aberystwyth, said that having endured an alien rule for so long the Welsh regard England's law as something which it is their duty to circumvent rather than obey. Leo Abse, the former MP for Pontypool, said, 'We wage guerrilla war. We avoid confrontation, we operate by nudge, by conspiracy. In Westminster the Welsh members wrest out of the English establishment a lot of prizes by calling upon the old cunning which has enabled Wales and its Welshness to survive.'

Wales works because it is relatively small and intimate, the lines of communication efficiently short. It is a country of well-placed brothers-in-law, useful uncles and former team mates. People in public life know each other well. They run the institutions and the Welsh version of home rule, the quango network operating under the eye of the Welsh Office. It is not surprising that Japanese companies feel at home with this way of doing things; they like the informal contacts and avoidance of confrontation.

'A musical nation, yes,' one of the brahmins told me, 'but also a nation of busybodies. We like to involve ourselves in each other's affairs. We are committee-minded.'

These brokers of influence are commonly seen at their feeding grounds, at eisteddfodau, international rugby matches and good lunches. Their heads nod conspiratorially. Their left hands may grasp a drink but their right hands are always free, extended like the claws of crabs, ready to grasp an elbow.

'You know,' said one of these crustaceans, his claw squeezing my arm, 'Wales needs a new image.'

Of course. A picture of thundering choirs, rugby, colliery winding gear and miners coming home to Mam persists even though mining has all but gone, the massed choirs have shrunk and the landscape itself is reshaped. Waiting to see what happens next, what new images emerge, is part of the excitement of the times. When people say Wales needs a new image they are looking forward to a future in which Welshness is relevant.

Meanwhile, stereotypes have their uses as reference points and they are, after all, rooted in history. The artist Pietro Annigoni was once being driven across the Welsh countryside by a Welsh friend who saw in front of him a coach taking a choir to a concert. The Welshman overtook the coach, flagged it down and spoke to the choirmaster. The choir disembarked and, smart in bow ties, against the backdrop of mountains at sunset, sang their hearts out for Annigoni, for whom a romantic and traditional Wales had come true.

Shakespeare's Head

I walked up the hill to Trellech, which almost rhymes with relic; and that is what it is. A town of significance in medieval times, it was reduced by the Black Death and by the rampaging impis of Owain Glyndwr.

A typed card pinned to the church door revealed the vicar's experience of fashionable, if tottering, young godmothers. 'Stiletto heels', his notice advised, 'are very welcome, but beware of the grille in the centre aisle near the font. Bless you!'

A carving on the font depicted a local curiosity, the Virtuous Well, and I went to find it. It lay in a meadow within sight of the church, a small clear pool in a stone recess. A handful of coins gleamed on the mossy shelf above the water. Jam jars were filled with wild flowers. In the canopy of hazel and blackthorn branches which sheltered the well small strips of cloth fluttered like prayer-papers in a Japanese temple. Striped and polka-dot, satin, silk and cotton, they were cut from the clothing of sick and troubled people in the hope of a cure. The well has been a source of solace and hope since pre-Christian times.

A few steps up the lane I leant on a gate and watched a farmer walking in a meadow, throwing food for his sheep from a bucket. His grandchildren, a small boy and girl, trailed behind him hand in hand, wandering among the sheep and buttercups, and I hoped they would remember this sunny day and store it up for their old age.

Sticks and leaves crunched underfoot as I plunged into woodland. I emerged into a meadow in front of Cleddon Hall where Bertrand Russell was born in 1872. His radical mother kicked up the local dust with her ideas on education and female emancipation; but the stir did not last long. She died when Russell was two, so did his sister; and his broken-hearted father died a year later. The owner of the house took me to the bluebell glade in the grounds where they had all been buried. Russell, his liberal upbringing ended, was raised by his sanctimonious grandmother who believed boys grew best on a regime of discomfort and reproach. I met him once, tracked him down to a hotel in the Isle of Wight when he was in the news during the heyday of the Campaign for Nuclear Disarmament. He gave me the quotes I wanted, ordered tea and cake, and told me about his grandfather's meeting with Bonaparte in Elba, marvelling at the way you can reach back through the centuries through a single intermediary. His eyes were sharp and bright, his nose beaky, his neck scrawny: it was like having tea with a talkative condor.

Years later, I went to north Wales to report his death at his home near Portmeirion. He had chosen the house for its prospect of mountains and distance from metropolitan distractions. He loved walking and complained, at ninety-five, that he was finding it more difficult to climb over gates. The evening he died, aged ninety-seven, he went to his bedroom to watch the sun set over Tremadoc Bay and took with him, as was his habit, a large tumbler of Red Hackle whisky. One of his staff showed me the bottle next day, as if it were a chalice. A group of Russell's admirers in America wrote to the suppliers of Red Hackle, asking where in the United States they could find the whisky which 'clearly did not diminish the mental or sexual powers of our lord'. I attended his funeral in Colwyn Bay. He had resisted clergymen all his life and did not want them to get him when he was dead, so the final act was just as he wished, a plain coffin, no words, no music, no service.

A dazzling parade of yellow Welsh poppies cheered my progress along the lane to Cleddon Falls. This native flower has a better claim to be the national bloom than the upstart daffodil introduced by Lloyd George in the flummery he orchestrated for the investiture of the Prince of Wales in 1911. I descended to the snaking coppery Wye, inspecting the changing panorama through embrasures in the trees. Poets have been moved to scribble about this spectacle, but I was born by the Wye and felt proprietorial rather than lyrical. A map on a parish notice board showed the river dividing the Kingdom of England from the Principality of Wales, a description without much meaning, for the Prince of Wales has no residence in Wales and he is not regarded as a particularly Welsh figurehead. The investiture at Caernarfon had its political uses, but there will probably never be another; the sentiment in favour is unlikely to be strong enough within the government, in Wales or, come to that, in Buckingham Palace.

The eighteenth-century parsons and dilettantes who invented tourism and swanned about the British countryside, sketching, philosophizing and admiring the girls, conceived the cult of the picturesque. They adored the Wye. Its limestone cliffs and curving course made it, mile after mile, an almost perfect picture. Tourists floated slowly downstream in pleasure boats furnished with tables for their drawing and writing. Many carried a Claude glass, popularized by the French painter Claude Lorrain, a mirror which obliged the spectator to stand with his back to the landscape and frame a view that could be improved with colour filters.

After idle days on the Wye in 1770 William Gilpin, a New Forest vicar, became an apostle of the picturesque, and wrote a book proposing that the countryside should be examined 'by the rules of picturesque beauty'. This became the handbook for connoisseurs who understood with Gilpin that nature was not perfect and could justifiably be improved in paintings and draw-ings. Gilpin mused that the sombre ivy-clad ruin of Tintern Abbey, the Taj Mahal of the Wye, could be improved by a few editing blows of a hammer. For many genteel tourists Tintern was made less of a pleasure by beggars and importuning crones, stinking bundles of rags that sprang frighteningly to life and offered themselves as guides. Gurus of the picturesque instructed that a view was an emotional experience, the spectator to submit to exhilaration, enchantment, awe and the pleasures of melan-choly and gentle despair. In the hotel across the river I leaned towards gentle despair. My room was so perversely small that with the bed, the chair and myself, we were a crowd of three; and there was no view at all of Tintern's claustral beauty.

I marched on downstream past churchyard walls, thick with maiden's navel, the path a glorious show of speedwell, forget-me-not, red campion and yellow archangel, all attended by sated boozy bees. As I climbed a woodland path, the air was heavy with the scent of wild garlic. By some standards my walk was paltry: a master of the Wye Valley Otterhounds marched fifty-two miles a day in these parts, but was rejected for military service because his tireless legs were bandy.

My path joined the walk created in the eighteenth century by Valentine Morris on his Piercefield estate, parkland that became Chepstow Racecourse in 1921. Morris, too, was devoted to the picturesque and the walk he designed was replete with artful vantage points and entertainments such as the 'giant's cave', an artificial cavern that still exists, guarded by a stone giant holding a boulder aloft. At one of the viewpoints Morris would fire a cannon to impress his guests with the echo.

In the heart of the woods I came upon a deep and mysteri-ous hole, like a shell crater, large enough to have trapped an ele-phant. Using a fallen tree as a ladder I scrambled to the bottom. The cavity was a curious memorial to the obsession of Dr Orville Ward Owen, a Detroit physician, who believed that Francis Bacon wrote the plays of William Shakespeare. He worked assiduously for years to prove it and constructed a decoding contraption, a primitive computer, to help him with his work. It consisted of two large spools with a canvas belt a thousand feet long. To the belt Owen glued hundreds of pages of various Elizabethan texts to enable him to locate key words in a cipher he was certain that Bacon had written. With the aid of this machine he persuaded himself that Bacon had hidden a number of manuscripts, proving his authorship of Shakespeare, in sixty-six iron boxes; and these were to be found in a cave somewhere in the Wye valley near Chepstow. As a grisly embellishment there was a story that Bacon had cut off Shakespeare's head and had stored it in one of the boxes.

In 1909, having squeezed money out of backers and persuaded the Duke of Beaufort to allow a search on his land, Owen began his treasure hunt. For three months he dug in a cliff cave near Chepstow Castle. He found nothing and retired to London to reconsider the whole matter, living handsomely at his backers' expense. After further thought he declared that the iron boxes had been concealed in the bed of the Wye itself. The Duke of Beaufort permitted him to dig in the river and a Chicago supporter put up the money for an expedition. In 1911 engineers and labourers built a dam and fought flooding and tides, to excavate a pit in the river-bed. At night they crouched over pumps and dug by the yellow light of spluttering flares, a hellish scene. After some months Owen admitted defeat and retired to America.

His Baconian fantasy, however, continued to tantalize. In 1920 one of his American disciples took up the spade again, digging in the foundations of Chepstow Castle until the owner became so alarmed, lest the walls were being undermined, that he ordered a halt. That was still not the end of it. For several years in the 1920s another of Owen's American followers turned mole and dug holes in the woods, searching for the sixty-six iron boxes, the Stars and Stripes fluttering above his hopeless muddy labours.

Twenty feet down, in the mulchy bottom of one of these holes, I poked around, hoping that the original searchers had missed something, that my stick might strike a rusty casket containing manuscripts or, failing that, the skull of William Shakespeare.

Nelson's Eye

Nelson embarked on a celebrated holiday in 1802. Far from being a quiet rest it was a personality tour of England and Wales, and he was accompanied by his brother, his sister-in-law and nephew, by Emma and her husband Sir William Hamilton, and by two servants. The party set off from the Hamilton–Nelson mansion in Merton, Surrey, and the objective was Milford Haven in Pembrokeshire where Sir William had an estate. This was managed by Charles Greville, Sir William's nephew, who had once been Emma's lover and had passed her on to his uncle with the recommendation that 'a cleaner sweeter bedfellow does not exist'. Greville planned a dockyard at Milford Haven and wanted his uncle to bring Nelson to endorse the scheme. The party drove to Blenheim, expecting the hospitality due to the victor of the Nile and Copenhagen. The Duke of Marlborough, however, offered only sandwiches at the gate, perhaps because he disapproved of Nelson's going about so publicly with a mistress. Nelson was furious, but that was the only rebuff and at every other stop he was enthusiastically mobbed. He was hailed at Oxford, Gloucester and Ross and spent lazy hours on the Wye, in a boat garlanded with laurel leaves, while Emma, no doubt, trailed her sensuous fingers in the water. The excursion ended triumphantly at Monmouth, Nelson baring his head as the crowd cheered, cannon boomed and a band played 'See the Conquering Hero Comes'.

From Monmouth, the tourists drove through Wales, reaching Milford Haven by way of Brecon, Merthyr Tydfil and Carmarthen. Nelson spoke in praise of Greville's dockyard and the party returned by way of Tenby, Swansea, Cowbridge, Cardiff, Chepstow, Monmouth, Hereford, Ludlow, Worcester, Birmingham, Warwick, Coventry, Althrop, Dunstable and St Albans. We are fortunate that Nelson was so prolific and assiduous a letter writer and compiler of notes: he kept details of the costs of the inns, drivers, horse-hire, repairs, carriage-greasing and boot-cleaning, the half-crown he paid for oysters in Wales and the guinea he gave to a Welsh ventriloquist.

Nelson's visits to Monmouth laid down a seam of gold. The

town has cashed in ever since. Every Nelson fan worth his grog makes the pilgrimage. The museum here has a collection of pictures, letters, medals, swords, plates and other pieces amassed by Lady Llangattock, an obsessed Nelsonian. Some of the letters in the museum are from antique dealers. 'My Lady . . .' they begin, asking politely when she is going to settle their bills. Lady Llangattock was the mother of the pioneer airman Charles Rolls, of Rolls-Royce. A statue in Monmouth shows him holding a model of the biplane in which he was killed in 1911, the first British aviator to die in a crash.

In the museum a pair of Lady Hamilton's black sharply-pointed shoes was displayed. The man next to me said, 'Big feet, eh?' Nelson's false eye stared out from its mounting in a kind of eggcup. But it was false in two senses, because Nelson never had a glass eye. The shell that burst in front of his face during the siege of Calvi in 1794 severely bruised, but did not blind, his right eye, and the deterioration of his sight may have been caused by a detached retina. He sometimes wore a shade over his left eye to shield it from the light. But it is impossible to eradicate the popular idea that Nelson habitually wore an eye-patch over his right.

I also examined one of Nelson's jam bills. It was a trivial detail that helped to bring the great man to life. Preoccupied with Bonaparte, the Navy, the shortage of English oak trees, his place in history and the delicate manners of a *ménage à trois*, he also had to consider the price of jam.

The Sacred Rhubarb

Churches and chapels formed my stepping stones as I headed into the folds of the Black Mountains. I paused first at Partrishow, a small shy oyster of a church whose pearl is a carved oak rood screen, one of the loveliest in the country, depicting a dragon eating grapes. Its other gems are wall paintings, concealed for years by limewash but now revealed, and painted memorial tablets with lettering by the Brute family of masons, decorated with golden-haired cherubs, like mischievous choirboys, with centre partings and impish smiles. Such churches stand among the real treasures of the country, works of art reaching out from the centuries, the records and reflections of ourselves, of faith that remains a matter of wonder, of local pride and craftsmanship. People are surprised to find these churches so accessible and I often saw in visitors' books the remark, 'Lovely to find it unlocked.'

I walked across the valley to Cwmyoy, to the church knocked askew by a landslip, so that it lies broken-backed with a tipsy tower and all its planes awry, like a cartoon church. From here, a little breathless, I reached the top of Hatterell Hill and picked my way through the bracken-covered stones of an Iron Age fort. The wind whooshed so loudly that I fancied a race of Stentors must have lived up here in ancient times. I watched the play of sunlight on the comfortable orchard shires of England to my right. The ruins of Llanthony monastery, enfolded in the arms of hills, lay to my left. I descended into the Vale of Ewyas by way of the Beer Path along which monks, laughing and stumbling, once hauled their ale from England.

I sat in the sunshine on the stump of one of Llanthony's stone columns. I read, in the Reverend Francis Kilvert's diary, his account of his visit here in 1870. Like many tourists, he did not much like other sightseers and was irritated to see two of them among the ruins. 'If there is one thing more hateful than another it is being told what to admire and having objects pointed out to one with a stick,' he wrote priggishly. 'Of all noxious animals the most noxious is a tourist. And of all tourists the most vulgar, ill-bred, offensive and loathsome is the British tourist.'

The serenity of the Black Mountains has made them for centuries a magnet for hermits, monks, artists, poets, hippies and dreamers who thought they knew the latitude and longitude of Shangri-La.

St David was one of the earliest pilgrims, living here in beerless piety, drinking from the Honddu stream and eating leeks, beginning the Welsh attachment to 'that sacred herbe'. Many followed his path. The Lord of Hereford rode into the valley early in the twelfth century and was so enchanted that he turned anchorite and ordered masons to build the magnificent monastery of Llanthony.

In earthly Edens, though, a garden rake lies in ambush for the unwary foot. The monks of Llanthony found the 'beggarly Welsh' worse than any scourge or penance, a thieving and irreligious lot, resentful of their Norman masters. After thirty years they packed their bells, books and candles and decamped to Gloucester to serve the Almighty in peace. The monastery decayed and its walls and fallen columns, echoing to the flitter of bats' wings, speak of the abandoned dream.

Walter Savage Landor, longing for contentment, a place to write his poetry, bought the ruin in 1807. Envisioning a Utopia he planted hundreds of acres of sycamores, chestnuts and beeches, whose splendour we enjoy today, and built an Italianate house on the hill above the monastery. I explored its ruins. Landor spent hardly any time in it, for he and the valley were never good companions. His anger was never far off the boil and, in common with his predecessor monks, he could not live in amity with the locals. He bickered constantly with builders and tenants, and was swamped by debts, rows and lawsuits. The vicar of Cwmyoy told me how Landor dealt with a Welsh butler who enraged him. He picked the man up bodily and threw him out of a window, roaring at him not to damage the flowers when he hit the ground.

'I shall never cease to wish', he wrote of his Welsh neighbours, 'that Julius Caesar had utterly exterminated the whole race of Britons. They are as irreclaimable as Gypsies or Malays.'

If it was not the 'rascally Welsh' who made him rage it was the Welsh nightingales, maddening him by disturbing his sleep. In the end the valley defeated him and he went to live in Italy where he died aged nearly ninety, possibly in a temper. As I ate my picnic in the monastery ruins a blackbird stole one of my sandwiches and dragged it away. Landor would have recognized it: definitely a Welsh blackbird.

I went down to the museum in Abergavenny. Frank Olding, the curator, took me to a store room, opened a box and extracted a framed square of glass in which was preserved what appeared to be a piece of shrivelled nylon stocking.

'Rhubarb,' he said.

It was a religious relic, the sacred rhubarb gathered by an

extraordinary man who, in the last decades of the nineteenth century, attempted to build his heavenly vestibule in the Black Mountains.

The Reverend Joseph Leycester Lyne, who called himself Father Ignatius, was a man of pure faith, a Christian extremist, a Bible fundamentalist who believed the earth was flat, a charismatic preacher, a holy fool no bishop in England or Wales would dare ordain. He believed that he was on a mission from God, and although many saw in him the characteristics of a March hare few doubted his earnestness. He devoted his life to reviving the Anglican medieval monastic tradition that had been broken by the Dissolution of the Monasteries three centuries earlier.

He started wearing a monk's habit when he was twenty-four, and cut a mystical figure. A belief grew up that he had miraculous powers. When he worked in the slums of the East End of London a story circulated that he had restored a dead girl to life. In another story, a woman jeered at his monkish tonsure and he placed a curse on her son. The boy's hair fell out; and when the woman apologized he restored the curls with a touch. Later, he was forbidden to speak in churches and Protestant thugs disrupted his meetings. In 1867, his spellbinding preaching drew huge crowds and caused riots.

He founded a monastic community in Norwich but it fell into disarray because of mutinous monks, money troubles and the scandal of a monk's love for a choirboy. During a trip to the Black Mountains he saw the ruins of Llanthony and vowed that here he would build his monastic order. The owners refused to sell. Undaunted, Father Ignatius decided to build his own monastery four miles away, at Capel-y-ffin. He journeyed there in a cart drawn by a wretched horse which appeared at one stage to be dying in the shafts. Father Ignatius, the story went, got out to pray and the horse, transformed into a veritable Pegasus, cantered the rest of the way. He laid the foundation stone of his monastery in 1870 and raised the money for it with electrifying evangelical sermons, packing every hall.

Ever the autocrat, he insisted on a rigorous monkish regimen, saying he wanted 'no more namby-pamby nineteenth-century-hearted men' and declaring his preference for 'openly downright, brave, faithful, medieval-souled Welshmen and Englishmen'. It was difficult to recruit postulants who could stay the rugged course, and Father Ignatius could not keep order because he was often away preaching and raising funds. On three occasions in 1880 monks claimed they saw an apparition of the Virgin Mary, but it was strongly suspected that there had been a prank with a magic lantern. Whatever the vision, the apparition was thought to have hovered over a rhubarb bush and a leaf taken from it apparently cured the diseased leg of a nun. Another leaf was the one I saw in Abergavenny.

Father Ignatius journeyed to America and preached among the defeated and pathetic Sioux. He died in 1908 and was buried in his monastery church at Capel-y-ffin. Before long the church crumbled. Perhaps the workmanship reflected the meagre wages Ignatius paid the builders. I visited his grave among the fallen stones, a few yards from a white figure of the Virgin commemorating the vision above the rhubarb.

The valley saw no more paradise-seekers until 1924. Then a lorry came snorting up the lane to Capel-y-ffin, carrying three families, an assortment of children, chickens, dogs and ducks, all led by Eric Gill, going famously into retreat to found an artists' commune.

Gill once said in exasperation that he would only secure peace for his stone carving, his engraving, and contemplation, if he moved to a remote part of Africa with lions to deter visitors. Although not Africa, Capel-y-ffin seemed to suit his idea of wild and almost inaccessible retreat. The tribe lived in the shadow of the conical mountain called Twmpa, also known as Lord Hereford's Knob, and passed the days working, brewing beer, making cheese, growing vegetables, cooking on open fires, bathing naked together in chilly mountain pools and enjoying 'heavenly picnics in sunny secluded paradises'. A visiting friend found 'as cold a spot as any anchorite could wish for', with the Gill tribe wrapped in overcoats at dinner.

Gill was charged with artistic and sexual energy: at times he seemed to be a phallus with an artist attached. He carved some of his masterpieces here and also designed, for the Monotype Company, the brilliant Gill sans-serif and Perpetua typefaces.

His Black Mountains adventure lasted four years. The bloom faded, the commune crumbled and Gill returned to England.

Tidy

Capel-y-ffin, the chapel on the edge, really did feel like an outpost. The church is lovely, little more than a white cottage, its louvred wooden bell tower tipped like a hat, seven great yews gathered around it like protective brothers.

I read the inscription on the gravestone of Noah Watkins who died aged eight in 1738. 'This child said he would not Take a hundred pounds in money for Breaking the Sabbath but keep it holy.' What a burden of piety for a young lad to bear. In the youth hostel nearby I was told a story which reminded me of poor Noah. A party of schoolchildren staying in the hostel were marked down by their accompanying teachers as vegetarian. When the warden saw that the noses of a couple of boys were twitching, Bisto-kid fashion, at the smell of sausages, she gently reminded them they were vegetarians. No, they said, wistfully, that was what the teachers said. A piety of nutrition had been placed upon their shoulders.

In the visitors' book in the church some young people had written 'cool' and 'brill'. A Welsh peer had written elegantly, 'On the frontier between the material and the spiritual; thanks for it.' Someone had remarked, 'Smells of my childhood', and another wrote, 'Eric Gill's been here' – and so he had; he had carved two tombstones in the churchyard.

One visitor had written the single word 'Tidy'. It did not mean that the church was swept and the hymn books were neatly ordered, though they were. 'Tidy' in south Wales has several shades of meaning. A tidy woman is respectable and a tidy man is reliable and mannerly. If you are admonished to talk tidy, you avoid slang and watch your ps and qs. 'Get home tidy,' says a wife to her husband, straightening his tie before he goes to his rugby club dinner. 'A tidy wedding' means the bride was not pregnant and the occasion was seemly and proper. 'There's tidy' means that something is done well. Tidy is a variant of nice and also an emphasizer, meaning substantial: a tidy dinner

139

is a slap-up meal. In Wales, always take note of the sign that
says, 'Park Tidy'.

Violet in her Realm

This part of the borderland seems to have its own life, an allegiance to itself, as if it were a third country. The Black
Mountains are penetrated only by thin capillary roads hemmed
by tall concealing hedgerows and often closed in winter by snow.
Enfolded by mountain walls, the Vale of Ewyas has the secluded
air of a cloister, an ethereal beauty. It has struck many an
imagination as a primeval place, spooky and enchanted, its
numerous neolithic tombs echoing a pagan past; and some feel
that the Twmpa itself is a brooding presence, a Welsh Ayers
Rock, elemental and compelling.

Cliff and Violet George run a flock of more than a hundred
sheep on seventy-seven acres of a hillside about half an hour's
walk along the narrow lane from Capel-y-ffin. Their whitewashed farmhouse, barely visible from the lane, is half-way up
the hill, a stone building, old and weathered, with thick walls,
standing among a huddle of outbuildings and evergreen trees
around a small straw-covered yard.

We talked in the lean-to parlour, under a ceiling of old and
rough white-painted planks. The wind tugged like a bailiff at the
door. Pale light entered through the window. A bible lay on the
table. The glass-fronted dresser housed glassware and china and
small picture cards with religious verses. An old wireless set stood
by the dresser. Cliff and Violet own no television, telephone or
car. I sat in the warmest place, by the Raeburn stove on which
stood a large black iron kettle. Cliff sat on a high-backed pew by
the table, wearing a tweed jacket, his hands as knotted as tree
roots, gnarled and purpled, large and strong. He was nearly
eighty, his face boyish, his hair a white thatch, his eyes cerulean
blue, merry and inquiring, his smile so ready that I doubted he
had ever known a surly moment. Violet sat in a chair, in Sunday
best of black. She had a quiet voice and a shy smile, and she was
not uncomfortable with silences. She was sixty-nine and her
skin was clear and youthful.

Violet's mother had recently died in this room at the age of ninety-seven. For many months she lay in a bed beneath the window, her hair streaming over the pillow, her eyes filled with the spectacle of the mountain and the valley in all its moods. Violet showed me a clipping from the local newspaper, the funeral report. It spread across three columns and began, 'We record with regret the death of Mrs Sarah Ann Lewis . . .', and gave the names of the many people who attended the chapel funeral service that marked the end of one humble life.

Cliff did not know the age of the house, though it was old when he was born in it. He had lived all his life on this farm and the boundaries of his existence and travels were marked by the town of Abergavenny, fourteen miles distant, and Hay-on-Wye, eight miles off across the wild Gospel Pass. He had never been to London, he said, and laughed as if to say why on earth would he want to do such a thing.

He worked for his father on the farm and drove cattle and sheep along the crooked lanes to market in Abergavenny or Hay, sometimes on foot, sometimes on a pony like a cowboy. He was on the road by four in the morning, whistling up his little grey dog and giddyupping the pony. He reached the market around nine o'clock, hoping to sell every beast, otherwise he would have to drive the unsold animals back. After the sales in Abergavenny he and his friends went to The Bear where 'Mrs Price cooked us a lovely dinner of beef, potatoes and peas, stacked up like a mountain, and we ate it by the open fire where our coats were put to dry.' He drove animals to market into the late 1940s, when his father hired a truck and brought Cliff's cowboy days to an end.

Violet had been to London once, for a day, in 1947, and saw St Paul's. In the winter of that year the snow lay so deep in the valley that she did not see a gate or a hedge for nine days. She was born on a small farm a few miles away, on the Breconshire–Monmouthshire border, and grew up helping her mother to churn butter and make cheese and eight- and ten-pound loaves of bread, salting freshly-killed pigs and making faggots and brawn.

Her grandmother was a midwife who made her rounds on

horseback; side-saddle, said Violet. Her father was crippled by polio and every Sunday for thirty years he walked with the aid of two sticks to chapel. At home after the evening service he read aloud to the family from his bible. Violet and Cliff met at the Baptist chapel in Capel-y-ffin. Violet had been taken there first in her mother's arms. When she was a young woman she embraced the faith. 'I was convicted of my sins,' she said, 'and, in need of a Saviour, I was baptized in obedience to my Lord on the eighth of June 1947.' She was immersed in the stream by the chapel. 'As I was going under the water the sun came out from behind a cloud and that was seen as good fortune.' It was around that time that she signed a pledge she had honoured all her life, that she would not eat fish, flesh or fowl.

She is devoted to the chapel and plays the organ during Sunday evening services. She has seen the congregation dwindle to a handful. She is also the organist at the church in Capel-y-ffin, at the Sunday afternoon service twice a month. 'Only a few people attend,' she said, 'but there's hope because two children from a farm are coming now.'

Violet had travelled to Cardiff and to Bristol to hear evangelists preach and said she hoped to see a religious revival, such as her mother experienced in 1904 when the charismatic Evan Roberts drew fervent thousands to his sermons. 'Mother was taken to Swansea in the revival and remembered the miners singing hymns in the streets and teasing her, saying they would brush against her new white dress with their black pit clothes. She remembered that even in the deepest snow the chapels were full and the people's tears dropped onto the pews.'

Violet got up to make tea. She had baked a fruit cake, a sponge cake and thick scones and brought these to the table with cheese and jam. She took a white loaf and, sawing horizontally, cut slices as thin as bank notes and buttered them. There was an insistent banging outside and a ram appeared at the window, wearing an imperious look. Violet said, 'He wants some food and a warm,' and she went to let the ram into one of the outhouses. While she was away I picked up her bible and saw that she had filled the endpapers and flyleaf with notes. One entry, neatly penned, said: 'John Wesley travelled two hundred and fifty thousand miles on horseback, and preached to thirty thousand people. He lived to ninety years of age.' Violet said she heard such things on the wireless and liked to jot them down.

Cliff said the pattern of their lives was set by their sheep which they worked with their Welsh collies Wally and Fly. 'Our favourite time of the year is the beginning of April when the lambs are born and we're often up half the night helping the ewes having difficult births.' They often heard the screech of vixens and the bark of dog foxes and expected to lose some of their flock when lambing started. Fox-hunting was necessary, Violet said, though she preferred that the foxes were shot. She and Cliff loved their animals so much, she said, that they had kept on a couple of cows, Sara and Cherry, because they could not bear to get rid of them. Cliff took me across the farmyard to the old cottage that served as his beast-house and let out the two cows for an airing. They bumped and lurched around the farmyard. 'They're like me,' Cliff said, 'pensioners.'

Violet said her brother took her once a week to shop in Abergavenny where she buys the two local newspapers. 'Our main entertainment is the wireless,' she said, although she and Cliff sometimes go to a concert in Cwmyoy or to a village pantomime. 'The trouble with modern music,' Cliff said, 'is that it's so loud that you might give the wrong answer because you didn't hear the question properly.' Outside in the farmyard we watched the cloud shadows scudding across the valley. Violet said, 'We've wished for no other life. We have our animals, pure air and water.'

We fell to talking of Francis Kilvert, the curate who lived not far from here, and who died of peritonitis in 1879, five weeks after the marriage he had longed for. 'Such a shame,' Violet said, 'such a good young man.' It was as if he had only recently passed away, as if his obituary, clipped from the local newspaper, might be on the dresser.

We returned to the parlour. On the bookcase in the corner of the room lay a copy of *Woman's Own* which Violet had recently bought in a second-hand bookshop in Abergavenny. She said she was looking forward to reading it. It had none of the stridency, breathlessness and urgent preoccupations of modern magazines. It was dated 1963.

The Photograph of Trotty

When I mentioned to friends in London that I planned to walk along the bank of the River Taff from Quakers Yard to Merthyr they thought it a decidedly eccentric expedition. In their minds the river ran black through a ransacked and worn-out landscape, the very picture of a Stygian south Wales. A few years ago the river did run black, as it had for more than a century, and walking along it would have been difficult. But the river and the land have been cleaned and there was a path which took me beneath trees along a river bank brilliant with bluebells. After a couple of miles or so I met an angler casting his fly for trout on clear water. He had good reason to hope, he said, that the salmon, the king in exile, would make his long-awaited return to this stretch of the river.

In its time this valley was an industrial carotid through which wealth poured in a torrent towards the sea. Merthyr erupted in thrilling violence and its coal and iron came down by canal and railway and transformed the small town of Cardiff into a world port. As I walked I saw the gigantic monuments of that age, bridges and broad-shouldered viaducts, soaring out of the jungle of trees and thick brambles of the gorge. The best of engineers, men like Brunel, flexed their muscles here and their stone structures have an imperial, Roman, feel to them, boasting of conquest and Progress with its Victorian capital P. This was once the busiest railway junction in the land. The path brought me to the birthplace of railway transport, a long stretch of ground beneath the trees where Richard Trevithick built his tramway in 1802, thirty years before Stephenson fired up his Rocket. I put my fingers into the bolt-holes of the stones that had held the iron rails in place. One of the Merthyr ironmasters bet five hundred guineas that Trevithick's steam locomotive could haul five wagons loaded with iron and passengers the nine miles from Merthyr to Abercynon. It did, at just over five miles an hour.

The path passed by the cemetery on the hill above Aberfan.

A single word can call a rush of images to the mind and Aberfan is such a word. It encapsulates horror, grief and anger. For every pound of coal mined in the pit in the village a bucketful of waste was added to the mountain of slurry on the hillside until it became an unstable, deadly mass. One hundred and twenty-eight children and sixteen adults died when it fell on the village school in 1966.

The inscriptions on the long rows of white memorials pierced the heart as they had always done, and I was reminded of what a man said to me at this place years ago. 'A word, a snatch of song, a shout, is enough to bring it all back. Sudden death was always a part of going into the pit, God knows we have learned that, but not of going to school.'

Aberfan was an unremarkable mining village. Its people showed remarkable qualities. There was a widespread assumption that they would leave after the disaster, flee Aberfan and never return, but most of them stayed. Within themselves they discovered resilience, strength, comfort and leadership. The public anger that followed the Aberfan disaster led to the concerted effort to rid all of south Wales of its industrial scars. Fujis of colliery waste were levelled, shaped and planted with trees. The reclamation teams saw that their task was to turn back the clock by more than a hundred years, to restore a former beauty.

Along the road, in Troedyrhiw, I came to St John's church, the mausoleum of a Valleys pharaoh, a symbol of his conceit and power. Anthony Hill, a Merthyr ironmaster, built it and decreed that no one else but he should be buried here. He died in 1862 and lies alone and secure in a vault beneath the altar, his coffin in a lead casket and that in turn enclosed within a coffin of thick oak.

The path followed the bed of the canal that for years was the most profitable waterway on earth, and took me to the outskirts of Merthyr and the substantial homes of the Victorian middle class. This was the monkey-puzzle belt. The trees were a vanity and status symbol popular with the Nonconformist clergy. A minister of substance could mark his status by planting a monkey-puzzle and sending his boy to Oxford.

I climbed into the hills above the town, into the land that

made Merthyr mighty, every square foot dug for iron ore, coal
and limestone. In parts, the land reminded me of battlefields in
Flanders, trenches and craters still discernible. Deep in the
woods, by rusty pools, I came upon a sixteenth-century char-
coal furnace, molten deposits of iron still adhering to the curved
wall. Further on, broken stone steps, velvety with moss, took me
down through the centuries to the ruins of a large ironworks,
half-concealed by trees and undergrowth. Massive walls and
archways furred with lichen stood like a lost temple in a jungle
in Mexico, raised to gods once all-demanding and now forgotten. The stones were eloquent: I imagined the noise, heat,
shouts, fumes and the teams of sweating horses. On its signposts
Merthyr calls itself the Iron Town, but there are few industrial
remains. It was partly because of Aberfan, partly from a wish to
expunge the past, that Merthyr tore down many of the monuments to its history.

Merthyr was made by faith as well as by iron, and the pulse of
religious dissent beat very strongly here. In a glade still hard to
find, I came to a ruined chapel where Nonconformists once met
in secret. The radical ideas that bubbled in this place and other
religious hide-outs gave power to political convulsions. The
workers' rebellion of 1831, which became an armed insurrec-
tion, remains a matter of pride in Merthyr. The descendant of
one of those who took part told me the story in fresh and grip-
ping detail, how the troops marched into town and opened fire.
This was where a banner was dipped in calf's blood, the first red
flag of revolt raised in Britain. This was where poor Dic
Penderyn was arrested in the aftermath, scapegoated and
hanged, an innocent remembered as a working-class martyr.
The landlady of The Three Horseshoes showed me the room in
her pub where Chartists met and argued, their debates heard by
a government spy who reported directly to the Home Secretary
in London.

For sixty years Merthyr was the largest town in Wales. It was
ruled by potentates. The first and greatest, a colossus, was
Richard Crawshay, a John Bull figure with a porcine face, son of
a Yorkshire farmer. He bought the Cyfarthfa ironworks in 1794
– its name means barking dog – and made it the largest in the

world, a roaring hearth gushing sparks, lighting the sky. Poets came to see the brilliant violence of industry, chewed their pencils and wrote that the sons of Vulcan toiled in the hills.

Merthyr grew rich on the wars with Bonaparte. Crawshay cast guns for the Royal Navy and his coat of arms included a pyramid of cannon balls. And who is this driving into town, in 1802, but Nelson himself? During his holiday he stopped to see how the guns were forged. Crowds besieged the inn where he stayed and the raucous welcome was punctuated by wild musket shots, one of which killed a boy. Crawshay was reduced to tears, not by this, but by the presence of his hero. He conducted Nelson around the ironworks and paused to present him to the workers. 'Here's your Nelson, boys,' he cried emotionally. 'Shout, you buggers, shout!' Nelson asked for his health to be toasted in Welsh and gave a guinea to the first man who called out.

Richard Crawshay sired a dynasty that bestrode Merthyr for more than a hundred years. No novelist could have composed such a saga of wealth, power, eccentricity and Victorian family values. All the Crawshay men fought bitterly with their fathers. One of Richard's grandsons, William Crawshay, built the mock-Gothic pile of Cyfarthfa Castle, today a museum and a memorial to Crawshay swagger. It commanded the uproarious and lurid town. The seething slums, though, in the district called China, were ruled by criminal chieftains who styled themselves emperors. Such was Merthyr's reputation that, told he was being posted to the town, a young curate in one of Anthony Trollope's novels fainted away.

Richard Crawshay's great-grandson, Robert, inherited the iron kingdom at the age of twenty-two. In his forties a stroke left him deaf and cantankerous and he cut his men's wages and shut down the ironworks rather than let them form a union. He withdrew into the solace of photography and made a virtual slave of his principal model, his daughter Rose, nicknamed Trotty. He summoned her to his presence by blowing a whistle and ordered her to pose in all manner of costumes, as a fishwife in a bonnet, as a Swiss maiden, as a gypsy, as a peasant girl with an urn on her head. He made her process the prints and the chemicals made her hands cracked and sore. She grew to detest the sight of a camera.

She was her father's prisoner. He forbade her to marry, forced her to swear that she would stay with him. Pouring out her loneliness to her diary she wrote, 'I would do anything to get away from this dreadful life.' She was twenty-nine when she met and fell in love with Arthur Williams, a barrister. Her petulant father refused to attend the wedding. He told her, though, that he would leave her one hundred thousand pounds. But he promptly sat down and wrote a codicil disinheriting her, a cruel stroke melodramatically revealed when the family gathered in 1879 to hear a lawyer read the will.

I went to his tomb in the churchyard at Vaynor, not far from Merthyr. Robert Crawshay lies in a grave fenced by iron railings, secure forever under a heavy red stone slab. As he commanded, it bears the words 'God Forgive Me'.

Recently a television crew went to Cyfarthfa Castle to make a film, and set up their camera on a heavy tripod in front of one of Robert Crawshay's portraits of Trotty. They moved to the other end of the room to discuss the next session of filming and the tripod and camera suddenly tipped over with a crash. They thought that one of the tripod legs had collapsed. It had not. There was nothing wrong with it. Everyone knew how much Trotty had hated cameras.

Jones Cape Horn

I left the Cnapan hotel at Newport in Pembrokeshire and tramped up the hill called Carn Ingli. Cnapan was an early form of bloodynose rural football, war by other means, played by teams of hundreds of youths kicking a slippery ball across country from one village to another.

The stones of Carn Ingli stood blue and purple in the distance. A snowcrust lay on the mountainside. The huddled sheep looked shipwrecked. The wind blustered this way and that and hissed among the rocks and gorse as if half the ghosts of Pembrokeshire were whispering malevolently that I should quit their place of convocation.

From the stark summit outcrop, a natural fortress, I looked out over the quilted Preseli hills, at the headlands and the sea. The land and weary trees ached for sunshine. I fancied that from this wind-blasted crow's-nest I could see almost to Cape Horn, for this is an evocative coast, once a kingdom of seafarers populated by captains and shipwrights, herring-netters and coxswains, where the schoolmarms taught navigation and showed boys how to find their way from the Falklands to Fishguard.

The little ports in bays and coves had their backs to the Welsh hinterland and the west in their eyes. Many of their men knew the quays of Valparaiso and Yokohama better than they knew the streets of home. In New Quay a boy sent to the harbour on an errand for his mother was taken aboard a ship which was short of a lad. It sailed at once to catch the tide. The boy's mother did not see him for three years. In Llangrannog, on the Cardigan coast, Geraint Jenkins told me that he did not see his sea captain father for years at a time. His mother would sometimes receive a message – 'Meet me in Antwerp' – and she would hurry across Wales and England by train to catch a ferry to Belgium.

In Llangrannog, as in many places on this coast, ships were built on the beach. When they were ready for launching labourers dug a channel towards the sea, the tide flooded in and teams of men and horses hauled until the vessel floated. In Tresaith, a few miles away, there were no jetties or quays, just a bare unsheltered beach; but the captains of sailing coasters ran their ships ashore at high tide, unloaded their cargoes into farm carts and, with luck, floated off at the next tide. Almost everything came by sea – furniture, and groceries – but the chief cargoes were lime, burnt in kilns near the beach to make fertilizer for the alkali-deficient soil of these parts, and fuel bricks made of coal-dust and clay.

Spring was turning into summer when I came back to walk the cliffs. The paths and cliff edges were brilliant with the blue and pink embroidery of squill and thrift, the flower that adorned the reverse of the old threepenny piece. I found numerous small places like Tresaith, some as shy as moles, just a hamlet and a pocket-sized sandy bay at the end of a long, winding glen thick with wildflowers. Most of them, like any self-respecting cove, had a legend or a story attached to them, about shipwrecks, smugglers, pirates and castaway princesses, with mermaids two a penny. Penbryn was such a place. A ship driven ashore here in 1816 was robbed by the local people of its cargo of wine, an act which moved the Bishop of St David's to order clergymen to 'preach once a quarter on the unchristian enormity of plundering wrecks – press on their consciences the flagrant criminality of this inhuman practice so disgraceful to them as Britons and Christians.'

At Cwmtydu, a little place where dolphins sported and sunbathing seals reclined like starlets, I was told that during the First World War a German submarine crew came ashore and roistered in a local pub. The legend was embellished in the Second World War: this time the Germans came ashore from their U-boat and went shopping.

On the cliff path I saw a young raven on its nest, its open pink mouth a beacon for its foraging parents. I watched fulmars about their business of raising their young on the cliffs. They spend most of their time at sea, rather like the sailors of the last century.

Far from home, seafarers dreamed of the villages and tranquil lanes of Wales and the houses they would live in when they at last returned. The chapel graveyard near Llangrannog is the final anchorage of many mariners. It is also where local poets have their last lines, some of the headstones saying simply 'Farmer and Poet'. These men made verses as readily as they breathed, composing as they ploughed, or when they met in competition. They wrote verses to order: just as people sent for the plumber or the vet, so they sent for the poet to celebrate a wedding or an anniversary; and the poets were paid a few shillings or given a chicken or a goose.

On the road out of Llangrannog I came upon a fine house with an anchor device incorporated into its front gate. The owner, John Harries, told me that the house was built by a sea captain for his retirement. 'But he never lived in it. He was killed in a brawl in a bar in Casablanca.' Casablanca! How far from dear Llangrannog.

I came down from the cliff path through a flowery way of meadows, on the sort of sunny day I wanted to eke out, and into pretty New Quay. In its Victorian prime the local people financed ships, buying shares of one sixty-fourth of the value, and they built them, rigged them and sailed them to the earth's ends; and the houses where master mariners lived still bear the names of local schooners, ketches, brigantines and barquentines.

A man called Reg, a resident originally from the Midlands, gave me his views about New Quay. More visitors would come for their summer holidays, he said, if the district stopped calling itself Ceredigion. The name of Ceredigion, an old Welsh kingdom, has been in use since the ninth century, and possibly since the fifth, but Reg thought it should be discarded because in his opinion Welsh names put English people off and were bad for business.

In New Quay there was no escaping Dylan Thomas. The town has not forgotten that during the war he lived scampishly across the bay in a bungalow. I was shown the steps down which he famously fell. I had a drink in the pub restaurant that bears his name and whose walls are covered with photographs of him. He used to drink here, as he drank everywhere else. In death as in life he supports local business. I was told that there had once been a plan to erect a mark or memorial to him, but a man objected, saying that Dylan Thomas had, on more than one occasion, taken a ride in a local taxi and not paid the fare.

The Beach Party

In a cartoon drawn during the height of his belligerence, Bonaparte threatened: 'In my seven League Corsican Boots I'll step across the water and pay you a visit Master Bull.' I walked to the beach at Carreg Wasted, near Fishguard, the only beach in Britain that bears the imprint of those Corsican boots. Here on 22 February 1797 the nightmare of invasion became reality.

It was originally part of a plan to destabilize the country by striking in three places, Ireland, Newcastle and south Wales. In Ireland the invaders were to help Irishmen throw off English rule, and in Newcastle and Wales they would spread terror and help the poor rise against the rich. The attacks in England and

Wales were intended, not to capture Britain, but to stir trouble and so divert attention from the invasion of Ireland.

Forty-five French ships, with fifteen thousand soldiers aboard, reached Bantry Bay in Ireland in December 1796, but the weather prevented a landing. Not a man got ashore. Meanwhile, five thousand men set off from Dunkirk aiming to cross the North Sea and attack ships in the Tyne, but retreated after a few miles because of foul weather and mutiny.

The third force did not sail in time. It departed in February because the authors of the plan felt that doing something was better than nothing, a hopeless spin of the roulette wheel. Called the Légion Noire because of its dark uniforms, it was a gang of desperadoes freed from jails and led by Colonel William Tate, an elderly anglophobe American. Landing on the rocky beach, Tate commandeered a farmhouse for his headquarters, while his ravenous soldiers plundered nearby homes, seizing and boiling every goose and chicken in sight. A wine ship had recently been wrecked on the coast and most houses in the district therefore had claret galore. The invaders were soon reeling.

At daybreak the Pembrokeshire lanes swarmed with men hurrying west to tip the French into the sea. They brandished sticks, scythes and muskets. At St David's, they stripped lead from the roof and melted it to make bullets. Throughout south Wales men took up arms. When the news reached the ironworks at Merthyr, Richard Crawshay called up a thousand of his men to march westward. They set to work at once to fashion pikes with iron tips.

The enemy, meanwhile, staggered from house to house, stealing food and money. The locals attacked with fists, cudgels and muskets. Several were killed on both sides. Jemima Nicholas, a brawny Fishguard shoemaker, captured twelve Frenchmen at the point of her pitchfork and earned a government pension for life. After two days the bleary French surrendered, and tradition says that they did so partly because they mistook the red cloaks of scores of women for a regiment of soldiers. Some saw the hand of God in the wrecking of the wine ship, the cause of the invaders' intoxication. After a surrender ceremony on Goodwick Sands the French were fed bread and cheese and marched, confused and laughing, to jail. Colonel Tate was sent to the prison camp in Portchester Castle, and was returned to France the following year in exchange for an English prisoner.

The sequel reads like a romantic novel. Two Welsh girls working as servants in Pembroke prison fell in love with a pair of French officers confined there and smuggled tools into their cells. With these the officers and thirty others tunnelled under the wall. They stole a yacht and put to sea, the two officers hugging their Welsh sweethearts as the coast receded. They all reached St Malo and the girls married their dashing officers. In the uneasy peace after 1801, one of the couples returned to Wales and ran an inn in Merthyr. Possibly they waved at Nelson when he came to inspect Crawshay's cannon foundry. When war loomed again they slipped away.

The Department of Nomenclature

In Aberystwyth I was introduced to a baby a few weeks old. Her father, Keith Morris, said she was called Ffion Jac Medeni. 'Ffion is a traditional Welsh name, Jac is in honour of my father and Medeni marks the fact that she was born in September. If you translated her name into English it would be Foxglove Jac Septemberborn, which would sound strange, wouldn't it? But Ffion Jac Medeni sounds natural, perfectly in tune with the country. Welsh is a wonderful language for names.'

It is as if the given names of Wales are the private property of the Welsh, for the English do not intrude on this domain and rarely choose Welsh names. If I think for a minute I know men called Alcwyn, Aled, Aneurin, Bryn, Cenwyn, Cynon, Deian, Dylan, Dyfrig, Ednyfed, Elystan, Emlyn, Emrys, Emyr, Geraint, Gerallt, Gruffydd, Guto, Gwilym, Gwynfor, Hywel, Idris, Idwal, Ieuan, Ifan, Ioan, Iorwerth, Islwyn, Iwan, Meirion, Moelwyn, Penry, Prys, Rhodri, Rhydderch, Rhys and Vaughan. I know women called Angharad, Awen, Bronwen, Carys, Ceri, Eirlys, Eleri, Elin, Gwenno, Heulwen, Leucu, Mair, Meleri, Menna, Nest, Nia and Rhiannon. Some of these names are ancient and others are legendary. They are a distinctive embellishment to the surnames of Wales, which are few and plain compared with English ones.

For many centuries the Welsh had no surnames. They employed the patronymic, using the connecting *ap* or *ab*, meaning son of, as in Dafydd ap Gwilym. They often added their grandfather's and great-grandfather's name, too. The Member of Parliament for Anglesey in 1541 was Richard ap David ap Hugh Ieuan ap Geffrey. Such names were more than a form of ancestor worship: they placed a man in society and were important in the settlement of land disputes. It was vital in law for a man to know his pedigree. After the Act of Union in 1536 the Welsh were encouraged, partly by English church and state administrators, to discard the patronymic and take on surnames in the English fashion.

'Content yourself with one name, like a Christian,' was the instruction given to Thomas ap Richard ap Howell ap Ieuan. Thus Dafydd ap Dafydd became David Davies and Huw ap Siencyn became Huw Jenkins. Men called ap Hywel became Powells, ap Richard became Pritchard and the term 'fychan', meaning junior, was rendered into Vaughan. Old Welsh baptismal names were discouraged in favour of plain ones like Richard, John and Robert. John, in its variety of forms, Sion, Ifan, Ioan, Ieuan, Iwan, was the most widely-used Christian name. In the English style, an *s* was added to turn it into a surname and, before long, Jones became the most common surname. The Registrar-General's report of 1853 noted that 'The name of John Jones is in Wales a perpetual incognito.' Of the eighty-four members of the modern Caernarfonshire and Merionethshire county council, twenty-one are Joneses and thirteen are Williamses.

Nicknames always answered the need for identification which stemmed from the paucity of surnames. Men were called after the pit in which they worked – Dai Navigation, for example – or after the coal seam in which they laboured. Others were iden-tified by their job: Dai Bread, Jones the Meat, Eddie Clickclick, the photographer, Dai Death Club, the insurance man, and Evan Stretchem, the undertaker. In modern times there is Dai Cuts, the film editor. Some recognizable quirk or habit was readily turned into a nickname, hence Billy Firingfart and Harry Greensuit. Thomas Thomas was forever Tom Twice. One Pembrokeshire schoolmaster is known, for his frequent use of the word, as Alun Hush.

In their search for distinction people traditionally adopt the names of their native districts. The poet William Williams was known as Williams Pantycelyn. The writer and broadcaster the Revd Gwyn Jones, from Llanerfyl, is known as Gwyn Erfyl. The Talfan Davies family take their name from the schoolboy who was one of six William Davieses in a class told by their school-master to add a distinguishing mark to their name to avoid confusion: the Talfan was a local rock formation. Similarly, many people distinguish themselves from others by adding their mothers' maiden names to their surnames, as in Parry-Williams or Vaughan-Thomas. Farmers are identified by their farm, as in Jones Cwm-du. Recently farmers in remote areas were asked to include a grid reference after their names when calling the emergency services, so that the fire engine does not hurry to the wrong Jones. In Welsh regiments the common surnames are augmented by the last two digits of the man's service number: Sergeant Davies 49, for example.

The parents of Ffion Jac Medeni registered Medeni as a surname because they wished their daughter to possess a unique title. As it happened, Keith Morris was deeply involved in the matter and mystery of names, particularly his own, and was caught up in his own idea of tracking down and photographing every other Keith Morris in Wales. At that time he had found nearly eighty. 'I've been intrigued by the name Keith Morris for years. It has to do with the influence a name has on your life. When I first encountered it in someone else, on an estate agent's board, it came as a shock, as if another person had my identity. So that's what I'm exploring. Who is Keith Morris? Is Keith Morris special in some way? How do I fit in with other Keith Morrises? I am fascinated by who I am, and this helps me define myself. It's a form of psychoanalysis. It is vital to me that my project is comprehensive, that all the Keith Morrises in Wales are included. I don't want to introduce any distortion by selecting only a certain number. Every possible example of Keith Morris is recorded. I am using my name to sample a group who have nothing in common but their name. Keith Morris is not rare, but neither is it as common as, say, Dai Jones. It is both familiar and limited. It has a cultural significance. It is anonymous in that it does not reveal class, status or linguistic background, as would names like Algernon Q. Fortescue or Idwal ap Siencyn. Keith Morrises form a manageable slice of modern Wales. When I photograph them I also interview them on tape and they talk about themselves and their family history. I started my hunt with the Welsh telephone directories, making contact with every K. Morris. One in five was a Keith. Some knew others and passed me on to them. When I go to their homes to do the pictures they are as curious to find out about me as I am about them. Although they are from all sorts of background, I see a common thread. Many Keith Morrises seem to be independent-minded, freelances, men working on their own, long-distance drivers, self-employed plasterers, people who don't do regular hours in offices. I'm in that category. I wonder if the name predisposes us to be men on our own. Many Keith Morrises are becoming as intrigued as I am by the phenomenon of Keith Morris.'

I wished him luck and said goodbye to Ffion Jac Medeni, as pretty as her name.

The Welsh in their Wigwam

From Abergynolwyn I walked into the Dysynni valley, still a remote place, never well-trodden. I climbed the rocky outcrop on which stands a ruined castle whose name is engraved in the Welsh imagination: Castell-y-bere. The rock stretched out like the tail of a mighty fallen dragon. Around this place, in 1283, the history of England and Wales turned decisively. The Welsh leader Llywelyn had already been killed in battle, and here his brother Dafydd defied King Edward I's army of conquest. It was the last place of Welsh resistance to Edward. Dafydd was captured nearby, hanged, drawn and cut into quarters. I stood on one of the towers and looked out at the sweep of blue mountains. Edward himself had stood on this spot, gazing around as if to satisfy himself that the dragon really was dead.

The castles of Wales are a striking and enduring motif, symbolizing both conquest and defiance, the ambiguity of the country. The Normans left Wales partly in the hands of lords who controlled the marches, the borderlands, and partly under the rule of Welsh princes. Edward smashed the princes and made Wales the first English colony. He ordered legions of craftsmen into the country, under armed escort, to build the castles that endure as monuments to English determination and Welsh tenacity. The debts he incurred to pay for them rose like a cloud over England's economy.

The conquered Welsh drew comfort from the myths of King Arthur and, as we have seen, Owain Glyndwr's uprising was partly inspired by prophecies of renewal. Later the Welsh saw fulfilment and redemption in the seizing of the English crown by their countryman Henry Tudor, Henry VII. His claim was shaky, but Welsh support at the battle of Bosworth was decisive. In the Tudor ascendancy Welsh gentry deserted Wales in flocks and fattened on the greener English grass. Soon it seemed that half the lawyers in London were Welshmen. The attraction of England as an economic and cultural alternative has always burnt brightly in Wales.

Henry VIII integrated Wales into political union with England. The bible was translated into Welsh to keep the country Protestant and safe from Rome and it was thought that, using their Welsh and English bibles side by side, the people would be weaned from their native tongue. Instead, they embraced the Welsh bible. It became a raft carrying their language into the future.

Into the ear of Elizabeth I, in 1577, the Welsh magus John Dee artfully dropped the wonderful tale of Prince Madoc of Snowdonia. In 1170, he recounted, Madoc and three hundred men sailed from Wales and discovered America, and Madoc became the patriarch of a new nation. It was more than a romance: the story had strategic importance. John Dee pointed out that this Welsh prince, a Briton, had landed in America long before Columbus claimed it for Spain; and the Queen, therefore, not the ruler of Spain, had title to America. John Dee coined the phrase 'British empire' and the legend of Madoc had a part in its origins.

The story assumed a more dramatic form when Morgan Jones, a clergyman, returned from America in 1686. Captured by Indians, he said, about to be put to death, no Pocahontas in sight, he uttered a Welsh prayer. The Indians stayed their hand, for, of course, they spoke Welsh. They freed Jones and told him of their illustrious ancestor, Madoc. The story persisted. Other travellers, too, claimed they had met blue-eyed Welsh Indians, and towards the end of the eighteenth century Welsh imaginations were aflame with the story of a lost tribe of noble savages, the custodians of Welsh greatness, wandering an Arcadian wilderness.

One of those struck by Madoc fever was John Evans. He set off from his home near Caernarfon in 1792 at the age of twenty-two and carried a Welsh bible to take Christianity to the Welsh Indians. His search for them was an epic of exploration. He reached St Louis where the Spanish governor jailed him for two years as a spy. Freed on the intercession of another Welshman he trekked for two thousand miles, exploring the Missouri almost to the Canadian border and meeting many Indians. In a letter in 1797 he stated his disappointing conclusion: 'There is no such People as the Welsh Indians.' He died of drink and fever at the age of twenty-eight in New Orleans. The map he drew during his journey reached the hands of President Thomas Jefferson and he gave it to Meriwether Lewis and Daniel Clarke. They used it during their epochal expedition of 1804 which penetrated the western wilderness, found a route to the Pacific and opened up the American West.

Edward Williams, poet, scholar and opium-taker, who once went on hands and knees to graze a field, to discover if men could live off grass, was another Madoc enthusiast. A dazzling spinner of tales, he found a ready and hungry audience among the influential London Welsh communities who longed for the romance of Wales. He presented himself as a new Merlin, a link between the Welsh greatness of the past and the Welsh brilliance of the future. Adopting the bardic name of Iolo Morganwg, he proclaimed himself the repository of legends and guardian of druidic mysteries. He plaited myth with history and forged manuscripts in support of his visions. His friend William Owen

158

Pughe, a kind-hearted mug, published Iolo's fabrications and himself compiled a Welsh–English dictionary filled with invented words which muddied the literary waters for half a century. Pughe was also a devotee of the prophetess Joanna Southcott; and on her death he was among those who opened her up and rummaged in her womb, looking for the messiah.

Iolo was a genius in his way. He perceived the importance of tradition, even if it had to be invented. He staged his first druidic ceremony at Primrose Hill in London in 1792 and created a guild of literati, the *gorsedd* of bards, replete with pagan pageantry of golden robes, trumpets, a horn of plenty and a mighty sword of peace, never bared. In 1819 he grafted this delicious pantomime onto the eisteddfod. Although derided from time to time, it has become entrenched as the eisteddfod's necessary ritual; and the champion poets of the land are enthroned and crowned to acclamation amid elvish dancing, the wheezy blare of trumpets, cries of 'Peace!' and some theatrical business with the giant sword. The eisteddfod itself grew as one of the institutional pillars of the new Wales which developed during the swelling of Welsh awareness in the nineteenth century. In 1866, in keeping with this mood, Wales adopted as its national anthem the song 'Hen Wlad fy Nhadau' ('Land of my Fathers'), written ten years earlier by a father and son, Evan and James James of Pontypridd. Lady Llanover, a rich Englishwoman devoted to Welsh culture and wife of Benjamin Hall, who gave his name to Big Ben, invented a female national costume of tall black hat and cloak, still worn by little girls on St David's Day. It is a mercy that no one invented a Welsh kilt.

Recognition of the importance of institutions led to the founding of the University of Wales, the National Library and the National Museum. Rugby football was established as the national game and was held to have a distinctive Welsh quality. The educationist and editor Owen M. Edwards had a profound influence on schooling, his numerous books and magazines revealing to children the history and traditions of their country. In this century more institutional pillars have been erected, broadcasting bodies and a department of state, the Welsh Office. A statue of Owain Glyndwr was erected in the city hall in

Cardiff, enshrining that mystical warrior and symbol of defiance as a national hero.

Victorian London looked down its nose at what was going on in Wales. Like Shakespeare's Pistol, some Englishmen have always grown qualmish at the smell of leek. *The Times* wrote that the eisteddfod was 'mischievous and selfish sentimentalism, a foolish interference with the progress of civilization. It is a monstrous folly to encourage the Welsh in a loving fondness for their old language.' *The Daily Telegraph*, too, complained that the eisteddfod was 'a national debauch of sentimentality'.

The view that the Welsh should anglicize and integrate themselves was crystallized in the report by a Royal Commission of 1847 which blamed the poor state of education in Wales on the Welsh language, chapel, and sex, especially on promiscuous women. In Cardigan it was found that 'want of chastity is the giant sin of Wales'. In Glamorgan there were were 'revolting anecdotes of the almost bestial indelicacy with which sexual intercourse takes place'. In drunken Brynmawr a woman's profanity made men 'turn away their heads in disgust'. The vicar of Talgarth said that 'it scarcely seems to be considered a sin, or even a disgrace, for a woman to be in the family way by the man to whom she is engaged'. A north Wales clergyman stated: 'In England farmers' daughters are respectable; in Wales they are in the constant habit of being courted in bed. In the case of domestic servants the vice is universal. It became necessary to secure my servants' windows with bars to prevent them admitting men.' The Bishop of Bangor's chaplain complained that 'fornication is not regarded as a vice by the common people. It is avowed, defended and laughed at . . . a man in bed with two women, night after night . . . the increase in bastardy a monstrous charge on our poor-rates.'

The evidence was remarkably detailed. Of course, the stories of drink and sex would hardly have been different in rural England; but it was Wales that was under the microscope. As well as finding poverty, lust, drunkenness, the Welsh language and religious dissent the commissioners, to their horror, discovered people reading the works of Thomas Paine which 'infected them with infidel and seditious principles'.

The report was published amid uproar. It was damned as an English libel. Its effect was to make many Welsh people wish to cast the slur and become English-speaking British; and others more determinedly Welsh.

The founding of institutions and growing national awareness in nineteenth-century Wales corresponded to nation-building in Europe and elsewhere. In Scotland a romanticized Highland culture, Sir Walter Scott, kilts and Balmoral emerged. The British monarchy was reshaped and made more popular. In America the notion of manifest destiny and the frontier helped to build the nation. In Italy one of the architects of Italian unification said that now Italy was invented, all that remained was to invent Italians. In establishing their own traditions the Welsh responded to the demonstrations of power and pomp of their neighbour. Like the Scots, they certainly wished to be part of the British Union and Empire and to play their full part in it. They also wished to be distinct. It is because of their certainty of the value of distinctiveness that Wales endures and is not a valley of bones.

Crossing the T

In Tywyn a wretched youth waited at the tables in the dining room. Tepid brown soup swept over the promontory of his thumb as he set down plates.

'It's not my night,' he muttered as he spilt the gruel.

'It's not hot at all,' elderly ladies said to each other as they tasted the soup. But they didn't complain.

'I've had worse.'

'You don't like to make a fuss, do you?'

'Not when you're on holiday.'

The waiter dropped the cutlery and forgot the orders. He rolled his eyes. 'I'm having one of those evenings.'

I went to see the two wonders of St Cadfan's church. The first was the weeping knight, a recumbent effigy of a fourteenth-century warrior whose right eye welled and glistened because the stone absorbs and excretes moisture; though I thought he was shedding tears over the incorrigible nature of mankind, or

161

the efforts of the waiter. The other wonder was the Cadfan stone, thirteen hundred years old, a memorial to a beloved wife. The inscription, 'Grief and Loss Remain', still touches us across the centuries. The words are the earliest written in the Welsh language.

John Corbett also left his mark on Tywyn, on granite and marble slabs recording his good works. He might have been invented by John Galsworthy, and there is more than an ounce of Soames Forsyte and Irene in the story of his career and marriage. A man of property, Corbett made his fortune from salt extraction in Worcestershire and built a magnificent and expensive French château in Droitwich in order to outdo the splendid home of his political rival. He became Member of Parliament for Droitwich in 1874 and tried to turn it into a fashionable spa.

Poor Corbett. He was haunted by the fact that his name was spelt with two Ts. He yearned for a connection with the ancient and aristocratic family of Corbet, with one T; but never found it. A fall in the Corbet fortunes enabled him to get close to his goal. He bought the Corbet estate near Tywyn and planned to make the town a resort. He built a promenade and it is still there, isolated and slightly forlorn at the end of Pier Road. The pier was never built. A writer at the time noted tartly of Tywyn that 'few spots were more ill-adapted for drawing the gay and gregarious and those to whom the negro minstrel is dear'.

Corbett had married the vivacious Anna O'Meara, but their relationship staled. He disliked her Catholic faith and denied paternity of her sixth child, declaring that her priest was the father. Anna was popular in Tywyn but in 1884 she left town under the terms of a banishment order drawn up by her husband's lawyers which forbade her to live within forty miles of his homes. John Corbett died in 1901 and in his bitterness cut his wife out of his will; but this particular Victorian saga had a curiously happy ending. Anna came back in triumph to Tywyn in 1906, twenty-two years after her exile, and the whole town turned out in welcome. The brass band oompahed and Anna sat like a duchess in a carriage, waving to the Tywynians, her procession led by a man on a white horse.

The Snowdon Lily

I set off for Snowdon's summit by way of the Snowdon Ranger track, a well-worn route. The mountain has been a tourist attraction and a challenge since the seventeenth century. Bonaparte had a hand in its popularity, for his wars closed much of Europe to British travellers and made them seek other resorts. They discovered the alpine grandeur of exotic Snowdonia and soon the bookshops bulged with accounts of their travels – Snowdon the forbidding abode of the gods, all its chasms fearful and every cataract stupendous.

Llanberis railway station resembled a railhead in India, swirling with pestering urchins, guides touting for business and police trying to keep order. Until the end of the nineteenth century most visitors hired guides to take them to the summit. These mountain goats in human form sometimes climbed the mountain twice a day, and the most famous of them dressed in a goatskin suit. Another advertised himself as 'guide-general and magnificent expounder of all the natural and artificial curiosities of north Wales, professor of grand and bombastic lexicographical words'.

The guides knew where to find the prettiest rock crystals and, during the Victorian fern-collecting craze, they led the way to the hidden crevices and the rarest plants. One of them lowered himself down a cliff to collect fern specimens and the rope broke. His death was reported in *The Times*.

Lord Tennyson hired Tom Ward to guide him and his wife up Snowdon but decided that the day was too chilly for the ascent and went for a walk by himself. When he returned he found the guide lying flat on his back and Lady Tennyson sitting on a chair, warming her bare feet on his chest: just one of many uses for a Welshman.

The early male tourists admired more than the mountains. Like the seamen on the *Bounty*, besotted by the maidens of Tahiti, they were enchanted by the creamy women of Snowdonia. They beheld a Celtic version of the noble savage and wrote lyrically of the girls' hair and their eyes, the curve of their bosoms and throbbing necks. 'And here', wrote one, 'let me pay homage to the finest girl I saw in Wales. Her beautiful ankle and well-shaped foot spoke for themselves.' Another noted 'pretty pouting lips ever ready to distend into a smile. The tendency to embonpoint, so characteristic of the Welch woman, was by no means displeasing in these young and elastic subjects.' It was little wonder that at least one Snowdon farmer kept the prettier of his two daughters out of sight when these English gentlemen, so plainly in need of cold baths, were setting out on their walks.

Snowdon's panoramas opened for me as I climbed in the sunshine. The going grew rough and stony as I crossed a desolate stretch, the pitiless terrain of another planet. I skirted the inky Black Lake of Arddu, guarded by the sentinel bulk of the Black Cliffs. Here in 1800 a Welsh parson and his English friend made the first rock climb, while searching for plants, the clergyman taking off his belt to help haul his friend to the top; and here in the 1950s the climber Joe Brown secured his reputation with pioneering ascents.

A little farther on, I saw a lean figure abseiling as delicately as a spider down the face of a cliff. Barbara Jones, a botanist, was at work: she had a special licence to search for one of the rarest flowers in Britain, the Snowdon lily. She was monitoring its survival. She said she would show me where it grew and we climbed a bit until she pointed to a little bouquet of blooms growing in a crevice. It was a privilege, for the lily flowers for only two weeks a year, and only on this patch of Snowdon cliff. Some people make a pilgrimage every year to see it. The flowers were the size of a sixpence, with pale yellow petals, fragile yet perversely stubborn, preferring to bloom in harsh rocks torn by the wind. I imagined heartless Welsh princesses ordering their hapless suitors to gather a bunch to prove their love.

As I climbed I met a young man and woman coming down. Since the man was wearing a dinner jacket and bow tie as well as walking boots, I felt entitled to ask him why. Because, he said, he and his girl had just exchanged vows of love on the summit. They had met on the mountain a year before and decided, as their romance grew, that they would marry on the top. Of course, they said, they would be having an official marriage, but they considered the vows they had just made to be their true wedding; and they smiled and walked on, arm in arm.

Silhouetted on a distant ridge a steam engine of the Snowdon railway, its chimney smoke streaming, hauled itself hand over hand up the mountain. There was something imperial about it, I thought, a slightly eccentric Victorian railway venture, an engineering feat combining conquest of a difficult landscape with a determination to make a profit.

It opened in 1896 after bitter argument between its promoters and conservationists. To the cultured mind of Canon O.H. Rawnsley, Snowdon was sacred and sublime, and when he read that businessmen were planning a tourist railway to the summit he was horrified. As secretary of the National Trust for the Preservation of Sites of Historic Interest and Natural Beauty, he protested.

A railway director retorted, 'Why should Snowdon be reserved for mountain climbers? Are there not thousands who would like to inhale the exhilarating air and look down on the glorious panorama?'

The canon said that the railway would 'vulgarise one of our grandest national possessions . . .'

'Your epistle', replied the director, 'is sticky sentimental dribble.'

Today the canon's successors in the environmental lobby would no doubt win the argument. But when it opened the railway had public opinion firmly behind it. Snowdon tourism and the infant sport of mountaineering were growing, and competition for the tourist guinea grew between the villages of Llanberis and Beddgelert. The worried leaders of Llanberis told the village squire that Beddgelert was winning the race to be the tourist capital. Let there be a railway from Llanberis, he said.

A company was formed and the bosses went to Switzerland and bought a rack-and-pinion mountain railway. Five miles of track were laid in an astonishing seventy-two days. Eighty passengers bought tickets for the inaugural trip and the locomotive *Enid*, built in 1895 (and still in regular service) hissed out of Llanberis, pushing two carriages at five miles an hour. The locomotive *Ladas* departed later with the rest of the passengers, and in an hour both trains were at the summit. Triumph, however, turned to calamity. On the journey down *Ladas* lost its grip on the toothed track.

'Jump for it,' yelled the driver to the fireman.

They landed safely. *Ladas* plunged over the cliff. A Scottish rambler, enjoying Snowdonian serenity in the valley below, was astonished to see the steaming engine fly past him.

Up on the track the carriages began to run away. Then, as now, locomotives were not coupled to the carriages. The railway manager applied the carriage brakes and stopped safely, ordering passengers to sit tight. But one, a Llanberis hotelier, panicked, jumped, and died later of his injuries. A year passed before the railway opened again, this time with a safety device to stop locomotives jumping the track; and there has been no serious incident since. The railway has become as much a part of the Snowdon scene as the climbers.

'It's still a Victorian experience,' Tony Hopkins, the general manager, told me. 'We have four locomotives built in 1895 and 1896 and three built in the 1920s. They are constantly refurbished, and we make a lot of parts in our workshops. The carriages are the original pattern. We use Welsh dry steam coal for the fierce fires we need. We also have diesels and diesel–electric rail cars with the latest computerized control systems, so we span a century of technology. The railway still does what it set out to do. It pays a dividend to its shareholders. There's a family feel about it and many drivers are the sons and grandsons of footplatemen. Most visitors don't mind whether they go up by steam or diesel, but some purists wait for a steamer. An Australian arrived recently and his ambition was to travel by steam. We were only running diesels that day, but when a chap comes all the way from Australia . . . well, we put a steamer on for him.'

At the summit the cloud closed in and cheated me of the view. It often happens. A Victorian couple who laboured to the top recorded huffily that they saw nothing except the absurdity of their expedition. The ugly café on the summit was built for wind and weather, not for elegance, and I was glad of its comfort. A train disgorged its crowd of shivering tourists who bought T-shirts and spent five pence in the lavatories to cover the cost of water, every drop of which has to be hauled up by train.

Mr Tod on the Phone

In the pale light of a frosty January morning I went out to a farmhouse in the hills of Montgomeryshire. Large logs burned in the hearth and firelight flickered on the blue and white plates stacked in the polished dresser and played upon the faces of the men and women who filled the room. It was ten o'clock and they were eating a second breakfast of mince pies and sausage rolls, laved down with coffee and punch. In the yard a crowd of farmers and villagers stood in faded jackets, corduroys, wool shirts with frayed collars, tweed caps and gaiters. They tossed back steaming glasses of punch, joshing and grasping each other's elbows, watching the horses which moved restlessly, hooves clattering on the stones.

Most of the riders wore black coats and caps, with white stocks pinned at the throat, and cream jodhpurs and black boots. David Davies, Lord Davies, the hunt master, a tall man on a supple chestnut horse, had a well-worn scarlet coat and was the picture of a nineteenth-century squire. The John Peel quality of the pageant was disturbed by a crash as a mobile phone fell from a huntsman's pocket. In the lane beside the farmyard, forty Welsh hounds waited, white and brown, long-legged, light and purposeful with solemn eyes. They sniffed and cast about, looking up constantly as if to say that good hunting time was being lost while foolish men laughed and stuffed sausage rolls. These were the David Davies hounds, a family pack started by Lord Davies's grandfather in 1905, and the descendants of hunting dogs kept by a Welsh prince a thousand years ago. At last a bleating, rasping and squeaking of hunting horns filled the air and horses and hounds jostled up the lane. We followed on foot, our sticks tapping the hard ground. The hounds soon turned into a winding valley, while a knot of us strode onto a hill to watch them work.

Since I had no idea where to go I was lucky to be with Clem, a hunt follower since boyhood, who knew every valley, line of trees, meadow, stream and stile for miles around. As well as his country nose, instinct and experience, he had a citizen's band radio. So did other followers. It meant that groups of them, scattered over the countryside, on ridges and hill tops, could follow the hunt and pass on news to the others, who would hurry to a new vantage point on foot or by car. There were bursts of excited commentary.

'I can see the fox!'

'Where?'

'Just down by here.'

'Where?'

'Coming out of the woods now.'

'Where?'

'Down by here.'

We stood panting on a ridge, leaning on our sticks. Below us the hounds streamed through a gap in the high hedgerow and raced over the rough grass. They dashed into patches of scrub and into gorse thickets, tails up and tongues lolling, setting up a yelping howl as they streaked across the slopes.

I had not yet seen a fox.

'There goes the fox!'

I saw him break from cover, sunlight gleaming on his red coat, running easily. Excitement crackled in the chilly air as a classic spectacle unfolded, the hounds hollering, a straggle of riders in vigorous pursuit, a distant cracked sound of horns. The fox vanished into a spinney and from the throats of the followers came primal caveman yells of 'Yoy! Yoy!' urging the hounds on. We marched across to the other side of the hill, over stiles and fences, and then marched back again, as if commanded by the Duke of York, to and fro, as the fortunes of fox and hunters see-sawed.

We lost the hunt for a while and stood eating sandwiches. We moved to another vantage point and saw a fox, a different one this time, flashing past an oak and into a culvert. Huntsmen appeared on a ridge, the hounds circling beneath them. The fox emerged under the noses of the hounds and fled.

The radios squawked.

'Where are you?'

'Down by here.'

'Where?'

'Down in the dingle – where are you?'

'On the hill.'

We roamed the slopes and lanes all day until the light began to go. The master called it a day. Four foxes had been chased and one had been killed. The manner of the death was as savage as it was swift, the spine broken in an instant by the jaws of the hounds and the body torn to pieces. There is no such thing as a fox left wounded by hounds. There are one hundred and ninety-one packs in Britain and they kill about twenty thousand foxes a year. But this is not enough for farmers. They use snares and go out in shooting packs to kill more than one hundred and twenty thousand a year; but shooting sometimes leaves a fox wounded.

Everyone said it had been a good day. For the hunters and followers there was the spectacle of the chase, vigorous exercise and the satisfaction of catching a fox. This is sheep country, a place of small hill farms, where foxes do a lot of damage to flocks and can make the difference between profit and loss. The hunt is therefore well supported, and I heard only one shout of abuse as the hounds passed through the lanes. 'Country people understand the need for it,' said one of the farmers following the hunt. 'Those against it are not locals, not country people, but newcomers, from the cities. There's very little debate because opponents don't want to learn. Their minds are made up and they have the arrogance of certainty. They want to take away a tradition without even trying to understand. It's town versus country and town thinks it knows better. Many of those against hunting think we're a wealthy élite, but most of us who follow the hounds are ordinary people, as you can see. It's a day in the fresh air with like-minded friends and neighbours. There's a rush of adrenalin. It is exciting to see hounds working well and there's a beauty in it. And the result is the death of a chicken-taker and lamb-killer, a pest.'

The hounds were tired. It had been a long day. At their peak they hunt for six or seven years and as they slow they are weeded out. Some have an extra lease of life as gun dogs, but worn-out hounds, unsuited to aimless retirement, are usually put down.

The hunt works from July to February, going out on foot two days a week and on horseback on Saturdays. The hunt committee meets twice a year to draw up a programme of areas to be covered on the advice of David Jones, the professional huntsman, who trains the hounds and keeps up a good relationship with farmers whose land is hunted and who provide fallen stock, dead animals, to feed the hounds. It costs more than twenty thousand pounds a year to run the hunt and the money is raised by subscriptions.

'What we do is useful. Killing foxes helps farmers,' Lord Davies said, 'but that is only part of it. I hunt because I love the pursuit, seeing a pack of hounds at work, the dramatic conclusion.'

The Coalman

On the roadside near Lord Davies's home in Llandinam is a statue of David Davies, his great-great-grandfather. It is unusual because the face is not looking steadfastly at distant hills, but is inclined downwards, studying a surveyor's plan. This is a man at work. Throughout his life he proudly bore the nickname of Top Sawyer because he started work in the 1830s cutting logs. Timber was cut by long two-handed saws, one man standing in the saw pit below the log and the other on top. The top sawyer was the senior man. He also avoided the shower of sawdust.

David Davies made one fortune building roads, bridges and railways, and another in the 1860s as a pioneer coal owner in the Rhondda valleys of south Wales. There was a novelettish drama about this. He prospected for so long that he ran out of money; but his men said they would work one more week for nothing. Sure enough, six hundred feet beneath a farm, they found dry steam coal, smokeless, easily ignited, rich in carbon. The Admiralty chose it for the Royal Navy, preferring it to Tyne coal. Mountains of it were delivered to coaling stations throughout the world. A century ago half the steamships in the world flew the British merchant flag, their boilers fired by roasted stokers shovelling Welsh steam coal. The Kaiser observed thoughtfully that the Japanese fleet which defeated the Russian

Navy in 1905 was powered by coal dug in Wales. The Rhondda was the most intensively-mined place on earth. As the historian John Davies notes, south Wales commanded the position in the world economy that the Gulf occupies a century later.

Young men flocked to south Wales. The excitement and clangour of the Rhondda valleys echoed that of New York. Welshmen swarmed from the neighbouring valleys, quit the farms, headed down from the quarry country of north Wales. Scots came, and Irishmen, so did Greeks, Spaniards, Germans and Italians. So many of the Bracchi clan migrated from the north Italian village of Bardi, and established so many cafés, that in south Wales the word Bracchi became a generic term for a café – 'I'll meet you in the Bracchi.' A man who worked in the Rhondda in the 1870s recalled that 'houses were built in hundreds and chapels were springing up in scores. There would be eight or nine men lodging in a house and when four got up to go to the early shift, the other four would get into their beds after the night shift: the beds were never empty.'

Gebuza Nungu, a Zulu warrior whose father had fought the British at Rorke's Drift in 1879, arrived in London in 1898 with The Savage South Africa Show which performed at Earl's Court. He eventually quit and sought work in south Wales. He went to a pub in Llanelli to enquire about lodgings. 'They were all ready to help me, although I was a black man. I was told to go to the café near the police station, but there, funnily enough, they refused to give me a room. So I went to the police station . . . a detective came across with me to the café and I was given a room.' His wife joined him and 'people treated us as one of themselves. They used to bring us home-made tarts.' He worked for twenty-four years as a furnaceman. 'I remember how disappointed the workmen were when they saw me sweating. They thought that because I came from Africa the heat would have no effect on me.'

So many Englishmen flocked across the Bristol Channel that miners sang a song in Welsh deriding the foolish youths crowding into the valleys: 'They come in hordes from Somerset, like an idiot band of thieves.'

My grandfather was one of them. He married a Welsh girl

and entered the Edwardian world of the Rhondda and its sister valleys, a civilization teeming, vigorous, young, sometimes unruly, united in the common experience of hardship and danger. It was outward-looking, education-minded, creative, cultured, musical; also raw and brutal. It bred boxers and singers and seethed with political argument. The small towns of the valleys, gathered in scrums around the collieries, strung together like beads, were garrisoned by chapels and irrigated by beer. The legends and idiom of south Wales were fashioned in pews, pubs and strike meetings, the human experiences laid down as a seam for the novelists who followed.

In the years of financial glory the coal and shipping barons made Cardiff a mirror of their prosperity, imposing on it its distinctive late Victorian and Edwardian appearance. It was still a small town in 1850. Half a century later it styled itself the Chicago of Wales. The Cardiff magnates built estates of handsome houses and ordered architects to ensure high standards and homogeneity. In sixty acres of parkland in the heart of the city the tycoons built the admirable baroque buildings, white halls and temples that established Cardiff as the capital of Wales. The Welsh Washington, some cried. No, said the romantic, Athens!

In 1918 there were more than two hundred and seventy thousand miners in south Wales. A third of the people of Wales owed their living to coal. In 1904 Admiral Jacky Fisher had suggested that the Royal Navy should run on oil instead of coal. The Admiralty responded: 'The substitution of oil for coal is impossible because oil does not exist in this world in sufficient quantities.' In July 1914, after Winston Churchill sent a team to evaluate oil reserves in the Persian Gulf, the British government bought a controlling interest in the Anglo-Persian Oil Company. The Royal Navy began to switch from coal to oil. It was the beginning of the long and bitter retreat from coal, of the years of slump, raised fists and mass meetings, hunger marches, emigration, evangelical socialism and government fear of miners.

By the time I went to Wales as a reporter there were about fifty pits left, and forty thousand miners. There was still a landscape my grandfather would have recognized, still mining com-

172

munities united by the rigours of pit life. I chronicled the steady dwindling of the empire of coal and of all its stubborn populations, wrote about closures and strikes and miners' meetings on cold mornings and observed the anger and puzzlement of proud people watching a way of life slip through their fingers. The libraries that educated generations of miners were sold off, the space filled by bingo and cabaret.

'If Nineveh and Tyre,' a friend said, 'why not Rhondda?'

At miners' conferences I listened to the passionate voices of their leaders. I could just see them through the tobacco smoke. There was always an ambivalence in their rage and sense of injustice. The miners were proud of their skills and the solidarity of their communities, yet the industry itself was always a focus of hatred. The cruelties of mining, the risk of disease and injury, led them to acknowledge that it was a terrible life, that they did not want their sons to follow them into the pit, that they would toast the glorious day when the last miner emerged from the last pit in south Wales.

They knew, of course, that this would never happen. Years later, it did – well, almost. When the National Coal Board announced the closure of Tower Colliery at Hirwaun its men raised the cash and bought it themselves and soon started making money from it. But this was a curiosity and the proud men of Tower were like the last cowboys of Texas, romantic in their way, a living and working reminder of a former greatness. In this final act of the Welsh coal saga the men of Tower realized the dream of the miners' leaders of long ago. The miners were now businessmen who owned and worked the coal themselves.

So there were no pits working when I returned to the Rhondda; and who could mourn? The brown-painted pithead winding gear and yellow brick chimney of the Lewis Merthyr Colliery still rose above the terraces of stone houses in evocative tableau. Beside the colliery buildings rested an iron tram. It was full of coal, large shining lumps, the last coal raised from the Rhondda, in 1986, one hundred and twenty years after David Davies launched the Rhondda frenzy. The colliery had a new life as a museum or, rather, as the Rhondda Heritage Park. In the winding house, smelling of iron and oil, a film was shown with a soundtrack of Rhondda voices. The faces of miners and their families, all the life of the valleys, looked out from photographs and from books of reminiscences of Rhondda's heyday. There were reconstructions of kitchens, cottages and grocery stores. It was a strange feeling to drink tea in the restaurant, in a colliery where I had drunk tea when it was full of noise, bustle and men's voices, the seriousness of winning coal.

A former miner had a job as a guide and he was dressed in pit clothes and had a coal-smudged face. He was a cheerful man and was perhaps surprised to find himself, still young, turned from a coalface worker into a teacher of history. Visitors donned helmets and entered the pit cage to make a simulated drop into the depths. They toured dark galleries and passages.

In the visitors' book there were expressions of appreciation: 'mega' and 'fab'. Someone wrote that the museum should provide subtitles so that people could follow the film show more easily, pointing out that 'not everyone is acquainted with the Rhondda accent'.

One visitor had written of his glimpse into the work and lives of Rhondda miners: 'Good, but dark.'

The Best Manhood of the Race

Out of Welsh coal came Welsh rugby. The game invented in English public schools entered the mining valleys and the imaginations of their people by way of Welsh colleges. It became a focus and social cement and for men who spent their working lives underground was an affordable and dramatic celebration of life in the open air. The managerial classes saw it as a means of channelling the energies of a simmering proletariat. Sometimes these energies boiled over and clubs were suspended because of the riotous behaviour of spectators. Cardiff Arms Park, which took its name from a pub, was closed as a punishment for five weeks in 1897 after a crowd manhandled the referee.

In many districts rugby was condemned by chapels as the devil's mischief, 'the twin sister of the drinking system'. In the Swansea valley righteous chapel-goers sawed down the goalposts before a game. Hopes ran high in 1904 that the religious revival would sweep away both rugby and the pubs.

But rugby became entrenched, a secular inspiration and expression of identity. It prospered on the rivalries of pit villages. Local loyalties were powerfully stimulating, and a man pulling on the red jersey of Wales was going out to fight for his village as well as his country. The quality of Welsh rugby was put to the test most famously in the greatest rugby match ever played. I can call it that because so much was at stake before the kick-off at Cardiff Arms Park on a misty December afternoon in 1905. Certainly, all of Britain caught its breath, and a good part of the British Empire, too. The match was more than a showdown between the best teams in the world. It was an epic contest between philosophies and racial and national theories.

One of the men who reported the match remembered years later that 'some of us were so affected we could hardly speak or write'. But write, of course, they did. They scribbled streams of short messages and shoved them into the hands of runners who hared out of the ground to the telegraph office where operators sent a record thirty thousand telegrams to newspapers and agencies who published as fast as they could. Breathless boys on bicycles dashed through villages shouting out the score. It was a kind of St Crispin's Day: those who saw the game talked about it for the rest of their lives. People still bathe in its aura. I have heard men boast, 'My grandfather was there', and, 'My father threw his hat into the air and never saw it again.'

The background to this fateful clash was the astonishing rampage of the New Zealand team during its tour of the British Isles. The players had sailed to Britain, by way of Cape Horn, and from the moment they landed they put British rugby to the sword. By the time they arrived at Cardiff station for the game of games they had won every one of their twenty-seven matches, had amassed eight hundred and one points to twenty-two, had beaten England, Scotland and Ireland.

These All Blacks were credited with almost superhuman powers. Some said they wore shirts of eelskin to make them slippery, that they drank magic Maori potions to make them faster. The New Zealanders laughed. Before each match they rubbed

175

on only a bracing embrocation of six parts eucalyptus, three parts whisky and one part spirits of ammonia. The fact was that they were superb players in the process of revolutionizing rugby. They had introduced the hipswing pass, used code words to originate moves, and played a fearsome forward game.

Their prowess and intelligence, however, raised disturbing questions in British minds. Were these Colonials, as they were called, a superior type of men? Had their breeding in the untamed and uncrowded lands of Empire, with plentiful food, fresh air and a rugged way of life, produced a more stalwart and more clear-thinking athlete?

A former England player asked, 'Is the Colonial born and bred on a higher mental and physical scale? It would really seem to be the case.' Many people looked at the rubble of English rugby and then at the All Blacks' stamina and quick wits, and wondered if Britain itself were in decline. Thinking along Darwinian lines they debated whether the pioneers who had gone overseas to found an empire were the brightest and the best of British stock. They expressed fears that the seed corn had been depleted, that overcrowded Britain was losing its virility and becoming stunted.

The question had been raised after the South African war, which ended in 1902. It had taken a long time to defeat the Boers and the evidence given to a Royal Commission revealed not only mismanagement of the war but also the fact that many young men who volunteered to fight were rejected as unfit and scrawny. Some British leaders wondered pessimistically whether an insidious canker lay at the Empire's heart. High infant mortality and the knowledge that thousands of children were sickly and rickety led to the creation of a national welfare scheme for children with the aim of developing a healthier imperial race.

Meanwhile, the New Zealand juggernaut rolled on in triumph. Only Wales offered any hope of stopping it. Welsh rugby was in its Edwardian golden age – Wales won the Triple Crown six times between 1900 and 1911 – and men talked of a 'Celtic genius'. Welsh half-backs and three-quarters flashed like sewin in a mountain stream. In the land of poets, some reasoned, there surely lay the intellect to overcome New Zealand's rugby brains.

176

The historian Dai Smith notes that 'the expectations swelled into a contest with reverberations beyond that year, or indeed, beyond rugby itself.' New Zealand was a young colony of sun-ripened brawniness. Like Australia it had participated enthusiastically in the South African war as a way of asserting nationhood and maturity. Wales was ancient, yes; but south Wales had some of the qualities of a young industrial colony.

To the humiliated English, Wales now stood for the honour of the imperial mother country – 'the last defenders of the prestige of rugby on this side of the globe', said *The Daily Telegraph*. Thus were the Welsh commandeered to cry God for Harry, England and St George, as well as St David. A newspaper cartoon showed a Welsh soldier confronting a dusky Pacific warrior and saying: 'I must fight for all I'm worth! The honour of the old country depends upon me!' Colonial supermen were matched against Celtic wizards.

Cardiff throbbed. Stepping from the train the god-like New Zealanders were mobbed by crowds. A newspaper declared that public enthusiasm was 'as fervent as on the morning of some great Waterloo when the destinies of Empires hung in the balance'. *The Western Mail* ran a photograph of the Welsh team: 'The Men on Whom the Reputation of British Football Depends'. If they cast their eyes from the rugby news, readers saw the reports of pit accidents and a lamenting of that particular Welsh brain drain, the migration of teachers to England – 'Good Men Lost to Wales. London Appreciation of Welsh Talent.'

Work stopped. The docks closed early so that men could see the match. Special trains arrived from Liverpool and London. Men too poor to pay the train fare walked fifteen miles or more to Cardiff. Leeks were pinned to thousands of coats. The ground, packed with forty-seven thousand spectators, was closed an hour before kick-off. Thousands swirled outside.

More than a hundred reporters sat at tables by the touchline. One of them recalled forty years later: 'Never before or since have I known anything like it. Hopes and fears were blended in an aching, choking anxiety.'

The All Blacks were led by Dave Gallaher, scarlet-shirted

Wales by Gwyn Nicholls. The All Blacks danced the *haka*, the Maori dance and song – 'It is Death! It is Life!' – the first time it was seen and heard in Wales. The *haka* is intended to intimidate. But the Welsh were ready with their riposte. The players broke into 'Hen Wlad Fy Nhadau' and it was picked up by the crowd in an awe-inspiring chorus, the first time the anthem was deployed against an enemy, an advance barrage of song.

And so it started. 'A terribly hard gruelling game,' reported *The Daily Telegraph*, 'a grim struggle, memorable in the annals of rugby.' The Welsh took the fight to the All Blacks. And then, twenty-five minutes in, the deadly Welsh backs struck, starting a feinting manoeuvre they had assiduously practised. From a scrum thirty yards out from the All Blacks' line, Bush, Nicholls and Llewellyn rushed to the right as a decoy, while, on the left, Owen passed to Pritchard, who passed to Gabe who whipped the ball into the hands of Dr Teddy Morgan who ran like a deer and touched down in a scene engraved on Welsh hearts. A Welsh selector jumped up and danced on the press tables while reporters scribbled frantically around his jigging feet.

The match remained as fierce as a medieval siege. 'Only well-trained athletes could have stood the strain,' wrote the *Telegraph* man. Ten minutes from the end, in the New Zealanders' last desperate endeavour, Bob Deans was felled close to the Welsh line. He and some of his team-mates, and Teddy Morgan of Wales, thought he had scored. The referee ruled that he hadn't. The try-that-never-was was energetically debated for the next thirty years. Nearly sixty years after the event Gabe said, 'I knew the truth.' Deans, he averred, had grounded short of the line and tried to wriggle over. 'I hung on.'

Teddy Morgan's was the only score. The final whistle squeaked through a gale of exultation. The pubs ran dry. The central market sold every last leek and triumphant fans tied onions to their coats instead and strutted the streets singing. A German visitor was put in mind of 'Rome in ancient days'. It was two o'clock in the morning when the mafficking ended in Cardiff. In London, it was reported, 'Cockney loiterers pondered the meaning of the newspaper poster: *Cymru am byth 3–0*.'*

* Wales for ever.

Reports described 'How Wales Won the Rugby Match of the Century' and effusively reflected a nation's gratitude. Wales, said *The Western Mail*, had rescued the Empire. *The Observer* declared: 'Enfin! Little Wales has immortalised herself and Taffy is the most popular man in Great Britain. Had the Irish done it we might have rewarded them with Home Rule. The panache of our football fez once more floats proudly in the wind.' A cartoon showed the Welsh goat butting a kiwi while John Bull waved his flag, Jock piped and Paddy jigged. A Welsh newspaper said the heroes of Wales 'embodied the best manhood of the race. We all know the racial qualities that made Wales supreme . . . It is admitted she is the most poetic of nations. It is amazing that in the greatest of all popular pastimes she should be equally distinguished.'

It was the New Zealanders' only defeat of their tour, and a cartoon depicted them leaving Wales in the abject manner of Napoleon retreating from Moscow. Wales was content: it had earned a place in the sun. A newspaper drawing showed Wales as a sturdy tree whose branches included the arts, sciences and rugby, the holy national game woven irrevocably into ideas of Welshness. For both countries '1905 and all that' was a landmark. Rugby isn't everything, but the events of that December day lit a fire at which the Welsh warmed themselves for most of the twentieth century.

Mrs Pritchard Jones and her Ladder

In his recollections of childhood in the Rhondda the author Gwyn Thomas joked about life on the steep gradients. Even goats, he said, had been known to knock on the vet's door with a worn-out gear-box. 'The lack of flatness between Porth and Trebanog was a thematic thing in our lives.'

From the top of the hill at Trebanog I watched buses grinding up the streets while women inched upwards, sherpas with shopping. On the narrow valley floor a train beetled along the line to Cardiff past shops and terraces, dead-eyed shuttered chapels and gaunt pubs.

Since there was no room to build new houses in the cramped

valleys, the local authority built estates like Trebanog, on bare mountain tops. Some of these places are treeless and tormented by the wind, like desolate reservations in South Dakota. Here were housed the hard-pressed and disaffected; up on the hilltop, out of the way. Unemployment in some families reaches into the second and third generations and there is a pool of deprivation and resentment. Some people feel, if only vaguely, that since coal-mining exacted a price in death, injury and poor health, and left a legacy of unemployment and loss of status, they deserve something: 'You owe us.'

Half-way down the hill is Cymer comprehensive school. In appearance it is another set of boxy school buildings. But the school itself is remarkable. Its eight hundred boys and girls are educated in Welsh. In an area where the tide of Welsh receded years ago, the overwhelming majority are from homes that are not Welsh-speaking. But, on the record of its examination passes, this is among the better schools in Wales.

Eirlys Pritchard Jones, the head teacher, was born and brought up in the Rhondda. Her grandfathers migrated from Cardiganshire at the end of the last century to work in the pits. Her parents fought to establish Welsh-medium education in the Rhondda in the 1950s. It was hard. After the first decade of this century Welsh declined rapidly under the influences of emigration, immigration, and a questioning of its value. In their struggles the socialist republics of the valleys expressed themselves chiefly in English, regarding Welsh as subversive, a stalking-horse for nationalism. The language divide ran through families like a geological fault and it was not uncommon for older children to speak Welsh while their younger siblings were disconnected from it. In the valleys, Gwyn Thomas wrote, 'the only binding things were indignity and deprivation. The Welsh language stood in the way of our fuller union and we made ruthless haste to destroy it. We nearly did.' When Eirlys Pritchard Jones was at primary school in the Rhondda she was the only Welsh-speaker in the class.

But since the 1960s, Welsh-medium education has grown steadily, most remarkably in anglicized south Wales. The motives of parents who do not speak Welsh but who send their children to be educated through the medium of the language are varied. A mother told me: 'My parents spoke Welsh but did not pass it on. I'm a missing link. I want my children to have their native language. I don't want them to miss out, as I did.'

'Parents just one generation away from Welsh feel they have lost something and want to restore a tradition,' said Mrs Pritchard Jones. There's something else. The high standards of Welsh schools are a significant attraction. 'We have dedicated teachers and encourage parental involvement. Parents like our emphasis on high academic standards, on discipline, school uniform, homework and pride.'

Cymer comprehensive was an English-language school until 1988, when a Welsh stream was established to meet an increasing demand. It became all-Welsh three years later, the first such secondary school in the Rhondda. It is fed by five local Welsh-language primary schools.

Mrs Pritchard Jones had no illusions when she became head teacher. Life can be rough on the estates and drugs are a serious problem. 'For a number of children around here this is a difficult time and place in which to grow up. Many see no future for themselves, living in deprived areas and lacking the will to achieve. In Welsh the word for school is *ysgol*, the same as ladder, and that is what we try to be. We emphasise respect – respecting other people is one of the most important things you can learn.

'The pervading culture of the school is Welsh and all subjects are taught through Welsh to GCSE level. It isn't easy for many children, but hard work and the atmosphere give them a sense of worth, confidence in their ability. Some come during the holidays for extra tuition and we run a homework club for two hours after school so that children can concentrate in a quiet atmosphere.'

Some councillors, she said, continue to view Welsh schools with suspicion. 'There's still flak, the sort of prejudice my parents fought. It's the politicians who are afraid, not the parents. We are sometimes called Rhondda Grammar, and that is not always meant kindly. As I see it, all children have the right to their own culture and I would like to see all Rhondda children have a bilingual education. It's not élitist, but a way into two cultures, a broadening of understanding, and it helps to make communities glad they are Welsh.'

In the 1960s and 1970s Welsh language campaigners sought official and legal recognition for Welsh and greater support for it in education, broadcasting and commerce. There were demonstrations, disruptions and battles in the courts. Scores of people went to prison. There was also pressure of a quieter kind. The language was a cause and to some minds it had the attributes of a secular revival. A question was posed – can you let a culture die without taking action? The demonstrations certainly caused hostility and resentment, but little would have been achieved had there not been a broad measure of agreement and sympathy among those who spoke Welsh and those who did not. Wales decided that the issue should be handled in a positive way. Hostility waned and, as it was put to me, Welsh joined motherhood and apple pie as a 'good thing'.

The Welsh television channel, bilingual signs on the roads and in stores, supermarkets, banks and public offices, and the growth of Welsh schools, flowed from a determination to give Welsh room to live. Lord Elis-Thomas, chairman of the Welsh Language Board, told me that the Board stands for the idea of making bilingualism free of controversy, spiced with tolerance. 'We have compulsory powers but we never want to use them. We want to go with the flow. I think people enjoy the identity of which Welsh is a part.'

The Welsh have something in common with the Polynesians. The history of the Polynesians was related to poetry, which was for them a religion. They too had a devoted interest in pedigree and at one time, unlike the Welsh, enumerated their ancestors with the aid of knotted strings: the knots were rather like the *aps* and *abs* in old Welsh names.

In his monumental *The Age of Arthur*, John Morris wrote that 'once the Welsh had learned to record their history, they took care to see that their known national heroes were not again allowed to lapse from memory, and enshrined the rest of their history in a continuing literature, deeper in their consciousness than elsewhere in Britain. Welsh literature has given the Welsh a saner and more balanced understanding of their origins . . . It has helped [them] to retain their identity, even when most of them have forgotten their language . . . from the sixth century onward it has continued to produce great verse and prose . . . the riches of many centuries give it powerful reserves, and when it finds translators worthy of its content, it is likely to enlarge the dignity of national sentiment far beyond the bounds of the spoken language, and to enrich the literary inheritance of Europe.'

There is no inherent reason why Welsh should survive simply because it has existed for fifteen hundred years. Laws and official policy can only go so far and the future of the language lies with people, not with governments. The language is spoken by more than half a million people, about a fifth of the population of Wales, and, because the number of young Welsh-speakers has been increasing, its retreat may have been halted. We do not know. Some have their doubts. It has a glamour now, and an economic value, and there is a broader sense of its worth. The coming generations may feel very differently about it. No one wants to preserve Welsh or make it a totem or something sacrosanct. Only when it is used, abused, absorbent, creative, slangy and relevant is a language alive.

6

Ulster Fry

The main line railway stations of London no longer smell of trains. To anyone raised on grime, dim light, dankness and the heartbreak of *Brief Encounter* they hardly smell like railway stations at all. The modern station is less a station, more a concourse, spacious and shining, with clean cafés and shops selling lingerie, and it smells of coffee from the cappuccino stalls and of hot chocolate, of pastries and croissants, baguettes, pizzas, pitta and quiche. Writers still joke about the British railway sandwich, conjuring a picture of dog-eared bread and a dubious filling, but most of these scribblers are pretending they have seen the dodo: they are too young to have spied the real beast, let alone eaten one and known the heartburn. Station sandwiches today are princely, stuffed with avocado, kiwi fruit, tandoori chicken, Italian sausage, French pâté, bean sprouts, prawns and brie.

In one respect, however, the main line stations have not changed. They are Babels buzzing and gabbling with the languages and accents of Britain. King's Cross speaks Highland, Morningside, Sauchiehall, Durham and York. Waterloo's voice is yeoman: Wessex, Dorset and Hampshire; John Arlott and Lord Denning. St Pancras speaks Leicester, Nottingham and Sheffield; and the talk of Liverpool Street is Cambridge, broads and black fens, cut through with Essex whine. Paddington's vowels are cider and sherry, Devon and Bristol; with an inter-strata of saw-tooth Cardiff and the English and Welsh of the southern valleys. Euston's tongues are Beatle, Birmingham, Lancashire, north Wales and Ireland; and Victoria speaks Sussex, Kent and French.

On the train to Holyhead I heard the flute of Snowdonia and the oboe of Dublin. By the time I had read half a book and dozed we were heading into north Wales, through a landscape of wintering resorts, desolate fairgrounds, a tattered pier and drab colonies of caravans interspersed with acres of bungalows, built too close together. At last the looming hills gave a sense of Wales and the promise was fulfilled as Conwy Castle came into view, and the train ran hard by the walls in a piece of railway theatre. It thrillingly crossed Robert Stephenson's Britannia Bridge, over the Menai Strait. A figure of Nelson kept a sentry's eye on the shore. Flat Anglesey, usually gentle and charming, looked forlorn on this sour day, the sparse naked trees like hunchbacks under the oppressor wind. We skimmed over gorse clumps, reedy swamps and outcrops to the knob of Holy Island, one of Christianity's first firm handholds, where the age of saints began thirteen centuries ago.

A rusted sign on a signal box announced Holyhead. Out on its limb in the Irish Sea, the town is a shared dependency of Euston and Dublin. In the eighteenth and nineteenth centuries stage coaches ran along the rough arterial road from The Swan with Two Necks in London to The Eagle and Child in Holyhead. The coach left London at eight in the evening and rattled overnight to Northampton, arriving, according to a timetable as precise as that of a Japanese bullet train, at 5.25 for a half-hour breakfast. It reached Lichfield by two o'clock, allow-ing threequarters of an hour for lunch, and was in Stafford by 5.15 in the evening, with a quarter-hour for tea; and jolted into Chester at five minutes after midnight, where a blessed hour was set aside for supper. The timetable called for the coach to be in St Asaph at six in the morning. After twenty minutes for breakfast there, it pressed on for three hours and twenty-five minutes to the banks of the Conwy, with a half-hour allowed for the ferry crossing. It arrived in Bangor at 12.40, and, after an hour for lunch and the ferry passage over the turbulent Menai, it clattered into The Eagle and Child at 5.13. Five-thirteen! With a tootle of the horn it delivered its numbed cargo to the pleasures of the packet boat and the malevolence of St George's Channel.

The mail coach rumbles through many a jolly English Christmas card scene, though one can guess at the passengers' aching backs, irritable bowels and malodorous company. Thomas De Quincey noted the strict demarcation between the four passengers who sat inside the coach, first class, and the three who rode outside, economy. The insiders shunned the outsiders and would not share a table with them at inns. It was like that decisive drawing of the curtain between club class and economy in an aircraft. De Quincey, though, mourned the passing of the stage coach and compared the splendour of the coach at speed to the new-fangled and vulgar steam strains. 'We heard our speed,' he wrote of stage-coach travel. 'We saw it, we felt it as thrilling, incarnated in the fiery eyeballs of the noblest among brutes, in his thunder-beating hoofs. But now iron tubes and boilers have disconnected man's heart from the ministers of his locomotion. Man's imperial nature no longer sends itself forward through the electric sensibility of the horse. The trumpet that once announced the mail has given way for ever to the pot-walloping of the boiler.'

Jonathan Swift, delayed by bad weather at Holyhead in 1727, scribbled: 'Lo, here I sit at holy head With muddy ale and mouldy bread.' I was delayed, too, the ferry from Dublin unable to enter the harbour because of rough seas; and the only refreshment available was in a small and fuggy snack bar. The ferry sailed at last and passengers stretched out with pints of Guinness and cigarettes as the ship punched across the sainted strait. In Dublin I had time for a stride around a Georgian square in the pelting rain and listened to the music and talk in a bar.

Next morning I walked through crowds of students jostling into Trinity, over the Liffey bridge and past the General Post Office to the gloomy cavern of Connolly Station to board the diesel train to Belfast. As it headed north the sea hammered at the coast and spray flew over harbour walls where coveys of fishing boats sheltered. The grey terraces and spires of Drogheda loomed from the wintry murk. Tall, disfiguring television aerials were pointed east, ear trumpets probing for programmes from Britain.

At Newry, just across the border, Union flags flew from lofty poles. In Portadown IRA slogans spoke from walls. Satellite dishes sprouted in profusion and sheets billowed on washing lines over the street by the station. The train wound through low hills and farmland dotted with new white bungalows. Moorhens skittered into the rushes as we rattled through marshland. At Lurgan a carefully-renewed slogan on a wall said 'Burn In Hell Bobby Sands' and the car park at the Crazy Prices store was nearly full.

Northern Ireland is small enough to be crossed by car in about an hour and a half, a small place made smaller by sectarian division, broken into fragments and enclaves. There was a sort of peace at that time, and people were still holding their breath, wanting to believe it would last; although it did not. For a while, anyway, the armadillo army vehicles were absent from the streets. No soldiers performed their balletic pirouettes, swivelling watchfully, covering each other. But the police stations still wore their crude Ned Kelly armour and widows' veils of bomb netting. The newspaper I bought when the train arrived in Belfast reported that more than a hundred Protestants had gathered to shout abuse at people attending a service of Christian unity in St Anne's Cathedral. They had taken the trouble to put on their hats and coats and pay the bus fare just so that they could stand and spit 'Popehead' at Catholic clergymen. The other side of the coin was that the cathedral was full.

I put up at a bed and breakfast house in Malone Road, a respectable middle-class area near Queen's University, and started walking. Belfast is set pleasantly among hills and on the edge of water and is another of those cities of the right size, intimate and accessible. Victorian and Edwardian houses and commercial buildings make it handsome in parts and many of the grander buildings are entertainingly furnished with distinctive embellishments and vanities. The heads of Homer and other sages, encircled by laurel leaves, look down on the streets like cruise ship passengers peering from their portholes. The Grand Opera House is a Victorian fancy, with Byzantine minarets and boxes supported by gilded elephants. Of course, there are dismal districts and shoddy structures, and the city has been damaged by bombers trying to cause maximum devastation and by vandalism. But generous compensation payments have helped to repair and rebuild the fabric, contributing to a feeling that storms can be endured. More than two-fifths of the working population are in the public sector and their earnings form a reassuring economic ballast. Belfast's commercial heart was beating strongly, with an after-dark bustle in the late-opening shops, restaurants and bars. Some of the stores in the new glass-and-glitter arcades were among the most profitable in Britain. The terrorist bombing had turned the city centre into a pedestrian district with steel fences and security gates; and when these defences were dismantled a pedestrian area it remained.

'So nice', a woman remarked, 'to be able to go into the shops without being frisked.'

I waited while a pint of stout was drawn in The Crown bar. It was like having a drink inside a kaleidoscope. Hexagonal wooden columns support a ceiling of arabesques, the marble counter, decorated with coloured tiles and divided by mirrored oak screens, faces ten carved and panelled wooden booths lit by stained-glass windows, made for canoodling. The doorposts of the booths are surmounted by heraldic lions and gryphons holding shields so that when you enter the bar you seem, in the smoky gaslight, to have blundered into a game of Belfastian chess.

The city hall in Belfast, a Victorian palace of splendent Portland stone crowned by a green copper dome, was raised as a statement of municipal pride and a declaration and embodiment of Protestant identity. The Protestant majority in the north felt threatened by the Catholic majority in Ireland as a whole, especially so after the 1880s as the demand for Irish Home Rule gathered strength. But their insecurity dated from the siege of Londonderry in 1689. The English fleet lay off the town for six

188

weeks and did not come to the rescue of the starving Protestants within. Eventually the Navy broke the siege, but the delay left Protestants suspicious of English attitudes. It planted the seed of uneasiness, a fear that Britain will one day abandon them, and this mistrust persists.

When all of Ireland was ruled by the British, Belfast was the second city, its people at work in the shipyards and linen mills. As the sentiment for Irish Home Rule grew, Protestants saw Belfast as their own town. When the twenty-six southern counties of Ireland were given independence in 1920 Belfast became the capital of the remaining six counties, the new Northern Ireland. Belfast city hall set the tone and for many years ninety-eight of every hundred people in municipal jobs were Protestant. From the 1920s to the 1960s the British government looked the other way as the Protestants, by gerrymandering and rigging the votes, ensured that Catholics were discriminated against in jobs and housing. There was hardly ever any common cause among the Catholic and Protestant working class: the tribal structure was too strong. The IRA, though small and not representative, fed upon the resentment that festered in discrimination.

In the city library I sat at a table covered with graffiti, the words heavily scored with ballpoint pens and knives. There were schoolboy and schoolgirl declarations, of the Debbie Loves Colin sort, and messages drawn from Northern Ireland's coarse and well-used lexicon: Kill All Prods, IRA Bastards, All Prods Should Be Gassed, Fenian Cowards, Murdering Scum. The table had been cleaned, perhaps often, but the old scratchings and gougings could still be discerned, a palimpsest of hatred.

In 1872 a newspaper reported that 'the streets around Shankill Road and Falls Road were in a state of utter desolation . . . pavements torn up . . . barricades . . . shops boarded against attack. In every street which bordered the Catholic and Protestant districts, pickets of armed police and soldiers stood guard.' There were riots twelve years after that, and again in 1886, 1907, 1909, 1920, 1922, 1936, 1964 and 1966, before the onset of the quarter-century of the modern troubles, the new chapter of a very old story.

After the 1886 riots an inquiry noted a dividing line between the Catholic Falls Road and the Protestant Shankill Road. In the 1970s that line, delineating the sectarian topography, became solidified in steel and is now a permanent high red-brick wall. In parts it has a yellow design to make it more pleasing to the eye. Here and there, a commercial development provides a buffer between Catholic and Protestant working-class territories. The heavily-defended police stations and army barracks amount to the most intensive fortification of a region in Britain since Edward I castled Wales. The city has become a case study, drawing town planners, sociologists, politicians and others from overseas to observe the normality of abnormality. 'I've no time to do my job,' some administrators say, 'I'm too busy showing foreign delegations around.'

In Shankill Road a man set out his stall of Protestant flags, badges, tea towels, bibs inscribed 'Proud to be a Baby Prod' and cassettes of loyalist songs like 'True Brits', 'Proud to be a Prod' and 'Songs of King Billy'. 'There's always a steady trade,' he said. I went up the road to eat in a steamy café where country and western music played and men addressed themselves to their Ulster Frys, much the same meal as the English breakfast, the Welsh breakfast, the Scottish breakfast, and the Irish breakfast that doctors frown upon; but the Ulster Fry was correctly completed by a mound of mushrooms and a thick potato cake. The breakfasters snuffed their cigarettes between finger and thumb and put the butts behind their ears, the canny habit of men who live in districts of high unemployment, where some families have had no wage-earner for two or three generations.

On both sides of the tribal line men and women are more than willing to show their scars and point with their umbrellas to places of murder – that lamp post, this street corner, that doorway: see what they've done to us. A butcher in Shankill Road guided me to the doorway of his shop. 'See that pub? Blown up. See that shop? Blown up.' But one of the customers remarked: 'In other ways it's not so bad here. There's less crime than in England, not half as much mugging and no immigration.' I paused nearby to watch a wedding party as they waited outside a church for the bride and groom to emerge. I fell into conversation with one of the guests. 'Well, look, we're not bad people over here you know. Write something kind about us, won't you?'

I had first been to Northern Ireland at the time the IRA bombed a Remembrance Day parade at Enniskillen and I went to the funerals and wondered whether that pale boy with a dark wound on his face, who buried his father and mother, would eventually wish to flee, or choose to stay because it was his home and there was no escaping its tormented history. Enniskillen was a well-to-do town of ten thousand, half Protestant and half Catholic, nice people everyone said. The *Fermanagh Herald* described the bombing, with its eleven deaths, and concluded, 'We can't take it any more.' People hoped in their sorrow that Enniskillen would be a watershed, but Northern Ireland has a way of digesting even the most horrible events.

I was struck on that first visit by the sheer vehemence with which views were expressed, by the way the argument raged in a small arena among people intensely fascinated by themselves and their conflict. I listened to bitter words in Belfast city hall; and I heard the thump of the Lambeg drum, thrilling to some, I know, but it is an ugly sound and goes to the bone. I noted how often you could see and hear the word 'No' in slogans and speech and thought it the land of No and not much Yes. I was struck, too, by the power of history, its capacity to imprison, and the presence of tormented ghosts. In The Crown bar in Belfast a man had stared at me over his beer and said, 'You'll never understand us. We don't understand ourselves.' It sounded like an old conceit, a claim to uniqueness, almost a boast.

Reticence is a significant part of life in Northern Ireland. People conduct themselves in a way unimaginable to most people in Britain. They inhabit a frontier subtle and intricate, full of pitfalls, where it is wise to post a sentry on the tongue; where, as the poet Seamus Heaney put it, 'Whatever you say, you say nothing.' People do not discuss politics in public places or with people they do not know intimately, and trust. There is something in this caution and ear for nuance that reminded me of the way people in the Soviet Union made their existence bearable, cultivating a private life, making oases of security among friends, gathering in the intimate safety of the kitchen. People use neutral language with strangers, and among themselves, too, euphemisms and evasions. They speak not of religion but of 'the two traditions' and carry in their minds the Protestant and Catholic vocabularies, just as they have a mental map of the streets and districts where Catholics and Protestants live, of the places and bars where it is safe to go, of the separate Catholic and Protestant taxi stands. In a land of litmus tests Londonderry is the right word for Protestants, Derry for Catholics; police station for Protestants, barracks for Catholics. Rugby and soccer are played by both sides, but Gaelic football and hurling are usually Catholic interests. In a segregated education system Protestants go mainly to state schools, Catholics to their own church schools.

Baptismal names and surnames can be tribal marks, but not infallibly. Bill, a university lecturer and a Catholic, said to me: 'My Christian name is usually regarded as Protestant. But you can have a Catholic called Bill just as you can have a Protestant called Sean. I was talking on the phone the other day to a man I didn't know. Probably he thought that my name meant I was a Protestant. Then he spoke of Londonderry, a word I would never use, a Protestant marker. You talk to people and wait for the clues. When you know what side people are on conversation becomes easier, you know where you stand. It's a matter of social sensitivity: you don't want to hurt, to make people feel uncomfortable. Discovering allegiance is really a matter of politeness.'

In common with almost everyone I met, Bill talked of Northern Ireland's magnetic qualities. Foreigners, he said, are quick to notice the strength of family support and social networks. 'In a small place you can't easily hide and that is often agreeable. I go into town and I'm sure to meet ten people I know. I switch on the television news and I know some of the people being interviewed. The other side of it is that it's hard to be anonymous; and that can sometimes be a burden.'

He said that it was difficult to be neutral in Northern Ireland. 'Some people will tell you that they don't care about religious allegiance, but, deep down, they do. It's important. You know the old joke – "Catholic or Protestant?" – "I'm a Jew." – "Catholic Jew or Protestant Jew?" Outsiders sometimes use the word atavistic to describe us and say we are trapped in history, that we live in a cocoon. I reject that. Religion became a badge because of the colonial experience. People found an identity in religion and that became the point of their community. History is important here because history is alive.'

The history of privilege and disadvantage created a pattern of employment that is hard to dismantle. For that reason most of the teaching staff at the universities are Protestant. But since the 1970s the law, the civil service and other professions have provided avenues for Catholics into the middle class. The law, in particular, has been significant. Catholics have always placed a high value on education as a way out of poverty, whereas Protestants found it easier to get jobs by virtue of their allegiance. If one member of a Protestant family had a job, in the shipyard, say, the rest followed. This has changed as the old industries have declined.

I wondered if the growth of the middle class eroded religious identity. 'No, not much,' Bill said. 'The middle classes are more subtle about it. They go to the same restaurants but that does not mean they become more intimate. Intermarriage is not increasing. Look at the difficulties – a Catholic marries a Protestant, but where do they live? Many places are excluded. If she lives with him in a Protestant area she may believe that because she is a woman she is safe. But he may be murdered for being a turn-coat. That has happened. And where do their kids go to school? They have to travel; and most schools have uniforms which identify the side they are on. On the other hand, intermarriage can work: my sister married a Protestant and moved into a middle-class area. She has friends on both sides and her children go to a Catholic school.'

Anna, who lives with Bill, arrived in Belfast in 1976, from her native Germany, to work as a peace and reconciliation volunteer. As a social worker, she has seen life in both Catholic and Protestant districts. She told me she had known fear on two occasions, once when she was in a Catholic street and was interrogated by soldiers, and again when she was in a Protestant house and heard that some toughs were looking for her in the belief that she was a Catholic.

'You learn quickly, how to converse, to understand the geography. I've stayed because I like the country and the people. It's a good life. Many books about Ireland are sentimental, but it is true that there is a genuine and attractive warmth here, as there is in Mediterranean countries. The street we live in has people of all ages, from newborn to ninety-six, and all the people talk to each other, and there is support for granny and for kids. That sort of community life is disappearing in Germany. I've never known a country where politics is so important, where there is so much political awareness, and yet where people do not talk about politics much. It is like the question of abortion: more than twenty girls a week go to England for abortions, but the subject is taboo.'

Evelyn, a lawyer, a Protestant, works for the Equal Opportunities Commission. She was in a bar bombed by the IRA in 1976. Two people were killed. She did not hear the blast, but felt as if she had been punched by it, and remembers the stench and the bloody casualty department where her injured leg was treated. She did not go out for a long time after that. Boys who knew of her experience would burst crisp packets with a bang to torment her, just in fun.

At school she wrote an essay critical of Cromwell's policies in Ireland and her history teacher, a stern Protestant, hurled it across the room saying that she had 'a very serious case of the hindsights'. In Birmingham, once, some youths jeered and called her a Paddy. She was shocked because, as she said, 'Northern Ireland Protestants don't think of themselves as Paddies, they think of themselves as British.' She has lived in England, Canada and Belgium. When she lived abroad people asked her to say 'How now brown cow', so that they could delight in her Belfast accent. She liked to meet people from Belfast 'so that I could talk fast and get into the Belfast shorthand'. She made a conscious decision to return to Northern Ireland because it is her root, because she wanted to contribute and not run away and because 'I love it, the people, the unspoiled countryside, the spirit of the place.'

She said she talked about Northern Ireland when she was abroad. 'But here we talk mostly about other things. I think maybe we have done our time, years of sitting up over the whiskies late into the night, going over the history of the troubles; and people feel a sense of futility about the political situation.' She has Catholic friends but is well aware that bigotry is still strong. 'A man I know complained of the way middle-class Catholics were moving into a Protestant district. He said it with disgust: "God, they're all around us." ' She told me about the row over a Protestant hockey coach who had been rebuked by the sport's authorities for saying to her team in the pre-match pep talk, 'For God and the Queen, let's go out and stuff the Taigs.'

Evelyn was on maternity leave when I met her, with a daughter aged three months. She said her child would go to a mixed nursery and perhaps to one of the integrated primary schools which have been started in an attempt to build bridges between Catholic and Protestant communities. Her view from her pleasant part of Belfast is that 'England seems softer and less interesting by comparison and I certainly enjoy a higher quality of life than I could in London. Like people everywhere you make the best possible life you can.'

Mike, a Catholic, grew up in a mainly Protestant town on the north coast. His mother ran a guest house and it was one of only two houses in the street in which a Sacred Heart hung in the kitchen. His father enjoyed whiskey and Irish music. Most of his drinking companions were Protestants and he took pride in knowing more verses of 'The Sash my Father Wore', the Protestant marching song, than they did. His mother and her Protestant counterparts were as neighbourly as landladies in any seaside town, helping each other at busy times with the loan of cutlery and pillow cases. Mike had a happy childhood, played with Protestant friends, and learnt early, by the osmotic process of Northern Ireland, how to tell from an address or a name whether a friend was from 'our side of the house' or 'the other side of the house'. He learnt that it was fine to write County Derry in a letter to a friend but that when he grew up and applied for a job it would be better to write Londonderry. In fact, he never wrote for a job in Northern Ireland because he moved to London.

Mike ('Always Michael in Northern Ireland, never Mike') was eleven when the modern troubles began. Many of the summer visitors who came to stay at his mother's guest house were snatching a respite from the violence of Belfast and elsewhere. He remembers the women's hands, fingers tarred brown from chain-smoking, the nails chewed to the quick.

One evening Mike's mother agreed to look after a boy of seven while the lad's mother went out. She dutifully looked into his bedroom during the evening and the boy was nowhere to be seen. She found him under the bed, his knees drawn up embryonically.

'You'd be warmer in the bed,' she said.

'I always sleep under it,' he answered, 'in case there's some shooting.'

Mike said he often thought of that boy. 'Perhaps he's a prosperous businessman in Derry. Maybe he became so fed up with the bloodshed and stalemate that he got out, followed relatives to England or Australia or Canada. Or perhaps, having been terrorized, he is now a terrorist himself, bombing and killing and making little boys hide under their beds.'

Another Country

At Belfast city airport on a Friday evening, I waited in the queue to check in for a flight to London. I was behind a group of Englishmen, engineers I imagined, returning home after a spell working in Northern Ireland. An announcement said the flight would be delayed for an hour.

'Going to call the wife?' said the man in front of me.

'No,' said his companion, 'I think I'll wait till I get back to the UK.'

7

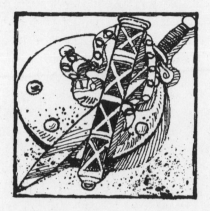

There's Nothing the Matter with Glasgow

For my breakfast in Glasgow one frosty morning I was directed to a café which served 'the best toasted sandwiches you'll ever eat'. There was no mistaking where the proprietor's heart lay. The tables were afire with red tartan cloths and the walls looked like a declaration of independence, abundantly decorated with maps of Scotland and lists of all the clans. On mustard-coloured banners the red lion of Scotland stood on his hind legs and squared up with pugilistic paws. Claymores, studded shields and battleaxes were hung in readiness, enough to furnish a punitive expedition across the border. A bagpipe was hooked on a nail, as limp as a shot duck; but, never fear, through the clatter of crockery and the splutter of frying came the skirly sound of 'Scotland the Brave', 'Flower of Scotland', 'The Skye Boat Song' and, inevitably, 'Auld Lang Syne'.

This tartanic spectacle had the imprimatur of the brave-hearted giant William Wallace, whose iconic portrait was mounted in a place of honour. In Scotland his defeat of the English army at Stirling in 1297 rings down the centuries, for it was under his rough and ready leadership that an idea of a united Scottish nation began to bud. Routed at Falkirk and on the run for seven years, he was betrayed to the Sassenach enemy by a Scottish knight, tried at Westminster amid medieval splendour and hauled to Smithfield for butchering. His head was piked at London Bridge, his quarters dispatched for display at Newcastle, Berwick, Perth and Aberdeen. Thus martyred, he does duty still as a hero of the wars of Scottish independence.

The café's menu offered an English breakfast of sausage, bacon, eggs and toast. It also proposed a Scottish breakfast, an altogether manlier feast, of sausage, bacon, eggs, black pudding, potato scone, beans and toast. Three men at the next table ordered Scottish breakfasts and attacked them vigorously. Between bites, they drew on their cigarettes, gulped their tea and talked in high-speed bursts punctuated with croaks of laughter. Filled and belching gently, they went to the cash desk to pay and the elderly woman in an overcoat behind the till presented each of them with a toffee from a basket and said, as a parting blessing, 'Good luck in the lottery.'

I walked across the green to the People's Palace, the museum which tells Glasgow's story. One of the exhibitions drew attention to the city's consumption of immense quantities of cakes and biscuits, and explained that the local diet helped to make Glasgow 'the heart attack capital of the world'. Indeed, Glasgow's diet is a matter of concern and morbid wonder. A Glaswegian I met in Edinburgh remarked that whenever she returned to her native city she was struck at once by the unhealthy appearance of many of the people. Poverty in the grim housing estates contributes to poor health and there are vitamin deficiencies and an increasing incidence of tuberculosis. It was pointed out to me that vegetables and fruit play only a small part in the diet of many people and there is a Scottish opinion that peas, beans and other greens are for cows and not for men. 'In English supermarkets the fruit and vegetable displays are large and accessible, but – do you notice? – in Scotland they are often small and distant, not easy to find.'

A popular dish in Glasgow is clootie dumpling, a sticky bomb composed of suet, treacle and sugar; and if any of it is left uneaten it is mixed with sugar and fried next day with the black pudding and sausage of the Scottish breakfast. An American journalist wrote an article from Glasgow describing the hellish greaseball diet and clinkered lungs of a city which serves deep-fried slices of pizza and Scotch eggs fried in beef fat, and where even the staff of health food shops are addicted to cigarettes. I imagined the gym-goers of New York and San Francisco reading the paper and recoiling with horror. Scottish health authorities became alarmed that the fatty and fruitless diet made Scotland one of the unhealthiest countries in western Europe and Scots much more likely than the English to die before reaching sixty-five. They launched a diet campaign supported by doctors, farmers and food retailers.

Many Glaswegians take a sardonic view of all this. There's a strut about them, a laugh in the face of dietary perils. Perhaps they like to feel that slight edge of danger that is part of living in a city with a reputation for being tough, quick-witted and exuberant, the big and battered town that everyone in the world has heard of. Like New Yorkers, they feel possessive about their city and can be stickily sentimental about it. 'We talk fast and we talk funny,' they say.

'Glaswegians love Glaswegians,' I was told over drinks in a pub called Babbity Bowster, 'and if they were chocolate they would eat themselves.'

Glasgow is special, Glaswegians say, because of its industrial past and the influence of thousands of Highlanders, many of them dispossessed in the mass evictions of the eighteenth and nineteenth centuries, who arrived as refugees and put down roots here. More Gaelic is spoken here than in the Highlands and the western islands; and perhaps it is because so many Glaswegians feel they are a transplanted people that they have a strong tribal and family feeling, a sense of continuity. It is all the fault of the Celtic gene, they say, that they are so colourful, affectionate and argumentative, so intimate and tactile. 'Women have well-kissed cheeks,' I was told.

It was not so long ago that barmen in the pubs close to the Clyde shipyards set up scores of whiskies on their bars in advance of the lunchtime rush. What a spectacle that must have been.

What men! Accounts of heroic drinking live on in nostalgic recollection and an idealizing of the era when the banks of the River Clyde were governed by cranes, crammed with workshops and lay under industrial smoke. For two centuries Glasgow drew its wealth, vigour and sense of purpose from the river; and also its transatlantic dimension. In the centuries of sail it was two weeks closer to America than London was, and its fortune was made first by the tobacco trade, cotton and sugar. The People's Museum displays a set of slave manacles as a reminder. At one time the city handled half the American tobacco crop and shipped it onwards to Europe. The first Scottish millionaires were tobacco tycoons. The world came to know Glasgow as a builder of ships and in 1914 its name was on the maker's plaque of a third of the British ships launched that year. Hammers pounding, steel blazing, Glasgow called itself the second city of empire, workshop of the world. In the 1930s the construction of the *Queen Mary* and *Queen Elizabeth* seemed to be a renascence of Glasgow's Victorian might. In fact the work was the last performance of the opera and was followed by a half century of decline, leaving Clydeside quiet and the river a memorial. With the fading of industrial vitality other passions have abated, too. 'You should have been here years ago,' I was told, 'and heard the roar of the crowd at the Rangers–Celtic matches.' The Protestant tribes of Rangers supporters and Celtic's Catholic legions still march in mutual hostility, the Irish tricolour is still waved furiously against the red, white and blue, the name of the IRA is still chanted and the Pope is damned; and the next Pope, too. There is still an edge of savagery, but people say the sectarian venom is less potent and the roar less deafening.

Modern cities do not collapse irrevocably and Glasgow is adapting, repairing, reinventing itself. The city has renewed its economy through electronics, insurance, banking and education. Handsome streets have been refurbished and there are prospering shops in the old merchant quarter and elsewhere. The disparities are all too uncomfortable. The east end is stigmatized by heart disease and premature death, by stabbings and a heavy traffic in drugs. But the west end is middle-class, cultured and growing, a good district to live in, plentifully supplied with restaurants, even if some romantics sniff that Glasgow's manly welders have become waiters. A taxi driver who took me to a west end restaurant warned me kindly that it was expensive and said there were cheaper ones nearby. He was right. It was expensive. It was also full.

The carved wooden bedstead in my hotel room was magnificent, solidly Victorian and handsome enough to have been looted from a laird. It seemed all of a piece with the statues of Victorian worthies and the red sandstone municipal temples I could see from my window. The splendour of these confident structures has been overlooked in the past, but today the tourists come to admire them. The city hall, for example, is a wonder of mosaics, Ionic columns, caryatids and marble staircases. The architecture contributed to Glasgow's winning of the title of European cultural capital in 1990, an accolade that took some Glaswegians by surprise and did much for civic swank. Glasgow and Edinburgh are rivals, and this feather for Glasgow's cap made Edinburgh grind its teeth. But, then, as Glasgow often says, turning up its nose, Edinburgh is all fur coat and no knickers.

A Matter of Sheep and Wolves

An obituary I read in a Scottish newspaper described a man as a good Scot. Another talked of a 'sound Scotsman'. Similarly, in Wales, a man may be judged by his peers to have been a good Welshman. But no one, in an English newspaper obituary, is ever called a good Englishman (a great Englishman is something else) because the matter does not arise in England. This is because, to a greater or lesser extent, Scottishness and Welshness are a cause, and Englishness is not. A man who earns the accolade of a good Scot is measured against his Scottishness. He is a patriot, not necessarily a political nationalist, who makes a contribution to his country and demonstrates his pride in it. He never makes excuses for being Scottish, never defers on account of his Scottishness. He is not necessarily a drum-beater but he speaks up for Scotland and puts his energy into Scottish culture or Scottish interests. As a good Scot he may have stayed on in his beloved country when he might have improved his career by leaving for London. Scotland is in his heart and Scotland is an ideal. A Scot may have his elbow gently taken and be asked: 'Do it for Scotland.' Certainly I know that in Wales one may be asked to 'Do it for Wales.' Englishmen may contribute in all sorts of ways to cultural life but they are not asked to 'Do it for England.'

The ideal of the good Scot resides in the quiddity of Scotland, in the Scottish difference. In 1540 it was noted that 'there is not two nations under the firmament more contrary and different from each other than Englishmen and Scottish men . . . they are as different as sheep and wolves.' In Edinburgh I talked with a Scot who recalled a conversation he had with an Englishman. 'I'm like a lot of English people,' this Sassenach had told him. 'I can't bear the Welsh but I like the Scots. What I can't understand is why the Scots don't like us.' The Scotsman said he wondered where he could begin, with history or geography. Distance, north and south, hard rock's contempt for soft chalk. I arrived in Scotland on one occasion after southern England had been lightly dusted with snow, reported in the English papers as a 'White Night of Hell'. A Scot brandished the headline at me, scorning this English weakness. When Scots think of the English they think primarily of the southern English: tall, confident, strident, braying and dismayingly numerous. Few Scots actively hate the English, but the English do irritate the Scots. The English hardly seem to know where Scotland came from. The air navigation maps of Papua New Guinea show large white spaces marked 'Limits of Reliable Relief Navigation'; and Scots feel that the English see Scotland, too, as a white space. It irritates Scots that the English do not understand that, like England, Scotland had a monarchy that ruled from the ninth century until 1603 when the crowns were united and King James of Scotland decamped with his court to London. When she was Prime Minister, Margaret Thatcher was taken to Edinburgh Castle to see the Scottish crown jewels, the symbols of a separate political tradition, and exclaimed, 'I didn't know you had all this.'

Scotland retained independence in medieval times because it believed in itself as a nation and because it fought hard. Ruggedness and distance were also allies, and the English spent so much energy and money in hammering Wales and building expensive castles there that there was not enough left to deal decisively with Scotland. But Scotland's independence increasingly came under question in the age of acquisition, when it was open season in the newly-discovered world and spices, tobacco and plundered treasure were unloaded on English quays. Excluded from England's burgeoning empire, Scotland was desperate to expand and trade on its own account. It sought, therefore, to lay the foundation of its own empire with a colony called New Caledonia in Darien, what is now Panama. The scheme laid out on merchants' tables in Glasgow and Edinburgh was to build a road across the isthmus and exact tolls from the Spaniards as they drove their treasure wagons, heavy with silver and gold and other loot, from the Pacific side to the Atlantic coast. This scheme was advertised as an Eldorado and Scots invested in it enthusiastically. Drawn by the prospect of riches, hundreds of Scottish migrants sailed for Panama in 1698, little knowing that they were bound for a malarial swamp. The venture collapsed in shipwreck, disease and starvation, a disastrously costly ruin, quite out of keeping with notions of Scottish financial shrewdness.

In 1973 the doughty Welsh voyager Tristan Jones, intrigued by the story of New Caledonia, sailed to Darien and walked in the ruins of Fort St Andrew near Punta Escoces, Scotch Point. He was told that in the jungle lived a shy, red-haired tribe, possibly the descendants of hapless Scottish colonials. Typically, since he never shrank from an adventure, he trekked for twelve days to find these people, cutting a path with a machete. When he reached their village they were not unfriendly and they did indeed have bright ginger hair, cut fairly short. Some had light blue eyes and the majority of them did not have the distinctive high cheekbones of Indians. The villagers served Jones a meal of iguana steak and their own brew of beer and fell into a drunken slumber.

The Darien adventure was such an eager assertion of Scottishness that its failure was correspondingly a most bitter dish. The humiliation increased Scottish detestation of England, not least because Scots believed the English had sabotaged the scheme. But it also hastened political union because many Scots concluded that only through England would they prosper. The notable survivor of the Darien business was the Bank of Scotland, which was founded to finance the colony and bobbed to the surface when it sank.

So the Scottish Parliament dissolved itself and was allied to the Parliament in Westminster, some of its members having been handsomely bribed: the 'parcel of rogues', as Robert Burns called them. With Scots as a whole the Act of Union in 1707 was unpopular and, here and there, a cause of fury and violence. There was rioting in Glasgow. The episode still rankles. 'A put up job, political chicanery,' I was informed, with some feeling, in Edinburgh, as if it had all happened a few months before. But those who believed that Scots would prosper in the Union were right. As the British Empire's frontiers widened, armies of dedicated imperialists, doughty engineers, canny administrators, indefatigable explorers, good doctors, tough soldiers and other leaders came out of Scotland to carry the flag and reinforce British influence. Hong Kong, for example, was famously run by Scots. The firm of Jardine, Matheson had its beginnings as a company of drug runners, supplying China with the opium on which the colony's early wealth depended. Scots migrated in large numbers, sometimes to escape poverty and the oppression of landlords, and built strong outposts of Scottishness in Canada and New Zealand. There is a Scottish view that since Scots ran much of it, it was really Scotland's Empire. The ending of the British Empire has changed the relationship between Scots and English. Many Scots feel that in the imperial aftermath Scotland needs a new direction, and that England is not as economically useful as it was.

The English made it clear when Scotland and England were joined that they, the English, were the ruling nation, the winners. Many Scots think the English have ever since shown arrogance in their dealings with Scotland and are annoyed by an English attitude of easy superiority and condescension. Scots grit their teeth when the English refer to England when they mean Britain, are annoyed by the way English newspapers show no knowledge of Scottish counties and write simply Wick,

Scotland, and Oban, Scotland, just as Americans do. After three centuries England remains the whetstone on which Scots sharpen their blade and resentment of English domination hangs around like a mist. Since the English are there to be blamed for Scottish ills, some pleasure is derived from English pain and humiliation. When they watch the England football team on television many Scots cheer England's opponents.

Scots who live in England know that the English find it hard to categorize them in the class and caste system. An Englishman can place another as soon as he opens his mouth, but it is not so easy with a Scot. Scots feel superior to the English in the matter of class because in their opinion there is less class-consciousness in Scotland and a greater value is placed on egalitarianism. This may be so, but in Edinburgh, at least, people are acutely aware of the caste distinctions of the city's schools. The answer to the question 'And which school did you go to?' is one of considerable social significance.

Many Scots take pride in speaking English well and to their ears certain English voices can sound painfully discordant. I was told several times that Margaret Thatcher's delivery had been as much a vote-loser in Scotland as her policies. Some Scots in England wince to hear their children's adopted accents. I met a father in Edinburgh who said that one of the considerations when he moved back to Scotland after years in England was that he did not want his sons to have north London voices. Another said that one of his reasons for returning was that he wanted Scottish schooling for his children, a better education than a London one in his view.

The attractions of Scottish life have been leading more than a few Scots resident in England to turn Dr Johnson's dictum on its head and state that the noblest prospect for a Scotchman is the high road back to Scotland. Giles Gordon, a literary agent, was thought to be an embedded metropolitan but quit London for his native Edinburgh after thirty years, to the pained astonishment of his boss who thought he had gone off his rocker; and the bewilderment of some of his friends who wondered how he could exist away from the centre of the universe. Sentiment played its part in Gordon's return, for Edinburgh is lovely and compelling, as black and beautiful as Prague, a city of comfortable scale. It has one or two carbuncles, but, on the whole, modern developers have not been able to get their hands on it. The old Edinburgh, dour, grey and Calvinistic, has largely been broomed away and replaced by a more liberal, sensible and easygoing consciousness. I saw a massage parlour next to a funeral parlour, a piquant juxtaposition of life, sex and death. The Edinburgh Festival, founded to celebrate a rebirth of the European ideal after the evil encroachment of Nazism, is simply the greatest arts festival anywhere. Its spirit has spread. The liberalizing of the pub opening hours has bestowed a benison upon the city and the bar life is sparkling. 'How staid London seems by comparison,' people said. 'It shuts so early.' A Glaswegian recalled that 'the Scotland I left in the 1960s was dour and dreary, whereas London was so full of life, swinging and utterly stimulating. But today it is in Scotland that so much is happening in music, writing, festivals and politics.'

Scots who go to England for the first time are often surprised at the differences. A young man brought up in a housing estate in Glasgow, who went to work in Buckinghamshire and Essex, said he had been impressed by the sleekness of England and the storybook quality of the villages. 'Scottish villages are a few houses in a glen, bleak places with a road running through them. But these English villages were just as I had imagined, with their churches, village greens and pubs. And what wealth – Mercedes as second cars, driven by wives in superior shell suits.'

English people, he recounted, would persuade him to utter the word 'murder' for the pleasure of hearing the rolled Scottish *r* – they would laugh and try it themselves. He felt obliged to hold a Burns Night party for English friends at his home; and he cut the haggis and read the poetry – 'something I never did in Scotland'. He enjoyed his years in England and found the people agreeable, but concluded: 'I could not have lived there for the rest of my life. I'm too rooted in Scotland.'

Scotland had become less miserable, I was told, though there are still plenty of old-fashioned, glowering, pessimistic Scots ready to say that whatever you propose no good will come of it; and plenty of Scots saying that if anything good were to happen, a price would have to be paid; and plenty of Scots whose education, as Muriel Spark has written of her own, seemed to pivot around the word 'nevertheless'. There is still a Scottish cringe, the cousin of anglophobia, the feeling that what happens in England is more important. And there is grating boosterism that boasts that the Scots invented this, built that and pioneered the other. Given history and proximity, Scots inevitably measure themselves in relation to England. Many believe that home rule is the medicine for anglophobia. 'There is a feeling that Scotland has to grow up and take responsibility for itself,' said Ajay Close, a Glasgow critic and novelist, 'and that we have to get beyond blaming England.'

Idylls of the Kings

I returned to Scotland some months later and on the road to Fort William I gave a lift to a Dutch couple. To their delight a *Brigadoon* version of Scotland swam into their view. They pointed out to each other The Thistle Bagpipe Works and Kilt Maker and a sign directing visitors to Whisky Tasting. They gazed at Loch Lomond. They gestured excitedly when they saw a kilted ginger man riding a bicycle.

After Fort William I had the sun in my eyes along the twisting road to Mallaig on the Sound of Sleat. The town makes its living from fishing and from the ferries to the islands. At ten o'clock in the evening it was still light, so that the moon seemed suspended in the mauve sky, for decoration rather than illumination. The latticed water of the harbour was clear to the bottom. Fishing boats called *Black Hunter*, *Minch Harvester*, *Nighean Donn* and *Twa Gordons*, all broken-nosed navvies of the sea, lay at rest after the day's labour, the saltire and the Scottish lion at their sterns barely stirring in the warm air. A fishing boat came in from the sound, trailing a mewing swarm of late-shift gulls in its wake. The food stall on the dockside offered fodder for hungry men: haggis, black pudding and pizza. I caught the scent of fish dinners drifting over the harbour and followed it to a table and had local scallops and haddock. I read the local paper and judged from the photographs that almost every bridegroom had married in a kilt, velvet jacket and bow tie. Afterwards I strolled round the harbour again and read, in a spirit of perfect idleness, all the advertisements in the post office window. The chimney sweep's card said: 'If your lum is needing done, call on Mr T to come.'

I took the ferry to Eigg next morning. Twelve miles from Mallaig, it rises from the sea like a tropical island, the massive grey lava rock known as the Sgurr punching dramatically through the surface like a fist through a plywood door. At thirteen hundred feet this is the largest pitchstone column in Britain and to my eye the Isandhlwana of the isles, though intoxicant breezes in these parts incline you to the fanciful. Porpoise outriders escorted the ferry past steep dark cliffs echoing to the cries of seabirds. A dozen seals lolled on their rock sofas and watched our arrival. Because the water was shallow the ferry could not berth at the island's stone quay, and the red island launch came out to take off passengers, parcels, stacks of groceries and a drum of oil. The arrival of the ferry is the important junction of the day for Eigg's seventy-five people. The quay was crowded with islanders watching the arrivals and picking up goods; and with walkers heading back to the mainland. I shouldered my bag and walked three miles around the bay to the farmhouse at Kildonnan where I stayed.

Most of the people who live on Eigg are native islanders and mainland Scots, and there is a handful of English people, white settlers as they are called in the Highlands, not always kindly. The island life is rugged, the economy precarious and few people have much money. The main business is the raising of two thousand sheep which are ferried to the mainland and sold. Some people live on crofts and grow vegetables; but much of their food is delivered by ferry. Scottish crofters no longer earn a living by crofting alone and contribute to highland and island life with the aid of subsidies and part-time work, repairing and building. There is little fishing in Eigg, though I found some adventurous young men diving for scallops which they sold to mainland restaurants.

For visitors the peacefulness is to be prized. They tramp the hills and heathery moors, go to the cliffs – a vantage point for seeing whales – and to the caves to see otters. They watch the buzzards, ravens and occasional eagles and climb the Sgurr, and peep into the grounds of the laird's Italianate mansion where palm trees grow. Some stay for bed and breakfast or eat cake at the tea shop on the quay and buy woollens and paintings in the craft shop. The island has a postmistress, a postman who doubles as a ferryman, a wildlife warden and a schoolteacher who supervises nine pupils. When they reach the age of twelve the children go to state boarding schools on the mainland, usually the first step towards leaving their native island. But in the meantime they have a chance to enjoy a childhood in an intimate community in a wild and lovely place where there is no crime and doors can be left unlocked. There is a general store and post office, but no police station and no pub. There are only four miles of road and no mains electricity. Diesel generators provide the power. A ceilidh is held from time to time, when a band comes from the mainland to play. It is attended by almost everyone, young and old, and goes on into the small hours, until the party is danced off its feet. There have been no resident clergy for more than forty years and the Catholic and Presbyterian churches are visited by priests and ministers. When an islander dies an undertaker sends a coffin on the ferry and the men gather to dig the grave and then carry the coffin in clockwise procession around the church. The people I stayed with at Kildonnan, Colin and Marie Carr, the parents of five children, were the very picture of resourceful, tough and hospitable islanders. Colin, a farmer, is Eigg's special constable and his wife the registrar. She conducts marriages in her large warm kitchen, and puts on a Black Watch skirt for the occasion; although, if the couple want informality, she wears jeans.

Christopher Tiarks, a dashing figure in his mid-fifties, is the general practitioner for all of the Small Isles – Eigg, Rum, Muck and Canna – and has one hundred and fifty patients. A flying doctor of sorts, he buzzes around the islands in a Zodiac inflatable, zipped into a heavy foul-weather suit that makes him look like a diver. He took me with him on calls to Rum and Muck, racing the swooping Manx shearwaters in a thirty-knot dash over the sea.

'I love this job,' he said, shouting into the wind, his mane streaming. He had found what he had yearned for. After a career in private practice and years in the National Health Service in England and Wales he wanted to be 'an old-fashioned family doctor with a pastoral role'. He had all of this, with a generous ration of the sea and adventure, too.

Distance and beauty lend magic to these Scottish islands. It is not surprising that rich men are tempted when they read the prospectus of an 'Island For Sale'. It brings out the laird in them, and such an island can be a kingdom of sorts. The romantic envisages silver sands and crystal seas, and white cottages and soft-voiced subject folk, and the lord in his castle. But the petty kings of Scottish islands and of Highland estates often find that their crowns give the devil of a headache. More often than not, islands, as idylls, are illusions; and wise men sighting the rocks of paradise put the helm hard over. Resentment, jealousy, insensitivity and bad humour may stew in an island's microcosmic pot. Kings start by seeing themselves as benefactors and all too often end up branded as tyrants while angrily viewing their subjects as Celtic ingrates.

A cloud brooded over Eigg. The islanders called it 'The Situation', the mutual disenchantment between many of the population and the laird at that time, Keith Schellenberg. When he bought Eigg for £270,000 he planned to make it a Hebridean Utopia. He was a charming, go-ahead Yorkshire businessman, well-intentioned and with ideas for making something of the place. He and the islanders got on well for a while, but the dream soured and some began to complain that he was a despot. 'He doesn't understand that people need to live in freedom, not servitude,' they grumbled. Many of the residents formed a trust to work for a change in ownership, saying that Eigg had been at the whim of landlords, most of whom failed to discharge their social responsibilities. Sounding like an independence movement they said they wanted to 'take charge of their own destinies'. The disappointed laird responded by calling them drunken, dangerous, rotten, barmy revolutionaries who thought that getting rid of him would be like liberating Haiti from Papa Doc. He was not disliked by everyone, though. One of the islanders told me that 'I respect my elders and betters and the owner is due respect. He is not a bad man. He has been kind. The old islanders were always used to a laird and they don't mind him.'

One of the sad aspects of this story was the shrivelling of the laird's relationship with the Carrs. The laird grew fond enough of them to give their eldest son an opportunity that they themselves could not dream of: he paid for the boy to go to Gordonstoun School. But over the years the friendship deteriorated into bitterness. The final wedge was driven when the Carrs learnt that he had stopped paying their son's school fees. The Carrs took over the fees because they could not take the boy out of the school at that stage of his education. 'It's a burden,' Colin Carr said. 'It was handsome of the laird to pay in the first place, but giving, then taking away, is playing with people's lives, playing God.'

A fire reduced the laird's prized 1927 Rolls-Royce to a charred chassis and ended any hope of *rapprochement*. He was convinced that it was started deliberately. He swung between weary disillusion and a determination to stay. Over a glass of wine, he reflected that he had become a hate figure and for this he blamed 'a handful of activists, a heavy mob'. By his own lights he was a generous man, and he was wounded by what he believed was ingratitude. 'Who else would send a shepherd's son to Gordonstoun for four years?' he asked. Owning Eigg had always been difficult, he mused, adding that he derived no pleasure from ownership. So why own it, I asked. 'It's a responsibility, but I always had a romantic idea of Eigg. I wanted to show that the private sector could conserve the island as well as any government body, costing the taxpayer nothing.'

Dr Tiarks said there was never a vendetta against the laird. 'He meant well but dissipated the goodwill he had. When you buy an estate you buy a community, and with it go rights, responsibilities, duties and privileges. If you take on privileges and rights without fulfilling responsibilities you get disaster. The heart of the problem is the system of ownership, which is sustainable only with an exceptional landlord.'

Some time later the laird of Eigg sold up. The new laird was an avant-garde artist from Germany. He did not last long, just long enough to irritate the islanders by selling off all the cattle; and the island was up for sale again.

Gunpowder Plot

I did not imagine I would find a link between Eigg and Nelson. Nelson never set foot here. But for many years the inhabitants of Eigg and other Hebridean islands harvested thousands of tons of kelp from the seashore; and Nelson had an interest in kelp. The seaweed was collected in baskets and carried to kilns for burning. The ash contained sodium carbonate, used in the manufacture of glass and above all in the making of gunpowder for the Navy. The Napoleonic Wars and the demands of the fleet created a boom in kelp prices. The owner of Eigg made a fortune. There was a widespread belief in those days that islanders were lazy people and so visitors to Eigg were pleased to see them bent in relentless and wretched labour.

This is the Place

From Mallaig I went to Knoydart on the ferry which runs three times a week with supplies and mail. It is a peninsula of melancholy beauty facing Skye, and since there is no road into it, it has the qualities of an island and is sometimes called by journalists the loneliest place in Britain. I put up at the guest house by the pier run by David and Jan Marriott. They were from Nottingham and chanced upon Knoydart while on holiday. They fell for it the moment they stepped ashore, looked at the simple whitewashed hamlet lodged between the mountains and the sea and decided: This is the place. They bought the guest house and quit Nottingham without regret. Bernie Evemy, once a plumber in Kent, was similarly entranced, left his business and became Knoydart's postmaster. Dave Smith was another, a Londoner who turned crofter. Most of the fifty people living in Knoydart can tell such a story. Not one of them is a native. Everyone is a sort of escaper who has dreamed of islands and has come to fashion a life around a small community

212

which has a shop, a post office, a pub, guest house, village hall, a school with three pupils and an estate management office. The people talked about the friendliness of the neighbours, the good air and the delicious local prawns. The Marriotts work the year round running their guest house and restaurant and David Marriott, a chef by profession, said: 'It's a holiday just being here.'

But, as I had found in Eigg, there was a frown on people's faces. Knoydart was one of eight large estates in Scotland advertised for sale at that time. It was in acute financial crisis. 'The trouble is,' I was told in the pub, 'these frequent changes of ownership make everyone feel insecure. People have no say in their future. Scotland is still feudal and owners can do as they wish.'

Dr Jim Hunter, an historian in Skye, said that communities should control their own destiny rather than face 'the awful lottery of new ownership'. A capitalist ogre is one thing, he said, but worse are owners who impose their fantasies in a locality they know little about. 'They have money and can muck about, but then they get fed up or run out of cash and the merry-go-round starts again. Some of the traditional landlords are far from happy with the situation because they feel that land ownership is blackened by loonies who come and go.' He proposed land reform in which the government would give crofting communities the means to buy out landlords. 'We need an agency to provide capital. The money would be paid back and reform need not be a socialist panacea. There is room for the state: to facilitate, not to nationalize. Interest in this sort of reform is growing. In the past people felt that a landlord had to be endured, like the weather; but younger people today are more articulate and a political solution will be forced sooner or later.'

Scottish estates swallow money. Buying them is one thing, maintaining them another. Some think that purchase by a conservation group is the answer, but there are doubts because environmental bodies do not necessarily have the local community interest at heart.

In the last century Knoydart supported more than a thousand people who lived by crofting and fishing. In 1853, in an episode typical of the Highland Clearances, the owner peremptorily shipped three hundred of them to Canada to make room for Cheviot sheep. The Clearances were carried out in the name of improvement and enlightenment and the lairds were supported by the majority of Presbyterian ministers who threatened the hapless people with the wrath of God if they did not go quietly. The banished people of Knoydart went to the emigrant ships and the slums of Glasgow. Some refused to go at first and their houses were pulled down before their eyes, and they watched without a sound. I saw the rubble of these houses, overgrown with thistles and foxgloves, the fallen stones not entirely speechless.

There were lairds good and bad, but none was hated more than Lord Brocket, a supercilious brewer who reigned over Knoydart in the 1930s and 1940s and came shooting twice a year. He was a Nazi sympathizer and a guest at Hitler's birthday party in 1939. In 1948 seven men of Knoydart, encouraged by the parish priest, carried out the last land raid in Scotland, seizing some of Lord Brocket's estate for themselves, to protect their homes and livelihoods. They occupied the land with the intention of working it as farms. Lord Brocket obtained a court order evicting them. A cairn on the waterfront notes that the seven men of Knoydart staked a claim for a place to live and work and that 'their struggle should inspire each new generation of Scots to gain such rights by just laws'.

Washing Up with a Hard Man

I first met John Ridgway in his kingdom of Ardmore, in Sutherland, twelve miles south of Cape Wrath, where the far north-west edge of Scotland juts into the Atlantic. As a great inhaler of cold air and a man suspicious of luxury he had constructed a life that offered him the correct measure of discomfort. His domain is remote, rocky, difficult and dramatic, reached only by boat or on foot. It lies three miles from the road, on a hillside stretching up from a sea loch of crystal water.

It was a sweat carrying my bags up the steep grassy slope to the house and Ridgway, who thinks life is not worth living if there is no physical struggle, was pleased to see the sheen on my brow.

214

'Hullo, old top,' he beamed. 'Bit hot?'

He took me into a shed and showed me *English Rose III*, the twenty-foot wooden Yorkshire-built dory in which he and Chay Blyth rowed across the north Atlantic in ninety-two days in 1966. Some of the six pairs of oars were still aboard, and battered clothing and goggles and the small gas stove used for cooking curries every evening, which were eaten with a shared wooden spoon. The boat seemed curiously old, like a relic from a Victorian expedition to the Arctic. Every plank spoke of fearfulness and fortitude. There was no cabin or shelter. I imagined Ridgway sitting there, bruised and swollen, plagued by salt-water boils, hands made claws by rowing, bracing himself, doggedly shaving his face. It must have been like scraping stone with a breadsaw, but Ridgway is a determined shaver. I resolved there and then that if he were to ask me whether I used an electric blanket on my bed in winter I would meet his gaze and lie.

Ridgway fashioned the idea for his adventure school during the crossing of the Atlantic. He reckoned that he and his wife, Marie Christine, could earn a living helping others to meet physical challenges. Thousands of people have been to the school to sail, climb, canoe, dive, walk, fish; confronting the elements and themselves.

Ridgway led the way up the ladder into his eyrie on the roof of his house. Here he writes his books and broods and prowls, not least in the hours before dawn, for he is a restless and questing man, impatient of slumber. From the window he indicated two kayaks flitting across the loch: he and his daughter Rebecca had paddled them around Cape Horn. His fifty-seven-foot ketch *English Rose VI* rode at her mooring. He had raced her around the world twice. On the second occasion, he walked out of the house, down the hill, climbed aboard the yacht with a friend, turned left and did not sight land again until Cape Horn; and he did not see land after that until he sighted Scotland. At two hundred and three days it was the fastest non-stop circumnavigation.

In his mid-fifties, as he was when I met him, he had no doubt mellowed, but he remained obsessed with testing himself and using every minute. He would have been fulfilled as a nineteenth-century imperial adventurer. *Carpe Diem*, seize the day, was the motto carved in large gold letters on a beam in his house; and he lived by it. He felt the march of the years, but this gave an edge to his battling. There was something of Ridgway in lines in Tennyson's *Ulysses*:

> I cannot rest from travel: I will drink
> Life to the lees . . .
> To strive, to seek, to find, and not to yield.
> How dull it is to pause, to make an end,
> To rust unburnished, not to shine in use!

Ridgway stared out at the hills. 'Adventure is to me the proof of being alive. I would not be true to myself if I did not construct a challenge and submit to it. You can't postpone such things. I don't want to be a waiting-to-die figure. I've seen too many people eaten by the worms of discontent.' He recited a favourite maxim: 'The opportunity of a lifetime must be taken in the lifetime of the opportunity.'

Ridgway had decided that he and his family would board *English Rose VI*, sail the Atlantic, transit the Panama Canal, cruise the south Pacific islands, walk the mountains of Peru, sail six hundred miles south of Cape Horn into Antarctica, then head to South Georgia, Tristan da Cunha, the Azores and home. 'The thing is, I've never particularly liked sailing,' Ridgway said. 'I don't like the sickness and I'm frightened of the dark and other things. But it's the price you pay for wonderful experiences. I'm still young and I want to see whales and dolphins and albatross again, trade wind clouds, islands.'

Ridgway and Marie Christine went for a run early every morning, returning wet and glowing. I do not run but I sensed that if I did not do something physical Ridgway might consider me a shapeless invertebrate, so I went for vigorous walks in the hills before breakfast.

Marie Christine and I walked to a rock high above the house, looking out to the mountains of Foinaven and Arkle. One of her challenges has been to assert her own individuality while living with a driven man determined to force a gallon of life into his pint pot. In Marie Christine the iron man had met his steel magnolia. 'Living with John can be like living with a lion. But he's a grand chap with immense humour, really inspiring. Of course, there are family rows. They start because we are all single-minded people and object to his self-appointed leadership. He can be severe and uncompromising, but never brutal. He's a frontiersman who has to carve an existence, otherwise he is diminished. He needs to be a general running a campaign. He springs vigorously to life in situations of physical danger. He's a man of such vitality that it is hard for him to accept that it all ends. A friend of his own age died recently and this shook John terribly. At the same time he puts himself into life-threatening situations, half-taunting death.'

Ridgway said, 'Wanting my own way, that's the trouble, not being a milksop saying "I'll just take the dog for a walk, dear." Jugs have been thrown in my direction.' He laughed. 'I've survived only by cowering back, you know. But Marie Christine and I have worked together for thirty years and she is the sunlight in the whole thing.'

Marie Christine met Ridgway at a roulette table and married him when she was twenty. He was a penniless paratroop officer. Their daughter Rebecca was born nine months after he landed in Ireland after rowing the Atlantic and she was brought to Ardmore in a fish basket when she was three weeks old. She has inherited her parents' resilience. She smiled and said she had learnt to stand up for herself. 'Yes, Dad can be annoying. He expects an awful lot of people, believes you don't grow unless you are stretched. But we know each other very well and we don't fight over important things. He has qualities I don't match up to, pays close attention to detail, leaves nothing to chance. He is meticulous and hates untidiness.'

After dinner that evening Ridgway asked me to help him load the dishwasher. I put knives, forks and spoons together in the stacking baskets. Ridgway sighed and patiently unmade my work, placing knives in one basket, forks in another and spoons in another.

'There's a wrong way, a right way and a Ridgway,' he said.

I caught a glimpse of his pirate's smile.

A Whack on the Head

Ridgway sent me a message. He was in the South Atlantic, roaring along, the spinnaker as taut as a drum. He asked me to meet the yacht in the Azores. He greeted me at the airport, his blue eyes merry in the weathered rock of his face. The grin revealed a missing tooth, lost in a struggle with a baguette, and the gap made him look even more the buccaneer. He extended his Cape Horner's paw.

'Hullo, old top.'

Marie Christine was waiting outside the airport building. Her smile lit her face. Her eyes, I thought, were on the horizon: just one more ocean and they would all be home. While we were having coffee at a bar in the port Ridgway glanced at the sky and said we might as well shove off. We walked around the harbour wall to the ketch. Within the hour we were under sail, shouldering the Atlantic swell in the sunset, the course set for Scotland and home, one thousand five hundred miles to the north.

After midnight Ridgway was steering *English Rose* and saw me pass the end of a sheet the wrong way round a cleat. His face took on the expression of an Easter Island statue.

'There's a wrong way, a right way and a Ridgway.'

By this time the Ridgways had been wandering the oceans for a year and a half and were aching for home after the long haul from Antarctica. Marie Christine yearned for a kitchen that stayed still and a chance to wear her black velvet dress. Rebecca longed for a reunion with her boyfriend. Her sister Elizabeth dreamed of her own bed after the cramped muddle of the fore-cabin with three crewmen. Ridgway said he was imagining breakfast. 'Bacon, eggs, black pudding, fried bread, tomatoes, mushrooms, kidneys and lots of sausages.'

He had found the satisfaction he sought. Under the stars one night, the sails as full as aldermen's waistcoats, we watched dolphins leaping, diving and torpedoing, escorting us across the grumbling ocean, and Ridgway summarized. 'We'll look back on all this and see a symmetry in it. The pieces have come together. It was our last chance for a voyage like this as a family. We are stronger for having done it.'

One purpose of the journey was to show Elizabeth her roots. She was then fifteen, the child of a Quechua Indian mother and a Norwegian–Quechua father. Her father saved Ridgway's life during an Amazon expedition in 1970. Fifteen years later the Ridgways trekked into the Peruvian mountains to meet him, only to find that he had been murdered by terrorists. His six-year-old daughter was cared for by her grandmother who asked the Ridgways to take the girl home with them and give her a future. This seemed to Ridgway the stroke of fate, for he himself had been an orphan, adopted at three months. Here was a way of helping someone in his turn, repaying a debt to the girl's father. The Ridgways legally adopted Elizabeth the following year. 'She is curious about her origins and knows she looks different,' Ridgway said. 'I wanted to show this vivid and volatile person from Peru that there is more to the world than a bleak corner of Scotland. I wanted her to see herself in context, to boost her self-confidence.' They took Elizabeth back, walking for three weeks in the Peruvian mountains, and showed her where she came from. She was content. The Ridgways felt she had crossed a bridge.

In a small town in Chile the Ridgways went to see a film, *The Piano*. Marie Christine loved it, Ridgway loathed it. Rowing back to the yacht, they argued fiercely and she pushed him out of the dinghy. When he tried to scramble back she whacked him on the head with a paddle. 'He was much better after that,' she said.

I shared the Ridgways' watches, six to eight in the morning, noon to two, six to eight and midnight to two. They were happy hours. I realized that one of my tasks was to be a storyteller and in the cockpit I related to Ridgway and Marie Christine all the news, gossip and stories I could recall. Towards the end of a watch Ridgway sometimes asked for a 'trailer' for the next story, something to look forward to in the next watch, and when we had settled into it he would say, 'Right, now tell us that story.'

Ten days out from the Azores, the island of Barra loomed out of the mist and gannets and fulmars circled in salute. *English Rose* sailed around Skye, into Ardmore and moored below the home the Ridgways had endlessly discussed, down to the last beloved cracked tile. In the yacht's saloon one of the family pinned up the word 'Happy', cut from a Happy Birthday streamer. Ridgway was moved. 'It says something when you've been with your family for five hundred and fifty-four days and they stick that up.'

The Ridgways and their crew of three walked up the hill to the house, took off their red ocean suits and sat down with a mingled sense of disbelief and triumph. Time was performing its trick of rendering what had seemed unending into a capsule of memory. Everyone drank a toast to survival. Marie Christine went out onto the mountainside and dug up a tin containing a small brooch she had buried there before she set off. That evening, indefatigable, she cooked for fourteen. Ridgway surveyed the jolly table, happy to be home. I wondered what he would dream up next to prove that he was alive.

Marie Christine said, 'Well, we've dealt with the monster.' She meant the restless ocean.

8

North of South

Hearing that the Secretary of State for Wales had resigned, and learning the name of his successor, the first reaction of many Welsh people was that another wretched Englishman had been foisted upon them. But gradually they became aware of a fact from which they drew some comfort. 'At least', they conceded, 'he's a Yorkshireman.'

So he did not seem so bad after all; and he played the Yorkshire card for all it was worth. He was English, yes, but another kind of English; for do not Yorkshiremen have a robust sense of place, of locality, a bred-in-the-bone feeling of difference? Is there not a Yorkshire voice more distinctive than a mere accent? What is the purpose of the *Yorkshire Post*, of *The Dalesman*, of the Yorkshire County Cricket Club, of Bradford, Leeds and Halifax, if not to reinforce and assert a Yorkshire identity? Are not Yorkshire women, when their pregnancies have reached full term, driven up from the effete south so that their children may be born within Yorkshire's rugged frontiers and thereby claim their tykeish inheritance?

It seems to many minds, inside Yorkshire and out of it, that for all the unifying influences of modern Britain Yorkshire is undeniably different, a region made by geology and Victorian industry, hard times and Nonconformist piety, individualism and local rivalries, the sound of its vowels and a jut-jawed attitude to the south of England. Yorkshire means something, in the same way that Texas means something different in the United States: it is distinct and it is large.

The special qualities of Yorkshire are not all myth. To many in the south it seems that northerners run up a flag as if to say 'I'm distinct and you have to take notice.' Some southerners object to this. George Orwell, for example, was irritated by the northern insistence on superiority, the assertion that northerners were the 'real' people.

On the other hand, many southerners like their northerners northern. They prefer them to be different. Harvey Smith, the show-jumper, was enjoyed by southerners because he behaved exactly in accordance with their ideas of a no-nonsense Yorkshireman. Fred Trueman was a satisfyingly glowering and pugnacious fast bowler and Geoffrey Boycott is admired for being a Yorkshire nationalist as well as terse. Similarly, Bernard Ingham, former press secretary to Margaret Thatcher, fits the picture of a pipe-smoking Yorkshire pundit with a properly gruff way of saying 'Balderdash'. It was in his birthplace of Hebden Bridge that a diner who asked a waiter for a cappuccino was told 'Nay, lad, if you want fancy coffee, you'll have to go to Leeds.'

There is a continuing conspiracy in which southern writers and others attribute supposedly 'northern' qualities to northerners, a constant southern reinforcement of the northern image. When they reach for words to fit their ideas of Yorkshiremen, southerners end up with dour, gritty and down-to-earth. The word 'Yorkshireman' seems underdressed without the adjective 'bluff' or 'blunt' attached to it. If a journalist writes of a Yorkshireman or a northerner without some gritstone qualifier it is very likely that a sub-editor will be minded to insert it, much as he will add the words 'shark-infested' to any reference to tropical seas or 'sleepy' to any story about an English village. Thus an obituary in *The Times* of a senior civil servant noted that he had 'a strong dose of Yorkshireman's common sense' – as if Yorkshire common sense were different from any other. A profile of a Yorkshire cabinet minister observed that 'his Yorkshire accent has survived Oxford and is put to effective use playing the part of the common-sensical common man.' A photograph of jockeys exercising their horses in the Yorkshire snow was captioned 'Yorkshire grit'. In an interview the playwright David Storey spoke in a 'fatalistic, phlegmatic Yorkshire monotone'.

For their own part, many Yorkshiremen believe strongly in their qualities of stubbornness and unadorned speaking. They think that the image is absolutely right. A Yorkshire businessman declared that 'there is a Yorkshire breed, based on self-help, thrift and old-fashioned values.' Another said of attempts by the Tory party to raise money among Yorkshire company directors, 'They'll have their work cut out getting money out of Yorkshiremen. There's a lot of miserable buggers up here.' A woman told a newspaper, 'Coming from Yorkshire, if I set my mind to do something, I do it.' An account of a garden-fence war between neighbours quoted a man as saying, 'My wife Wendy is a typical North Yorkshire person. She is blunt and likes to call a spade a spade.' Similarly, a Yorkshireman told *The Times*, 'We are Yorkshire born and bred, which counts for something, and we have a strong Christian faith which sustains us.'

Yorkshire is often taken in the south to be an exemplar of English northness. It does not, of course, have a monopoly of northern attributes. A woman was described in *The Daily Telegraph* as having 'a level-headed Lancashire pragmatism' – possibly different from Sussex pragmatism. A report in *The Times* said that 'the Lancashire temperament is not sympathetic to change', suggesting an immovability that would not be found in lower latitudes.

It may be that it is easier to sound blunt with a northern accent. A friend of mine recalled that when he went to live in the north he invited his new neighbours in for drinks. 'Lovely house,' one of them said starkly, 'terrible carpet.' A northern businessman working in the south agreed at an industrial tribunal that his plain-speaking manner ruffled southern feathers.

'I come from the north where it's practice to say what you mean and mean what you say,' he said. 'Bluntness is perfectly acceptable in the north – it's regrettable that it causes offence in the south.' You half expect that when you meet a Yorkshireman and ask 'How do you do?' he will say 'You daft booger', or 'You're nowt but a great girl's blouse.'

Northerners speak of the soft south, the spoiled south, and detect a southern condescension. In a reunion with his wartime comrades in Yorkshire in 1933, J.B. Priestley, the great English voice, met one of his old officers. 'Unlike most of us there,' Priestley wrote, 'he was not a West Riding man at all, but a South Country schoolmaster, whose character and reputation were such that through him the whole affected tittering South Country was forgiven everything.' The northern writer Colin Welland noted that when he first went south he became very defensive, hearing a patronizing inflection in every remark. Thirty years ago, he said, there was contempt for anything north of Watford. 'People imitated your accent at the drop of a hat and socially you were an oddity.'

The Yorkshire-born Member of Parliament Austin Mitchell wrote of the long war of attrition waged by 'southern governments' against the north and recalled that when he was a child 'all our jokes and hatreds' were directed at southerners.

At the Sunderland football ground in 1987 two men were heard discussing the great hurricane that had just caused immense damage in the south of England.

'Hell of a wind down south.'

'Aye, serve the buggers right.'

Northern speech is the most obvious identifier. Many northerners are proud of their accent. Others, over the years, have striven to rid themselves of it and have sent their sons south to have it educated out of their throats. An obituary in *The Times* recorded that a certain Yorkshireman spoke with no trace of a Yorkshire accent. Austin Mitchell was humiliated when he spoke for the first time outside Yorkshire, at an English literature seminar. The class laughed when he read Chaucer.

The Yorkshire broadcaster Wilfred Pickles was at the centre of controversy during the Second World War when he was asked by the BBC to read the main news bulletins. The Minister of Information suggested that listeners were tired of the standard 'Oxford' accent of newsreaders. More importantly, it said, the Yorkshire accent could not be copied easily by German broadcasters hoping to fool the British with false information. The Germans had successfully imitated Polish broadcasters to mislead the Poles.

When he reported for duty at the BBC Pickles observed other newsreaders at work and noted that while at the microphone Alvar Liddell rubbed his stomach throughout the bulletin. Pickles did not follow suit. Possibly he thought it a southern idiosyncrasy. At the end of his first twenty-minute bulletin, Pickles said: 'Good night to you all, and to all northerners, wherever you may be, good neet.' No chance of the Germans copying that. The announcer who followed Pickles played a record of the Yorkshire dialect song 'On Ilkla Moor Baht 'At'. Letters poured in to the BBC, defending and attacking Pickles's Yorkshire cadences. Newspaper cartoonists, reacting to the controversy, depicted Pickles in a muffler and cloth cap. Some people said the news read in Yorkshire tones was less believable. Many northerners wrote that Pickles's short northern *a* gave them comfort, but it was clear that other northerners disliked his reading of the news because they were embarrassed to hear their own regional voice: they were gripped by the northern cringe.

People still complain to the BBC about Yorkshire accents, and about other accents, too. George Bernard Shaw said in his preface to *Pygmalion* in 1912 that an Englishman cannot open his mouth without making another despise him. There is still truth in this, though not as much as there was. Radio, television and films have made us more accustomed to regional sounds, more aware of the variety of Britain and the persistence of dialect and accent which is part of British resilience.

Dracula's Landing

I travelled over the north Yorkshire moors to Whitby where, in the seventh century, Caedmon, the inveterate diner-out, was miraculously blessed with the gift of song and composed hymns in Old English. In Bram Stoker's novel, Count Dracula arrived here at the start of his expedition to convert England into a realm of the undead. I sat on the Bram Stoker memorial seat on the western headland, a favourite place for Dracula enthusiasts who flock here, and opened the local newspaper. The editor's lively commentary column included a scornful complaint about London's ignorance of the north: a national paper was upbraided because it couldn't even spell Teesside – did it suppose the river was called the Tee?

Whitby's heady nose, a sharp smell of the sea and of fish, rose up from the River Esk. It was a lovely morning and the red-roofed town spread below me was a picture. Houses nestled in the sheltered gorge and climbed the slopes alongside cobbled streets. Across the river, on the eastern headland, the road threaded up to St Mary's church above which brooded the dark and spiky skeleton of Whitby Abbey, ruined even more by the pointless potshots of the German Navy in the First World War. I walked down to the stone quay where fishing boats lay berthed, a haddock-throw from a number of fish and chip restaurants. Oysters, prawns and mussels were sold from white-painted cabins. Predictions were dispensed from a little wooden hut in which there sat a True Born Romany fortune teller, swigging from a bottle of mineral water, possibly having failed to foresee the need for a glass.

I had fish and chips for lunch and also for supper. There seemed little point in ordering anything but the succulent local catch. It was the freshest I had eaten since a dinner in Japan which included a little fish, presented on my plate alive. It observed me with a reproachful eye, like Walter de la Mare's fish that talked in the frying pan.

My hotel, a rambling pile with long corridors, rose from the top of the cliff as if it had grown there. Most of the guests were pensioners, brought by coach for their summer holiday. Notices in the lobby advertised a tea dance every afternoon, Eyes Down For Bingo every day, a country and western evening 'with resident hillbillies' and wrestling matches once a week.

On this particular evening the entertainment was an Old Tyme Music Hall. The ballroom was full, with tables set around the dance floor, all laden with drinks and ashtrays. The master of ceremonies was singing a George Formby song, 'I'm Leaning on the Lamp-post', in a Lancashire accent, while the audience tapped their feet and lightly slapped their thighs. He was a versatile man and he sang, danced and clowned and arched his eyebrows. He belonged to that tireless infantry of showbusiness, the backbone corps of vocalists, jokers and cheeky chappies who perform at resort hotels and at the end of the pier all over Britain.

After his song he bowed and skipped away and a vivacious commère clapped her hands and called everyone to dance a square tango. The spotlit floor quickly filled. White-haired men left their years upon the tables and swung their partners into the dance, each a Fred to his Ginger, their feet lightly treading the winegum spangles scattered by the faceted ball revolving above them. Girls darted from table to table, like Tinker Bell, lighting candles to create a romantic glow. The band played a syrupy waltz and then a rumba. The dancers knew a secret code of enjoyment, the steps and the skills, and they glided around the floor with their elbows at the proper angle, their feet in perfect harmony, survivors of the days when dancing was a commonplace social grace. It reminded me of an evening in Sokolniki Park in Moscow, when I had heard a distant saxophone and followed the sound through the silver birches, my feet crunching in the snow, until I came to a dance floor in the woods lit by a corona of coloured lights, and saw old Muscovites swaddled in their coats and fur hats so that they looked like elegant dancing bears as they waltzed beneath the stars; and the elderly gentlemen bowed to the ladies like young officers at a ball. Not everyone in the ballroom at Whitby could take the floor. Some sat with bandaged legs or had swollen ankles or a leg brace or had a walking stick at hand. But they hummed the tunes and swayed to the music.

The master of ceremonies emerged to lead the singing of 'Mademoiselle from Armentières', 'I Do Like to be Beside the Seaside' and 'Maybe It's Because I'm a Londoner', during which the coach drivers and some elderly chaps standing at the bar succumbed to sentiment and put their arms around each other's shoulders and ticked from side to side like metronomes, their pints of beer sloshing gently in front of their paunches. The master of ceremonies took the floor in a tail-coat, top hat and false moustache, to play the part of a music-hall chairman, sitting at a table with a gavel. Two pretty girls in Edwardian dresses sang romantic songs and a thin young man wearing a kilt sang 'Donald, Where's Your Troosers'. In front of the kilt there dangled, not a sporran, but a paintbrush on a string. The master of ceremonies made pop-eyed faces, raised his eyebrows, allowed his moustache to drop off and fell from his chair, his legs waggling like a beetle's; and the audience laughed to see such fun.

Next morning the pensioners were up early and the dining room was as full of white heads as a sheep pen. After breakfast they bustled into the coaches which waited in the sunshine. The seaside day seemed full of promise. A coach driver shouted: 'Any more for Durham?' Stragglers hurried out and the hotel lobby was suddenly empty.

The Whitby Cats

To my left the bronze statue of Captain Cook, one of my heroes, looked out over the North Sea, facing south-east, dividers in his right hand and charts rolled under his left arm. Whitby lies in the heart of the Captain Cook country, a heritage industry invention generating income from remembrance of the greatest British navigator. Although Cook was born and raised in Yorkshire, his achievements are better known in Australia and New Zealand, lands he put on the imperial map, and his memory is honoured more in Sydney and Auckland than in Britain. Many Australians and New Zealanders make a pilgrimage to Whitby and its blustery hinterland to satisfy their curiosity about their British discoverer. It was fitting that Cook's boyhood home should have been dismantled stone by stone and shipped to Melbourne in 1934.

The charts that this painstaking pathfinder made during the first of his three voyages, between 1768 and 1771, were so accurate that they served mariners for many years. It was only recently that Cook's name was removed from one of the New Zealand coastal charts, his work on Dusky Sound superseded by a modern electronic and satellite survey. He sighted the scrubby south-east coast of Australia in 1770, named it New South Wales and went ashore at Botany Bay. He charted the continent's east coast on his northward passage. More than two centuries on, I find in Cook's three Pacific voyages more to marvel at than in modern space travel. They were, in their way, interplanetary. Cook and his men felt they were journeying from their own world to explore others. As he set out on his second voyage Cook wrote to a friend at Whitby: 'I should hardly have troubled you with a letter was it not customary for men to take leave of their friends before they go out of the world, for I can hardly think myself in it so long as I am deprived from having connections with the civilised part of it.' Cook was fifty when he was chopped to pieces by islanders in Hawaii in 1779, and a bundle containing his skull, hands and feet was retrieved by his officers.

Several places on the moors have staked a claim on him. Middlesbrough styles itself the Gateway to the Captain Cook Country and names Cook as its most famous son, adding, bathetically, 'you may have heard of Middlesbrough in *Heartbeat*, the popular TV series'. There is a birthplace museum in the Middlesbrough suburb of Marton, Cook's schoolroom in Great Ayton is also a museum, and there is a Cook Heritage Centre in Staithes. I walked up to heathery Easby Moor to see the Cook monument, an obelisk commanding a view of the hills, with an inscription commending 'a man in nautical knowledge inferior to none . . . admired benefactor of the human race'. The Cook Museum in Whitby is in the fine house where he lived as an apprentice to shipowner John Walker, having undertaken in his indentures not to play dice, cards and bowls or to fornicate or marry. Cook was so conscientious and austere that it cannot be imagined that he contemplated anything but the last. He learnt his seamanship in Whitby, in tough, workaday colliers, devoid of ornament, known as cats, employed to transport Tyne coal to warm the houses of London. Cook admired their qualities and all the ships he chose for his three voyages of exploration,

Endeavour, Resolution, Adventure and *Discovery*, were robust Whitby-built colliers.

In St Mary's church a notice said, in answer to questions asked frequently: 'Sorry – we don't know where Captain Cook sat when he was an apprentice. And – No! Dracula never was here!' In Bram Stoker's story Dracula wrecked a schooner at Whitby and killed the crew, leaping from the vessel in the guise of a lupine dog, later transforming himself into a huge bat which flew across the harbour. Stoker's imagination was stirred by the eerie atmosphere which hangs like mist about the dark eroded gravestones; and in his book Dracula waits in one of these graves.

Like Captain Cook, Dracula earns money for Whitby. Students of the legend follow the tourist office's Dracula Trail pamphlet and build an appetite for lunch. You see them sinking their sharp teeth into fish as white as a virgin's neck. I visited the Dracula Experience, a seaside chamber of horrors tricked out with rising corpses and ghostly howls. When I emerged I found a small boy holding his sister's hand and looking worried. 'Did you see my Mum in there?' he asked. 'Yes,' I said. 'And Dracula didn't get her.' The shadow flew away from his face.

Tall Bold Slugger

J.B. Priestley was in a foul humour when he arrived on Tyneside in 1933. He had a cold; not an ordinary cold but a cold that 'seemed to be of gigantic size and strength'. Like most men in this condition, as women well know, he felt pathetically sorry for himself, right poorly, and he spent a page or so of his *English Journey* describing the symptoms in detail. He dosed himself with extract of belladonna, deadly nightshade, and, not surprisingly, the combination of this drug and his high temperature made Tyneside wobble and bulge 'like the world we know in dreams . . . things looked very queer indeed and were a little larger and wilder than life'.

It was raining when this boggled Priestley reached Newcastle. 'The whole city seemed a black steaming mass.' He sat in a dismal hotel room. His pipe had no taste. He had just seen squalid shanty housing that 'a Kaffir would not have envied'. He had also taken against the local accent. 'To my ears it sounds a most barbarous, monotonous and irritating twang.' And he damned it even though 'as a rule I like local accents, and have kept one myself' – as if he were describing a pet.

I was luckier. I had no cold. The day was crisp and the winter light was bright and encouraging. Instead of deadly nightshade I took sips of Newcastle Brown Ale, the local myrrh, invented in 1927 and known to Geordies as 'Dog'. On the evening I arrived I went to the Bigg Market and its web of neighbouring streets and wandered through the pools of gaudy light and in and out of the effervescent crowds, absorbed in the Newcastle tradition of the 'good neet out on the toon'. This revolves around more than one hundred and fifty pubs, night clubs and restaurants and spills onto the pavements, bubbling and noisy. It is a famous nightlife and an American travel company recently rated it number eight in the world, in the same league of revelry as Rio de Janeiro and New Orleans. Coach parties drive up the motorways from Sheffield and Birmingham and down from Scotland to take part in it. It is popular with expeditions of young people from placid Sussex who hear rumours of northern bacchanal and come to see it for themselves. It is also a magnet for commandos of Icelanders, and for numerous Norwegians who follow in the longships' furrow and feel a Norse kinship with Geordies. Late in the evening, Geordies are under the impression that Norwegians understand their language.

The night on the town is an engaging *paseo*. Hundreds of sparky young women with stylish haircuts and manicured nails walked up and down, arm in arm, breezing into the former male fortresses, the pubs. The good night out belongs to the emancipated young women as much as to the men. Although it was cold, with a chilly whip of a wind, the women wore no coats. In their exuberant parade of fashion they showed off miniskirts, exiguous bare-shouldered dresses and cutty sarks revealing their navels, pierced by rings, the pavements echoing to the roulette click of heels. They seemed to lack any protective plumpness, and, for the most part, looked slim enough to suggest a diet of plankton, but they did not shiver. Many of the men, too, were in short-sleeve rig, refusing to acknowledge the cold. In my coat I felt overdressed and rather southern.

Crowds queued to get into the popular pubs. In the window of one of them a young man sat in his underpants in a bathtub filled with cold baked beans, though no one could say why. In another pub I asked for whisky and the vision behind the bar said, 'It's cheaper if you buy a triple.' Neon lights coruscated and the thud-pubs throbbed. It might be thought that this kind of carnival would disintegrate into trouble, but it hardly ever becomes unruly. More than two hundred doormen, who hate to be called bouncers, and who have to be licensed, proficient in first aid and self-defence, help to keep order and steer away scruffy dressers. The police set out to be firm but not heavy, avuncular. Flashy young men, I was told, avoid trouble that might spoil their new and expensive trousers.

I walked down the hill to the quay which lies beneath the city's icon, the Tyne Bridge, Newcastle's iron shoulders, theatri-cally-lit, and presiding over a cluster of brother bridges. People flocked to the quayside restaurants and pubs. Berthed on the far bank of the Tyne was a ship, a reminder of what Newcastle used to build, now a floodlit night-club. Dance music echoed across the river. In a restaurant I asked a waitress if she joined in the night out. 'Every week,' she said, 'without fail, but I can only afford the one night. I save up for it. I love it. It's our Geordie tradition. People dress up and go out on the toon however hard things are; and, I can tell you, it really is tough for many people. I know men who haven't worked for years and despair of ever working again.'

The night on the town flourishes on Fridays, Saturdays and Sundays, a tribal ritual over a century old. A temperance society observed the heavy consumption of beer in the 1890s and erected an ornate drinking fountain in the Bigg Market bearing the admonition 'Water is best'. The surging crowds swirl merrily about it.

The revelry is all of a piece with Newcastle's assertion of the Geordie spirit. I was dubious about such a thing, and thought it would have much to do with nostalgia for the industrial past, or would be a fluctuating football loyalty powered by brown ale. But people talk of 'the Geordie nation' and if that seems fanciful I can only say that on the bracing streets of Newcastle I was persuaded that there was something in it. There is nothing in the south like the north-east's brand of local patriotism. No one, after all, says 'Surrey and proud of it', or 'Berkshire for ever'. Sir Jeremy Beecham, chairman of Newcastle's development committee, said: 'We were always a frontier territory and still are. People feel a strong identification with the region, that they are different and special.' A Geordie sense of place, and defiance, grew in an industrial economy that has so often risen and fallen, in a series of deaths and resurrections, that its people have had little choice but to be resilient, taking a pride in staggering to their feet after knockout punches. Priestley, during his visit, noted the shipyard cranes on the Tyne and said that 'these Geordies, stocky toothless fellows in caps and mufflers, cursing in their uncouth accent, could do a grand job whenever they were given a chance.'

Newcastle's swagger is not at all unattractive, although northness and distance from London contribute a little chippiness, too. I had an impression of a place with a strong sense of itself, a city-state almost, the most northern city in England, the metropolis of the north-east and the true source of Geordieness. Several people had given me different explanations about the origins of the term 'Geordie', so I went to the library to ask for an official ruling. It is a question that is often asked. The librarian handed me a sheet of yellow paper, headed Fact Sheet 5, which said that a Geordie is anyone born in Northumberland, Durham or Tyne and Wear. It offered four explanations for the origin of the word, two of them concerning George Stephenson, inventor, engineer and local hero, whose statue stands in Westgate Street. The librarian also gave me Fact Sheet 3, a piece of Geordie boosterism which noted that the northeast had the first public steam railway, the first railway bridge, first steam turbine, first house lit by electricity, the first beauty contest, the first windscreen wiper and the first flavoured potato crisps: vinegar, as it happens.

The first thing I saw in Newcastle's museum was a half-ton boulder of coal, hard, glinting and evocative. 'This', children are

233

told, 'is what coal looks like.' It was not so long ago that the Tyne quays were known as the Black Indies for their transhipment of coal. Near the boulder was displayed the Tyne-built turbine-driven *Turbinia* which a century ago was the fastest vessel in the world and revolutionized marine propulsion. These were symbols of the masculine working-class world of shipbuilding, coal, iron and engineering in which the great majority of men in the north-east earned their living. A southerner who went to work in Newcastle in the 1970s found it still very much a man's world. A Geordie he overheard complaining about the difficulties he was having with his wife was told by a companion, 'You can always smack her gob, man.' A department store assistant who telephoned his home to give a price for new furnishings would not discuss the matter with his wife, preferring to wait until the man of the house was available. But the male dominion has shrunk.

Catastrophic decline would make material enough for sad songs, but Newcastle and its hinterland do not sentimentalize the vanished heavy industries; or, at least, not very much. Hand-wringing is not the Geordie style and Geordieness is not backward-looking. People feel let down by the government, disappointed but not bitter. The 1980s were particularly cruel. No one tries to minimize the burden of twenty-five per cent male unemployment. 'There's no doubting the effect this has on health and crime,' Sir Jeremy Beecham said. The tradition of early school-leaving continues even though the supply of teenage jobs does not. No one forgets the anger which erupted in riots in 1991. But the optimists say that the Geordie is out to transcend the disintegration of the industries that once defined him.

The glory of Newcastle is its nineteenth-century heart, one of the finest townscapes in Europe, laid out by men who knew what they were doing and what they wanted. It has kept its shape and proportions and looking at it makes you feel better. From his lofty fluted column the second Earl Grey, architect of the 1832 Reform Bill, gazes out on substantial curving streets of tall and spacious buildings which exhibit that combination of muscle and elegance you see in heavyweight boxers in expensive suits.

Within Earl Grey's purview there is all the intensity and concentration of a walled city, fortified against the marauding Scots in centuries of border warfare. Everything is at hand. Within a few minutes' walk of each other are teeming shopping arcades, university colleges and restaurant belts. Close by is the brewery, source of the brown ale, and next to that is the Newcastle United football stadium. On Tyneside everyone is caught up in Newcastle United's fortunes. When 'The Toon' is playing at home thousands of men and boys sport black and white shirts. Girls wear black and white microskirts and babies grow up in black and white romper suits and boys in black and white pyjamas get into black and white beds and cover themselves with black and white duvets and dream of goals. All of the passion for football is symbolized by the statue of Jackie Milburn – 'Wor Jackie: 1924–1988. In Honour of John Edward Thompson Milburn, Footballer and Gentleman': one of the last, some say.

The convenient human scale of Newcastle, the fact that it is not an incoherent sprawl, helps it to work. In a population of two hundred and seventy thousand its decision-makers know each other well. Education is the city's growth industry and there are more than forty-five thousand students in two popular universities. Their money and youth are good for the civic complexion. I asked some students from the south what they made of Geordies. 'Well, they're not stuffy – they're a different sort of Englishman,' they said.

Dave Johns, a Newcastle comedian, said: 'I feel we really are a state on our own and humour is part of the essence of it. Unemployment is high but we are used to adversity and when things are hard you have to dig deeper for your laughter. In any case, Geordie humour does not allow people to feel sorry for themselves. It is irreverent and pricks pomposity. It goes down well in the south. My accent gets me halfway to making people laugh and I can get away with things a southerner can't. I like to think my Geordie aura protects me. I went to perform in Londonderry and when the compère introduced me he said: "It's all right – he's a Geordie, he's one of us." I suppose that because I have a Geordie accent they did not think I was really English.'

The morning after I had seen the night on the town I found myself in the fried–food fug of a café, standing in a queue behind a young man who had on his tray a breakfast mountain of eggs, bacon and sausage coated with a slurry of baked beans.

The girl behind the counter picked up a large white loaf and asked the man, 'Thick or thin?'

She hardly needed to ask. 'Thick,' he said.

She grasped the loaf, raised her knife as if it were a chainsaw and hacked off a slice that would have done duty as a flagstone. The spectacle was in keeping with Newcastle's brawniness and gusto. This is a town of big trousers and large appetites where *nouvelle cuisine* shrivels in a gale of derisive laughter, a town which boasts more than an echo of Carl Sandburg's lines about Chicago . . . 'a tall bold slugger set vivid against the little soft cities'.

Where the Wild Geese Go

Redstarts and wheatears, blown in on the east wind, darted among the bushes on the snaking pathway to the shore. From a hummock of sand I saw the beach, as bare as a bleached bone, stretching away in a long curve, the sea a cobalt disc inscribed with a thin white line of surf, and utterly empty of ships.

Nelson first smelt the sea and saw sail on this part of the north Norfolk coast. He was born nearby in the rectory at Burnham Thorpe and his father, the rector, lies buried in the chancel of the medieval church. Nelson once said that he would like to be buried here himself unless, he added artfully, his good eye cocked to posterity, others took the matter from his hands and decided that he should rest elsewhere. The lectern is carved from a piece of oak taken from HMS *Victory*, timber which shivered under the broadsides at Trafalgar. For its connection with Nelson the church has the right to fly the white ensign of the Royal Navy. This is 'Nelson country' and you can buy a guide in the form of a cassette tape for your car, a commentary on the hero's life. 'Push the start button and hear about the exploits of young Nelson . . . hear about his love for two different women.'

In the church visitors' book a man who added 'ex-RN' after

his name had written: 'A sailor's pilgrimage.' Someone had urged 'Come back Nelson, England is in need of you.'

A notice on the church door said: 'All who enter, of your charity, pray latch these doors lest a bird enter and die of thirst.'

This stretch of coast is not quite land and not quite sea, a marshland mystery made of tidal creeks and mudflats, reed beds and water meadows and dunes secured by tangles of marram grass. There is no grand drama of high cliffs in conflict with pounding breakers. It is understated country, a place of reflection perfect for long lonely days and a single set of footprints in the sand. Narrow paths run along dykes. A windmill makes a navigation mark. Churches and their villages are reached through a maze of lanes.

It is a wistful land, robbed of its inheritance. Many of the villages once belonged to the North Sea and the tides were their pulse. They felt affinity with those whose coasts lay on the same waters and who fished and traded as they did, the Dutch, Danes, Swedes and Norwegians. 'I noticed', a villager ventured, 'that when I was in Denmark there was a bit of a Norfolk accent in the voices.'

Over the years, the scouring sea and longshore drift piled up silt and built immense shingle banks so that today, between the villages and the North Sea, there lies a mile or so of marsh, the dominion of swans and geese and dibbling waders. The birds draw their own pilgrim flocks of birdwatchers who have made the Barbour *de rigueur* hereabouts, so much so that I half expected to see a Barbour dinner jacket in the hotel. From time to time the sea delivers a harsh reminder of its old mastery. Driven by storms, it rampages over the marshes to flood the old quaysides of villages which have felt bereft ever since it deserted them.

I walked to Stiffkey church and pondered on a cryptic entry in the visitors' book. 'Still no answer, still no peace', was all it said.

On the edge of the churchyard I found, beneath a rose bush, the grave of Harold Davidson, who was rector here from 1906 until he was unfrocked in 1932 for associating with prostitutes. His is a sad and English story. He frequently travelled to London on a Monday, returning on a Saturday. His interest in the women he met there may have been Gladstonian, a matter of rescue and reform, and he said: 'I have been known as the prostitutes' padre, to me the proudest role that a true priest of Christ can hold. If He were . . . in London today He would be found constantly walking in Piccadilly.' During the church court hearing Stiffkey was a place of prurient pilgrimage. The rector protested his innocence – 'There is not a single deed that I shall not do again with the help of God, a little more discreetly maybe' – but was sacked. In 1937 he went into a lion's cage at Skegness to preach a sermon, and as the gaping crowd looked on he was killed by a lion called Freddie. A board near the font in Stiffkey church lists the names of village men who went to the war in 1914, and the rector's name is on it. The church guide I bought had a loyal and compassionate note about him: 'He was loved by the villagers who relished his sermons, recognized his humanity and forgave him his transgressions.'

Down the road to the east, in the thirteenth-century parish church in Blakeney, the brass-cleaning rota and the ladies' dusting schedule were posted in the porch. There was a brown dog bowl, filled with clean water, and a notice saying, 'Well-behaved dogs on leads are welcome in church.'

'So English,' said an American woman to her husband. He looked the sort of visitor you often see around here, an air force veteran making a nostalgic journey among the villages and aerodromes of East Anglia he knew as a young man in wartime.

Blakeney, I thought, could be the bottled essence of modern rural England, with its sense of the past and of loss, of change half-concealed by what appeared to be unchanging. Many an easel is set up by the creek where boats at low tide lean nearly on their beam ends. The light is limpid and the outlook agreeable, the village a distinctive pattern of cottages and narrow streets, shops, pubs, a primary school and busy hotels. The cottages, many of them the former homes of fishermen, are in sympathy with the landscape, brick faced with flint. Most of the newer houses have been built in the same fashion, as if on the orders of an enlightened despot of design, and the village has been spared the blight of much modern British house building.

The handsome church, standing on a low rise, has a small second tower, like a rudder. A beacon light burns in it at night, a reminder of Blakeney's former relationship with the sea. The village traded with Europe and the east coast ports into the early years of this century. The Blakeney lifeboat was frequently in action and a tablet in the church records a rescue in 1918 when the lifeboat crew 'in a northwest gale with frost and heavy snow' saved thirty people from two ships. The inscription notes that the lifeboat's crew of eighteen was well-weighted with experience, with an average age of fifty-five, the oldest man being sixty-eight and the youngest thirty-five.

Blakeney is the largest village in the Glaven valley and its sister villages are Cley, Wiveton, Glandford and Letheringsett. All are pretty and have lovely churches and all retain a lingering sense of rivalry with Blakeney and with each other. When Blakeney church was chosen as the setting for a *Songs of Praise* television programme the rector, with a keen appreciation of local sensitivities, insisted that the occasion involve the entire valley, not just Blakeney.

As with almost any village the postcard appearance of an idyll is misleading. Blakeney divides into the relatively well-off and the relatively hard-up and there is not much middle ground. Jobs are scarce. Farmers, who used to have a dozen or fifteen men, now employ one or two; and seasonal work is done by fewer men or has largely disappeared. There are jobs in the shops and hotels and work for gardeners and cleaners. Some men fish for crabs and a few dig for bait in the mudbanks, hard work on winter days.

Blakeney's population of eight hundred doubles in the summer and complaints about traffic and cars obstructing the lanes are subjects high on the parish council agenda. But, give or take a grumble, holidaymakers are welcomed, for the income they bring. The permanent incomer creates different problems. For many years Blakeney has attracted weekenders and retired people from Leicestershire; and at one time it half-jokingly referred to itself as Leicester-by-sea. It drew a number of what the locals called 'the fast set' and 'smart people' and Christmas midnight mass at the church was as much a social highlight as a religious festival.

Some who come from outside to make a home in Blakeney want it to be like the England they knew, or thought they knew, a gentle village in a painting, Morris Minor country, a place of 'character'. They want yesterday, the attitudes and standards of the England of thirty or forty years ago; and hope that these will last for the rest of their lives. They have little wish to see change and often resist it. But reality sometimes intrudes rudely: a house is burgled, car windows are smashed by hooligans, a drug-user's needle is seen on the quay.

At the same time some of the local people resent the way that many incomers, as soon as they move in, set about changing the appearance of their houses with extensions. What makes it worse is that some incomers can conspicuously afford to do so. 'On one hand they bang on about the traditional appearance of the village and on the other they want to change their bit of it,' a villager said.

Some of the people who move in have led competitive professional lives and have no wish to take on new duties, to be the treasurer of this or the secretary of that. Others do, of course, although there is sometimes a muttered complaint when an incomer is appointed a churchwarden.

Morris Arthur, the vice-chairman of the parish council, poured me tea in his kitchen and said that people in this part of Norfolk form a sort of Sicilian society; and perhaps there is some truth in his joke. 'They're quite reserved and treat incomers with caution and if incomers are sensible they'll take things slowly and not fly their colours straight away. Some of those moving in are looking for escape and a way of living in dignity, in harmony with their surroundings, but a few of them want to dominate. A businessman from the city, for example, may be accustomed to being served and flattered and he'll get terribly worked up when he finds that all his power and money won't get a village trades-man to drop everything and deal with him immediately. Incomers tend to lose arguments in the villages. They'll make a point and often they'll be in the right; so they are puzzled when the locals win. But the incomers lose because their attitude to the villagers is wrong.

'Locals don't like their freedoms eroded by those who want

to manage the countryside, to rebuild it in their patrician way. Around here, for example, we know how to go on and we don't disturb the birds and the seals. I was on the beach with my family once, quietly watching the seals nearby, when a woman came running up, ordering us away, saying that we would disturb them. Naturally, her shouts frightened the seals and they slipped into the water straight away. Now, we don't want that sort of person trying to organize our lives.'

Morris Arthur's grandfather was the youngster of thirty-five in the Blakeney lifeboat exploit of 1918 commemorated in the church. Morris, the sea in his blood, has designed, built and raced boats, and sailed around Britain and across to Norway, his wife's home. Men from these parts, he said with a smile, learnt how to sail fast because in the old days they had to show the Revenue cutters a clean pair of heels. Smugglers were not necessarily ruffians, but ordinary men who smuggled Dutch gin, brandy and tobacco or went hungry. The trade was often carried on with the connivance of men in authority, who took a cut of the profits. 'How else could it have worked?'

Morris went away to Norwich when he was a young man, to work as an engineer, and came back to Blakeney after thirty years. 'The notion of growing old in Norwich did not appeal to me. People in cities don't live as long as country folk. It took me a while to get used to the disciplines and pace of a city. City people are trained to city life and I saw that the kids in Norwich were quicker than country boys. I noticed the impatience of the people in cities: they never had peace, never sat quietly and thought. People around here, you know, just sit and go off into a dream.'

A branch of his family settled on Tyneside in the years when ships took corn from Blakeney and brought coal from Newcastle. 'The North Sea was full of ships then. There's nostalgia for those times, of course, but they weren't the good old days. People counted for very little and there was exploitation and poverty under an oppressive and hierarchical structure. The clergy, the doctor and the landowners had the authority and matters were referred to their judgement, for they had the education and the money. A landlord had almost the power of

241

life and death and, of course, there was deference, that English thing. For many men the sea provided freedom from that tyranny because the hierarchy of seafaring men was different: it was founded not on who you were but what you could do, on the skill and experience on which men's lives depended.'

I asked Morris about Norfolkness. 'It's a bit artificial, but it's true there is a tribal instinct. The thing about it is this: when you are away from Norfolk you feel uncomfortable. And when you go to Suffolk you notice that it's different. For a start, it's tidier.'

Blakeney people have been determined to keep their village alive. It is a balancing act. The English village, as an institution, exists in the popular imagination as 'traditional' and peaceful. It is thought of as unchanging but the arguments in villages usually revolve around change, the need for it and the opposition to it. For all the sentiment, the lyrical poems and paintings, villages and the countryside itself have ever been a crucible, a place of continuous and sometimes painful development in agricultural practices, land management, machinery use and human relationships. In setting out to be a village with a self-sustaining life, a 'real' village, Blakeney had to bring together the imagined village and the reality. It had to reconcile the past with the future, accommodate the conflict between town and country, find equilibrium between those who wanted to settle and those on the inside who resented such immigration and replenishment. Above all, it wanted to avoid being an eaten-out husk, a village of holiday homes with no organic life. It wished to keep the school going, and some shops, and have a reasonable congregation both in the church and in the pubs. There had to be some organization and leadership. Blakeney has succeeded in its conscious effort to create a village life. There is an amateur dramatics society, a football team, the British Legion branch, indoor bowls, a sports centre at the village hall, a playing field and tennis courts. The school and church are focuses of activity. Local doctors set up a network to care for elderly people in the valley so that they are not lonely or frightened. It includes a day centre, an ambulance, physiotherapy, chiropody and visiting nurses who give baths and other help, the whole scheme linked with the social services. Another group raises money for good works,

242

provides a Christmas lunch for the elderly, sends cards to villagers in hospital and helps in emergencies, such as replacing a load of coal stolen from a house.

A decisive action, a necessary piece of social engineering, was the founding of the village housing society. Its chief purpose was to provide cottages at an affordable rent for local people so that they would have homes in the village and not be driven out by second-home owners. It set out to ensure that those who come in search of the past do not push out those who want a future, that the village has a core of locally-rooted people working, raising children and sustaining village life. Another aim was to keep Blakeney's characteristic appearance of brick and beachstone. Many cottages were restored. This was not always popular locally. A number of villagers felt very strongly that restoration was mere sentiment and they suspected that those promoting it were imposing their patrician views. Many wanted the old cottages demolished and replaced by new council houses. But the housing society persisted. Today it owns forty-one cottages, many of them bequeathed. The incidence of rent arrears is low and no one has ever been evicted. 'The scheme has helped village life to flourish,' Morris Arthur said.

In the church a kettle was set up on a table and a notice encouraged visitors to make tea and help themselves to a free pot of marmalade or seedlings from local gardens. No donation was requested. Nicholas Martin, the rector, told me that this was part of his welcome policy, to throw the doors open. 'I dislike the signs you see in many churches saying that they need thousands of pounds for this or that. The Church of England has a reputation for being a grabbing church, rather than a giving church, and we are trying to change that.'

He said the church needed to be open in other ways. 'I never insist that parents who bring a baby for baptism should be churchgoers. People need to mark significant moments in their lives in church and I believe that they should be able to do so, otherwise the church risks putting itself in a ghetto. In the forty years I have known it the church has become too judgemental. It should take a moral lead, of course, but rather than preaching at people it should persuade them to take responsibility for their

243

own actions. Morality does develop, though it is not easy to say that it is always a religious thing. My observation is that a great number of people try to live with integrity, but it may be done in different ways compared with forty or fifty years ago; living together, for example, rather than marrying.

'For some the church seems to be a place of condemnation. The result of that is that when it tries to give encouragement its words fall on deaf ears. The church is not attuned to reality in the way that people are. It becomes bound by dogma and rules and fails to teach forgiveness, acceptance and hope. It is in danger of becoming a society of the smug. I remember that when I was a chaplain at a detention centre in Oxford I was told by a clergyman there that "these children are in trouble because they don't get the Ten Commandments read to them every Sunday".

'I try to get through to people by listening rather than preaching at them. People want to worship and to link with the church, but they can't stand being made to feel got-at when they come into the place. My parishioners value the church, and not just as a building. They talk about "our church". They like it to rise to meet their needs.'

All of the five parishes in the valley had their own clergy until the 1950s but today Nicholas Martin covers them all with the help of two retired clergymen. 'Because I do so many services in the villages everything is set up for me by helpers, the chalice, candles, microphones and so on, and so I just drive in. It would not have done for my father. He was a clergyman who liked to do all his own preparations. Clergymen were more feared in his day. He was an autocratic man and said, "This is what we do" and it was done. I see myself rather as a team leader, one of a number of leaders in the community. I'm not feared but I think I am respected.

'The joy of the job is its variety, writing sermons, visiting, comforting the sick. I am involved. People know that if they need me I will be there. They ask my help for many reasons, when they are bereaved, when they have marriage problems. And I am often with people when they die. Recently, I was called to see an old lady and arrived just in time to speak to her for five minutes before she died; and one of her family said, "She was hanging on just for you."

'It is hard to make ends meet on a clergy income with two children. Had it not been for my wife's parents we would have been sunk. They gave us the car which we use to visit the children at school and we dread anything going wrong with it. We know what it is to shop carefully, to replace items on the supermarket shelves because we cannot afford them. Nevertheless, being a country parson is my fulfilment. I love village life and each of my five villages has a different character. I like the people. They are in touch with reality, they value the soil and there is not that veneer of pretence that you find in cities. In the city I dealt with a much smaller number of people.

'Indigenous Norfolk people are reserved and difficult to get to know at first, but they are down to earth and honest and a friend made in Norfolk is a friend for life. As a parson, I hear about bad and disappointing things, people not behaving well. But I also hear a lot that is positive. There is much unsung work, people putting themselves out to help their neighbours. I live among good people in a good part of England.'

9

The Naked British

To the gigantic countries, Russia, China and the United States, it has always been a wonder that the people of a small archipelago occupying one thousandth of the world's land made so profound an impact on the world's story.

The Chinese word for Britain is *Yingguo*, the land of the brave or the land of heroes. It is a back-handed compliment, an early nineteenth-century term reflecting the respect the Chinese had for British military power, a force they saw deployed with brutal effect in support of Britain's opium trade on their southern coast. It was also applied to distinguish the British from the other big-nosed European barbarians encountered by the Chinese and known to them collectively as the *falang*, the Franks.

Thoughtful and politically aware Chinese wonder not only how we acquired an immense empire but also by what process we came to lose it.

In their ponderings they also conclude that the British are guilty of *xuwei*, hypocrisy, for they believe that British self-effacement, modesty and deference amount to a sham, that people could not possibly live with themselves if they honestly believed in these qualities; and perhaps they have a point.

Nevertheless the ideal of the *shenshi*, the British gentleman, is admired; and the absence of it in China is regretted by some Chinese. When the Chinese Communists looked for a stinging insult to throw at the British they recalled that they had seen them running around a field in white clothes on hot days in Shanghai and they therefore described cricket as 'imperial buffoonery'. They could not know that any British gentleman would rejoice in such a delicious description.

The identikit portrait of the British assembled from the perceptions and experiences of foreigners contains a strong idea of the British gentleman. A Russian teacher in St Petersburg told me that by her observation the British were reserved, courteous and good at achieving compromise; and that was also the belief that had come down through her family. A woman I met in Moscow remembered the polite schoolboys in London in the 1920s who raised their caps and offered their seats to adults on the bus. She asked me if London were still like that. Since she was over ninety and had spent many years in the gulag at Stalin's order, for the simple reason that she had once been married to an Englishman and was therefore the object of suspicion, I assured her that London remained populated by gentlemen; and was rewarded by a sweet smile.

An Indian friend complained that fewer and fewer British men said a courteous Good Morning and Goodbye. They used Hi and *Ciao* instead; and in his eyes were somewhat diminished. In India I was often reminded that the British were expected to behave better than any other people in the world, including Indians themselves. The British were idealized as men of their word, as gentlemen. Indians always assumed that other nationalities would behave badly from time to time, but if the British did not live up to their reputation for decency Indians felt betrayed. During a quarrel between India and the British government, an Indian newspaper wrote: 'Perhaps without an empire to lord over, the British have reverted to what they basically are – a small, little people with small, little minds, inhabiting a small, little island.' The editorial wondered whether Britain had 'discarded even the pretence of fair play that was once the hallmark of the British'. It was this virtuous belief in justice, decency and fair play that Mahatma Gandhi saw in the British and which he patiently exploited in arguing with them that they should depart from a land that was not theirs.

Americans writing about Britain rarely fail to mention the extent of our class-consciousness. The suggestion is that we are hamstrung by it and, ridiculous idea, that there is little or no class division in America. Many Americans like to hear a Limey accent and recognize 'your famous British understatement'. But they sometimes detect an assumption of superiority in our voices and are irritated by it. As for that famous understatement, they often suspect an unwillingness to say what we mean.

Americans are not alone in finding us, at first encounter at least, cool and stand-offish. It has been observed of us since the eighteenth century that when we raise a newspaper in front of our faces we close an oaken door. A number of Americans at Oxford University in the 1960s found British students icily unwelcoming, not gentlemen at all. 'The British undergraduates were snotty,' it was said, 'and this had the effect of making some of the Americans anglophobic.'

In her poem 'The White Cliffs', published in the 1940s, the American Alice Duer Miller noted that her father had told her that the English 'do think England is God almighty'. She reflected that

> The English are frosty
> When you're no kith or kin
> Of theirs, but how they alter
> When once they take you in!
> The kindest, the truest,
> The best friends ever known.
> It's hard to remember
> How they froze you to a bone.

A booklet published for migrants from Barbados to Britain in the late 1940s warned 'You will find that the people in the United Kingdom are less inclined to join you in conversation than your own people in Barbados. This is not meant to be a slight on you but is merely one of the characteristics of English people. The British are said to be hard to get to know. They . . . consider that too much talking is a waste of time. This does not mean they are unfriendly.'

Nirad Chaudhuri, who left his native India at the age of fifty-seven and wrote a shrewd study of the English in *A Passage to England*, said he had heard of English reticence before he arrived; and, sure enough, the streets of London appeared to him to be like scenes in a silent film and the restaurants were quiet compared with the noisy eating houses of India. In a club one evening he tried to start a conversation across the table 'and I admired the skill with which the intrusion was fended off without the slightest suggestion of discourtesy'.

Englishmen, he said, 'are not unaware of their habit of taciturnity, which they call understatement. They are even proud of it, as if it was one of their titles to superiority over other nations, and overdo it at times.' But he drew a distinction between public and private manners; and in private he encountered no chilliness or formality.

American servicemen posted to Britain are told in an official briefing: 'They guard their privacy carefully. This reserve is sometimes misunderstood as unfriendliness.'

The French writer Philippe Daudy commented on 'the silence so loved by my English friends, which they compare to the cacophony of foreign languages. They cherish it as an expression of calm in the face of futile agitation. It is their antidote to excess of emotion. The British hold out their hand in a parsimonious gesture that maintains distance more than it expresses cordiality. This reassuring silence, made up of shared culture and certainties, is not always as comfortable as the English like to believe. At times it feels like the muteness of a prisoner who has forgotten how to speak after years of incarceration.'

Karel Čapek, a Czech writer who toured Britain in the 1920s, found himself longing for the Continent – 'noisier, less disciplined, dirtier, madder, subtler, more passionate, more affable, more amorous'. He was appalled by the 'joyless and reticent'

British. 'In the place of taverns where one can drink and talk, they have invented bars where one can drink and hold one's peace.' In spite of this silence he discovered that 'if you get to know them closer, they are very kind; they never speak much because they never speak about themselves. They cannot get out of their skin, but it is a solid and excellent skin. They are as hospitable as St Julian, but they can never overstep the mark, the distance between man and man. Sometimes you have a sense of uneasiness at feeling so solitary in the midst of these kind and courteous people; but if you were a little boy, you would know that you can trust them more than yourself, and you would be free and respected here more than anywhere else in the world.'

Čapek thought our food had something to do with our temper. 'English cooking lacks a lightness and floweriness, *joie de vivre*, melodiousness and sinful voluptuousness. English life also lacks this.'

Many foreigners have examined our dinner plates for clues to our character. The cult of our national dish asserted that English beef made English men. Deriving its unique flavour from sweet pastures, beef 'ennobled our veins and enriched our blood'. The French long ago dubbed the English *rosbifs*. 'As English as a beef-steak,' Nathaniel Hawthorne wrote. Washington Irving described part of the City of London as 'the stronghold of true John Bullism . . . roast beef and plum pudding are held in super-stitious veneration.'

Aboard Captain Cook's *Endeavour*, as it laboured in the bleak ocean off New Zealand in 1770, the botanist Joseph Banks sensed the homesickness of the seamen and recorded the most telling symptom of it – 'they begin to sigh for roast beef'.

Nikolai Karamzin, from Russia, who, by the by, met Banks in 1790 and thought him 'quite friendly, for an Englishman', endured a dinner served in the English style. 'We ate nothing but beef and cheese. I ordered salad, but they brought grass saturated with vinegar. The English do not like vegetables. Roast beef makes them melancholy and unbearable to themselves – and, not infrequently, suicides.'

Karamzin saw Englishmen sitting in coffee houses reading newspapers and drinking port in silence. 'You are lucky if, in the course of ten minutes, you hear three words. And what are they? "Your health, gentlemen!"' But he thought Englishmen generous, sensitive and brave. They were real men, he said. But he added that if he were to define them in a word he would call them morose – 'just as I would call the French volatile and the Italians crafty.' He put this down to gloomy weather and heavy food. A French friend told him that the English were a volcano cloaked in ice, but he himself saw no flame. 'My Russian heart likes to pour itself out in animated conversation. It likes the play of eyes, sudden changes of expression. It is said that the Englishman is more profound than others. Is it not because his thick blood circulates more slowly and this makes him look thoughtful when he is not thinking at all? The gloomy Briton greedily devours the sun's rays as a cure for his illness, spleen. Give the English the sky of Languedoc and they sing and dance like the French.'

The Belgians, on the whole, like the British, seeing some similarity in national character, stoicism and self-mockery; and they share a suspicion of the French. Belgians have not forgotten that in the First World War we fought to push the Germans out of their country; and, in remembrance of British soldiers, buglers sound 'Last Post' in Ypres every evening at eight o'clock.

The French Foreign Legion does not like British recruits because they tend to drink too much. But the Frenchman who founded the famous Crazy Horse cabaret in Paris paid a compliment to the British that is to be treasured. He said that he preferred to choose British girls as his nude dancers: for their willowy beauty, naturally, but especially for their punctuality.

A Handful of Earth

Edward Thomas, the essayist and poet, born in Lambeth, London, of Welsh parents, devoted much of his writing to the countryside of southern England, to Kent, Sussex, Hampshire and Wiltshire, to the high chalk downs, steep-sided valleys, streams and woods of a landscape in which for him lay the essence, antiquity and poetry of pastoral England. He converted half the study at his home in Hampshire into an apiary so that

251

he worked amid the hum of bees and the heavy smell of honey, an inhabitant of the hive.

When the First World War broke out he formed the belief, expressed in one of his short essays, that he would not be able to look at the landscape he loved so much unless he were willing to die for it. In 1915, just after he enlisted in the Artists' Rifles, one of those peculiarly English bands of brothers-in-arms, a friend asked him what he thought he was fighting for. He reached down and scooped a handful of English earth and rubbed it in his fingers.

'Literally,' he said, 'for this.'

A shell killed him in the battle of Arras on Easter Monday of 1917.

He was right, of course, about the handful of earth, for earth and stone have an elemental significance. Stepping ashore at Bulverhithe, between Pevensey and Hastings, in September of 1066, William the Conqueror stumbled and fell headlong on his proud Norman nose. He knew that his superstitious troops would see his tumble as a grim omen. With the acute presence of mind that marks out the true leader, that instinct for the moment, he scooped up a fistful of sand. Rising to his feet, he shouted: 'I have taken possession of the land with my hands, and by the splendour of God it is mine – it is yours!'

Edward Thomas's handful of earth, the residue of time and the distillate of history and myths, lies at the heart of the enigma of allegiance, a mystery central to my own experience as a foreign correspondent. I am fascinated by loyalty, the adherence to family, faith, clan, caste, tribe and nation, the emotional and territorial imperative that is as fundamental and natural a force as hunger or sex. It has been my occupation to witness and report the passion and immense power of allegiance in many parts of the world, in Asia and Africa, in the old Soviet empire and Europe, in north and central America and even in the Arctic.

I remember Mikhail Gorbachev's look of astonishment in Vilnius, when a Lithuanian waved a placard under his nose, demanding freedom. While Gorbachev prated about an empire that would last a thousand years, this upstart in the crowd was

252

demonstrating allegiance to a patch of conquered soil. It lay buried beneath the Soviet concrete, yet was still fertile. I remember, too, the outcome of this confrontation, the courage of ordinary people who, like Edward Thomas, could not look upon their landscape unless they were willing to die for it. I watched them link arms and sing songs about their own handful of earth and face the tanks and soldiers' guns; and later I saw their bodies on a hospital floor.

Edward Thomas touched the mystery and power of landscape, his mind a mirror of water meadows, new-turned clods and new-cut hay, stands of oaks and hedgerows in their seasons. It is not difficult to rouse an English sentiment with images of evensong in country churches, primrose glades, rookery nooks and the smell of woodsmoke. In the same way, a Scot's spirit soars at the spectacle of glen, crag and salmon streams; and Welsh hearts rise at the prospect of mountain, nant and cwm.

Some parts of the world remind you of the landscape of Britain but nowhere is there a landscape exactly like it. Its cultivated shape, scent and coherence is unique and unmistakable. In many places it seems to be a garden made of gardens. Love of it, of the handful of earth, invigorates opposition to brutish schemes. The wind in the willows is summoned up against the bureaucrat and his bulldozer. A Londoner told me he never feels English in the streets of London, but as soon as he walks the lanes of Kent or ascends the chalk downs of Sussex and bows to the boisterous winds of Beachy Head he is suffused and feels Englishness rising in crescendo. He vanishes into the mists and myths of England, and, metaphorically at least, picks up the earth as if it were a sacrament.

The rock itself, sandstone or granite, limestone or clay, claims allegiance and fashions the people. The fertile heartland has always been soft, easily travelled, readily ploughed, amenable to conquest; but other parts are hard, resistant and independent. Voices, too, seem shaped by geology: they are flinty, brittle, graunchy, flattened, squeezed, open, rounded, soft, hard. In spite of the homogenizing and levelling influences of education, broadcasting and social mingling, the accents and dialects hold their ground with remarkable tenacity. At the same time, anyone

253

travelling in Britain is struck by the way accents change every twenty or thirty miles. The country is a jigsaw of local loyalties, voices and tribal words; and some of the accents are almost mutually incomprehensible. It reminds me of Papua New Guinea, a land of more than seven hundred languages, where tribes existed for centuries without ever meeting their neighbours, or knowing of their existence, even though they lived only a few miles distant.

A young woman who cut my hair in Newcastle said to me that her beloved city was a complete world, all she wanted. Her chief anxiety was that her impending marriage would take her across the bridge to Gateshead, on the south bank of the Tyne, her *terra incognita*. There was no such concern for the girl whose wedding was reported in a local newspaper under the headline 'Swansea Girl Marries Swansea Man in Swansea'.

The attachment to neighbourhood puts the ginger into English village cricket: rivalry supplies energy to the bowler's arm and sharpens the cheating instinct. Until recently, in many villages, endogamy-minded young men felt proprietorial about their home-grown girls and chased off predatory boys from neighbouring parishes. English villages are part of an idealized world, where many of us think we would like to live. When someone is murdered in a village newspapers affect outrage because the illusion has been soiled; as if passion, madness and evil exist only in cities. I have seen how tight and jealous villages can be, kraals run by godfathers and informal hierarchies, where it may take a newcomer ten or fifteen years to earn acceptance.

For all that Britain is small and easily travelled, many English people have never seen Scotland, Wales, Ireland, Cornwall or Yorkshire, have been to mighty London once or never, have not travelled much more than Queen Elizabeth I who never ventured west of the Severn or north of the Trent. Americans are eighteen times more likely to move house than the British. I heard in Scotland of men and women proud that they had never set foot in England. A Welshman I know, who travels frequently between north and south Wales, will not take any short cut that leads him into England: it is a matter of honour with him to keep his lungs charged with Welsh air.

The attachment to their roots is so strong that when they are away from them many people consider themselves internal exiles, form themselves into associations and gather for tribal corroborees. Caledonian and Cymric societies abound and consenting adults gather for haggis-cutting and leek-gnawing on feast-days; but other tribal groups are rather smaller, collectors' items almost. In Cardiff there was once an association of Rhondda exiles, though Rhondda itself is only sixteen miles up the road. The London Bidefordian Society used to meet to celebrate that north Devon town, which it considers to be a cut above Barnstaple, and its members ate an annual dinner of turkey with bread sauce and listened to a performance of the Bideford anthem 'The Little White Town' and finished with a chorus of 'The Lads That Are Away' . . . 'Send them kindly greetings From the West Countree.'

Bureaucrats and metropolitan politicians often burn their fingers when they play baron with local pride. Given the loyalty and sentiment which attach to native rock, it was not surprising that the people of Rutland, the smallest county in England, plucked victory from defeat. Rootless administrators, lacking any sense of land, history and human nature, erased Rutland from the map in the interests of 'efficiency', leaving its people under the alien rule of Leicestershire. The dispossessed Rutlanders made trouble and won back their county. Similarly, the natives of the East Riding of Yorkshire fought their way out of the invented county of Humberside, though it took them nineteen years to do so. It is no surprise that, every few years, the Isle of Wight feels restless and thinks it would like to be independent, a tax haven, a banana republic like the Isle of Man. It is amazing what a strip of water does for a sense of sovereignty.

Every day the newspapers remind us of the British sense of place. Towns and villages everywhere are alarmed by threats of intrusion into their 'traditional' way of life. The word 'heritage' is invariably mobilized for the defence. Our favourite cliché is that a home is a castle. The garden fence or privet hedge, delineating territory, is a potent British symbol. We fight over inches. Transgressions drive householders to obsession and violence.

255

Neighbourly feuds over fences are a staple of newspaper reporting and of the income of lawyers.

Although jealous of our privacy we are also determined to have as much access to the land of Britain as possible, to get close to the handful of earth, to know it and thereby know ourselves better. Perhaps it is because it is such a small cake that we feel we have a right to every crumb of it. Long-distance walking is an activity that has grown phenomenally.

'How would you like it if I came walking in your garden?' landowners grumble. We would not like it and in any case they would not be interested in doing so. It is not the point: to many minds the right of access is a tradition, part of the British essence, an unwritten deal or social contract between the landowner and the rest of the people. There exists a passionate belief in the privilege, or right, of access, a feeling that the land is to be shared. The walkers are sometimes regarded as pesky subversives but they spring from a British tradition. The landowner, too, continues a tradition. Usually there is good will, an acceptance that each side has a proper view of what the land is for, though sometimes the traditions clash and there are disputes. During my travels I met Americans who had come to walk our footpaths for their holidays. They admired the extent of our access to the land. To them it was an enviable freedom, an aspect of British civilization.

The British curiosity about their landscape goes far beyond the mere quest for a view. They need to know more about themselves. Surveys reveal an ignorance of history, and a recent one showed that a quarter of the people interviewed did not know the significance of 1066 and many did not know how Charles I met his end; but that does not mean there is a deep lack of interest. Edward Thomas had it right, I think, when he wrote that 'because we are imperfectly versed in history, we are not therefore blind to the past. We are not merely twentieth-century Londoners or Kentish men or Welshmen. We belong to the days of Wordsworth, of Elizabeth, of Richard Plantagenet, of Harold, of the earliest bards.' George Mackay Brown echoed the point. 'We cannot live fully without the treasury our ancestors have left to us,' he said. 'Without the story – in which everyone living, unborn and dead, participates – men are no more than bits of paper blown in the cold wind.'

We carry our history in a hod. Concluding his *English Journey* in 1933 J.B. Priestley said: 'We stagger beneath our inheritance.' There is even more of it now. Hardly a British acre lies free of historical connection and you cannot round a corner without banging into the lintel of legend. We feel our age. Britain is not, like many countries, a logically-constructed frame with a written constitution and a manifesto of idealism arising from a fresh start, from the ruin of war or the overthrow of an old order. It has grown organically, sometimes haphazardly, accruing mosses, lesions, wrinkles, warts and patches. Ours is a library of well-used books. We have come to lean on habit, ritual, precedent and the knowledge that we have seen and done much. This experience has made us pragmatic, resistant to change, sceptical, sometimes lazy, ad hoc, sardonic and ironic, and very likely to resist fanaticism and fundamentalism.

In the post-imperial time of slack water, we dig increasingly in the seams of experience to uncover more of the mysteries of ourselves. The museums have never been so good, the castles, palaces and great houses never so popular. Fresh histories spill from the presses every week. History, nostalgia and commerce combine in the the White Cliffs of Dover Experience, the Blitz Experience, the Viking Experience. The countryside is divided into historical and literary districts unknown to the Ordnance Survey: Shakespeare country, Hardy country, Wordsworth and Austen country, Constable, Cook and Nelson country. Brontësauruses have long made pilgrimages to the parsonage at Haworth and tourists follow the paw marks into the Beatrix Potter country and make the rounds of the Herriot country of Yorkshire. I met people on their way to explore the Cadfael country of Shropshire, the setting of the medieval detective stories. People walk the Cobb in Lyme Regis in the footsteps of the French lieutenant's woman and flock to country houses used as a setting for a television period drama. Boatmen offer trips to the River Hamble and call it the *Howard's Way* country, after a gin-and-seawater television series. In my visits to East End pubs I began to believe that the people were not genuine noble-savage

East Enders but, rather, were basing their behaviour on the East Enders they saw in *EastEnders*.

Hundreds of men light their pipes and follow in the footsteps of Sherlock Holmes and Dr Watson, to the extent of dressing in Holmesian costume and staging the final showdown between Holmes and Moriarty at the Reichenbach torrent. Groups dressed in Victorian costume are seen at railway stations, setting off to visit the scenes of Dickens's novels, Broadstairs, for example. Occasionally, I see people processing through the streets wearing wimples and codpieces, on their way to 'fayres'.

For a people supposedly chilly, reserved and shy, disapproving of showiness, the British enthusiastically dress up. We famously excel at pageantry, full-bottomed wigs, plumes, tabards, men in tights and buckled shoes. When a Clerk of the House of Commons suggested that the Clerks might do their work in suits and not in wigs and gowns the suggestion was promptly flattened. As a hobby, men dress as Roman soldiers, and thousands of members of the Sealed Knot and its rival, the English Civil War Society, don seventeenth-century costumes and clash pikes in re-enactments of Civil War battles.

It may be eccentric, but the British have an immense capacity for eccentricity, tolerate it and enjoy it. No doubt it springs from confidence and freedom. Ralph Waldo Emerson said, 'I know not where any personal eccentricity is so freely allowed.' Nikolai Karamzin commented on the whimsy, playfulness and 'inane folk farces' he observed, adding that 'the British take pride in the fact that they can make fools of themselves to their heart's content without accounting to anyone for their caprices. If in England it is permitted to play the fool, in our country it is not forbidden to play the wise man. But often the latter is more ridiculous than the former. This unbounded freedom to live as one wishes . . . has produced in England a great number of peculiar characters and a rich harvest for the writers of novels.'

Cool and formal, the British stand on ceremony and on their dignity. But they also skip around maypoles, makes asses of themselves in morris dancing troupes and roll cheeses down hills. Admiral Jacky Fisher was a tough naval officer in the starchy Victorian Navy, but he was a joyous spectacle on deck or dance floor, whirling vigorously in a dance with anyone who came to hand, man or woman. The British see nothing odd in a tradition that insists that elderly men, sometimes at risk to limb, if not life, walk backwards from the monarch at the State Opening of Parliament. Only foreigners think it funny that we have officials called Black Rod and Gold Stick. We are accustomed to our Parliament's badinage, raucous scenes and curious customs and we hardly notice that a member has to put on a ridiculous hat at certain times to ask a question. It seems perfectly normal to us that a haggis, a stuffed gut, should be played to the table by a piper; that raw leeks should be ceremonially crunched while the eater places one foot on a chair; that the Second Battalion of the Royal Regiment of Wales go on parade with a mascot, a white goat with the rank of lance-corporal, looked after by a soldier designated the Goat Major.

A particularly British strain of humour and comic writing has grown out of our tradition of eccentricity and fantasy. It has enabled us to survive the business of being British. Unpricked, our pomposity and preposterousness would otherwise have stifled us. Our playwrights and novelists have invented a tribe of bizarre and wayward aristocrats and clergymen for our entertainment; though seeing how many there have been in life, we have scarcely needed the fiction. In his Beachcomber column in the *Daily Express*, J.B. Morton published a stream of farce and fantasy for fifty-one years; and given the realities of British life he sometimes seemed close to the truth. The BBC, a serious public service institution, which once insisted that its radio announcers read the news while dressed in dinner jackets, pushed the frontiers of comedy and encouraged the anarchic and creative *Goon Show*. Later, the flights of fantasy and subversion soared in *Monty Python's Flying Circus*. To most foreigners such humour is impenetrable; and notwithstanding the common language, British humour is often too subtle and too ironic for Americans, and also too vulgar. One facet of our chilly and taciturn nature is our belly-laugh, the coarseness of comedians and seaside postcards.

The vulgarity is a tradition. From the seventeenth century, satirists and cartoonists have savagely lampooned monarchs, princes, aristocrats, political figures and their women; and many caricatures have been obscene and scatalogical. Even heroes like Nelson did not escape being drawn as ludicrous figures. In robust self-mockery, John Bull was often depicted as beefy and warty. Naturally the scorn extended to foreigners. Oliver Goldsmith, in 1798, deplored the prejudice of men he encountered in a coffee-house, one of whom avowed that the Dutch were 'avaricious wretches; the French flattering sycophants; the Germans drunken sots; the Spaniards surly tyrants; but that in bravery, generosity, clemency, and in every other virtue, the English excelled.' The British, of course, jeered at Bonaparte, the Kaiser and the posturings of Hitler.

An American journalist wrote in the 1840s of British scorn. 'The high are brought so low that the lowest can laugh at them,' he said. 'The proud are pulled down to where they can be scorned by the basest. A register is kept of Bishops, Peeresses, Dukes, Ambassadors, charged with being swindlers, buffoons, panders, sycophants; and this is one way of keeping Englishmen in mind that all men are brothers.'

The tradition of derision is energetically maintained in newspaper attacks on politicians, peers, the royal family, the clergy and business tycoons. On Tower Hill, the slope above the Tower of London, there is a small paved area where seventy-five dukes, knights, lords and high officials were beheaded. The executioner always held the severed head high to show it to the mob. In his *Crowds and Power* Elias Canetti wrote, 'Whoever the head belonged to it is degraded now. Though it may have started on the shoulders of a king it is made level with [the crowd] by this lightning process of public degradation. The impact of his downfall is tremendous.' Modern Fleet Street is Tower Hill. When it comes to a cabinet minister's affair, a peer's drug-taking and the scandals of celebrities, the pages of popular newspapers are the scaffold, editors are the executioners holding up the heads and readers are the mob.

As well as responding to, and reflecting, all our prejudices and hypocrisies, the press mirrors our fears. Fear is part of its stock-in-trade. It is an element of a much larger and significant theme of our times, the belief that Britain is in a process of decline, that there was a time when British civilization was better and that we have allowed opportunities to slip through our fingers. Columns, letters and discussions reflect regret, wistfulness and a sense of loss. In the pages of newspapers we mope. When we look around, so much seems to be diminished. We think we can hear the ticking of the death-watch beetle in HMS *Britain*. The 'good old days' are everywhere apostrophized. Pundits and correspondents assert that in years gone by men were mannerly and courageous and put women and children first. We are encouraged to believe that we are uniquely oppressed by crime, that terrorism and the trade in drugs are corroding our foundations. The murder of a child is held as evidence that our society is irreparably 'sick' – whatever 'sick' may mean. After another murder, the question is asked, 'Is nowhere safe?', which suggests a huddling in foxholes. After a riot the wringers of hands ask 'Is time running out for our cities?'

The idea that Britain is in decline is virtually unchallenged. It is accepted as a given, as obvious as rain. 'The national decline' is a phrase kept permanently in type and has become the emblem of our moroseness. It is shorthand, a term encompassing the ending of the greatest Empire, the shrinking of industrial power and the pain of economic evolution. But entangled in this is the idea that there is a continuing failure of morals and morale, that there is a spiritual collapse. 'The national decline' is a cliché written without thought. It is anything you wish it to be, from the ending of the Empire, to the manners and music of young people, to the closing of the village pub, to the littered streets of dreary suburbs, to all of society's ills, injustice, crime and squalor.

I cannot rue the end of Empire. It was a marvellous and splendid adventure and took the British from their crabbed northern confines and put the sun on their pale backs. But its time was up and there is nothing to grieve over. The contraction of the great industries was inevitable, too.

The trouble with 'the national decline' is that it posits a golden age that never existed. Nostalgia is an agreeable condiment and reminiscence a proper pleasure. But nostalgia is corrosive if we set the past against the present and really believe the past was better. History shows that crime is not worse today and we do

261

not live in an especially immoral time. On the contrary. The death of a single teenager from a drugs overdose is not a matter of indifference but of public concern and debate. The murder of a child makes us sad and angry. When a schoolteacher or a clergyman is stabbed we are appalled. Our reactions spring from a fundamental goodness and decency, a clear idea of right and wrong. We have a moral view in a world of pressing and difficult moral dilemmas. Given our choices and circumstances, our fathers and grandfathers would not have behaved any differently.

As far as the golden age is concerned, I certainly met people who believed that times were sunnier thirty or forty years ago. An English couple had moved to a village in rural Wales because, they told me, it was like the England of the 1950s when everyone was more courteous. I lost count of the times I was told of the good-natured era when you could leave your doors unlocked. A new magazine with a high nostalgia content asked: 'Remember the days when the train journey was the best part of the holiday, when villages were more self-sufficient and there were few "incomers" competing for cottages, when everything revolved around the seasons and the crops?'

On the whole, though, it was the older people I met on my travels who instructed me that there never was a golden age. I went in search of it all the same, and returned to that supposedly sunnier time by turning the pages of *John Bull*, seeing what lay behind those optimistic cover paintings. An editorial in 1949 declared: 'Dishonesty, hooliganism, rank bad behaviour: today in Britain it almost seems as if some people don't know right from wrong.' An article wailed: 'Lost, at some time during the last ten years, a valuable moral code, property of the people of Britain', and expressed anxiety about the moral situation and an alarming increase in crime. A judge at the Old Bailey complained of 'this distemper of dishonesty which has swept over the country'. The magazine reported 'incredible mob behaviour' and wrote of 'an immense and sinister mass of moral indifference drifting about under the surface of everyday life'.

In another golden age, when Victorian values flourished, crime was worse and more violent, Irish nationalists were bombing London, child prostitution was rampant, cheap gin was a ruinous dope and London police officers were assaulted much more than they are today. The streets reeked of dung and smoke and people stank. If you bumped into a poor man you went home and checked your clothes and hair for vermin. Of twelve thousand men who volunteered for the army in 1899 in Manchester, only a tenth were found fit for service. Of course, things grew better: at the time of my grandfather's birth the age at which a child could be put to work in a factory was raised from ten to eleven.

We are seeing evolution and calling it decline. Indeed, we have made a fetish of 'the national decline' and created a cult of self-pity and pernicious nostalgia. But all of these are part of an historic process, the slow and painful sloughing of a skin. This is a time, not of chaos, but of disorientation, as the people of Britain search for identity and new definitions and wrestle with myths and history. The thread I constantly picked up in my travels was the desire of people to be distinctive, to have a purpose, to be able to say what they are. 'Who Cares Who We Are?' asked *Country Life* in an article bemoaning the sacrificing of red telephone boxes and the arrival of 'foreign imports such as French lavatories'. But only a German word would do when it declared that 'our national identity will cause growing angst'.

Identity is the question of the times. The English imperial enterprise created the United Kingdom and gave it a purpose for more than three centuries. Now that the Empire has joined history, and we have returned home from the world, the value of the United Kingdom's political construction is questioned. After all these centuries the Scots, the Welsh and the Irish have not been subsumed and have not forgotten that they are not English. There is an echo of the Arthurian age, the time after the long Roman peace when the future nations of England, Scotland and Wales were defined. Nothing stands still, and the limits of the British unitary state may have been reached. It is very likely that the United Kingdom will change, though the substance of it may well prevail. For the bulk of the British people, the English, the search for a new definition within Britain and within Europe is subtle, complex and bewildering.

We have reached a hinge of history. As at every turning point, trepidation rides alongside excitement.

A View from the Tomb

The bones of Vice-Admiral William Bligh rest at old St Mary's church at Lambeth, close to the curve of the Thames and not far from where Bligh lived at 100 Lambeth Road. I thought his tomb would make a bollard to which I could secure the narrative of this journey.

Modern planners with their blunt pencils have done their worst around here, crushing the heart of the old cockney republic of Lambeth under sullen concrete and grim buildings. The churchyard, though, is a surprising oasis, sheltered from the noise of traffic behind a wall of dark yellow brick, a peaceful garden where you can hear the song of birds, a place where the longshore drift of history has heaped up its sediment. It stands hard by the red and purple brick of Lambeth Palace, the home of archbishops of Canterbury since the twelfth century. As such it has been a place of incident, attacked by London mobs on three occasions. In 1381 Wat Tyler's angry men burnt its books and smashed the wine barrels and the floors ran with claret. The chapel was turned into a dance hall in Cromwell's time, although you do not associate the name of Cromwell with such an activity; and during the same period the body of Archbishop Matthew Parker, who had died seventy-five years earlier, was dug up and thrust into a dung heap.

A stone tablet on the church wall is an informative footnote and encapsulates the vanity, generosity and prejudice of an eighteenth-century English gentleman. It states that in his will he endowed apprenticeships for two boys, on condition that they did not become chimney sweeps, watermen or fishermen; and it adds that the rector should maintain the lettering of the tablet in good order. The will was drawn up in 1711, only four years after the union of England and Scotland which created Great Britain, the British state whose pillars were Protestantism and the accumulation of wealth; and the tablet notes the benefactor's insistence that 'no Roman Catholic should enjoy the benefit' of his endowment.

St Mary's church fell into disuse in the 1960s but was rescued and turned into a museum of gardening honouring John Tradescant and his son, who both lie here. They designed and planted gardens for Charles I and Charles II and brought many popular foreign trees, shrubs and flowers to Britain; also the pineapple. So the churchyard celebrates the genius of gardeners and the British devotion to gardening; and it is part of its symmetry that 'Breadfruit' Bligh rests here, for his expedition to the south Pacific in the *Bounty* was a horticultural one.

The admiral's tomb is a vantage point from which there is a view of the centuries and the world. Across the Thames, in Fleet Street, both Bligh and Captain Cook attended the Thursday Club at the Mitre Tavern, where explorers, geographers, naturalists and navigators gathered to discuss the marvels of discovery. Unrolling their maps, they poured claret and carved themselves venison and slices of the world.

Spread out the charts that Bligh himself drew as a trail blazer of the expanding empire and you can see his prints on shores and straits: Bligh Water in Fiji, Bligh Island in Alaska, Bligh Sound in New Zealand, Bligh Entrance between Australia and New Guinea, Bligh Street, in Sydney, commemorating his troubled reign as governor of New South Wales which ended with his overthrow in a *putsch* by the colony's rum racketeers.

The inscription on Bligh's tomb salutes 'the celebrated navigator who fought the battles of his country'; and fight he did, against oceans, storms and mutineers. He fought the Dutch at Camperdown and the Danes at Copenhagen, after which battle he was personally congratulated by Nelson.

In the quiet churchyard you might just hear the distant thunder of naval guns and catch the faint sniff of hibiscus and hear the proud admiral grumbling 'D—— you, Mr Christian!' And through your special spyglass you might see the river full of ships, thicketed with spars and as teeming with boats as a pond is with insects. The Thames is a river in retirement now, quiet and grandfatherly, its embankments lined with imperial memorabilia. Those noble witnesses of merchant and naval tradition, *Cutty Sark* and *Belfast*, rest like model ships in glass cases.

At Bligh's tomb the river has flowed from the Cotswolds, through the middle-England landscape of woods, water meadows and lion-coloured fields, past the stones of Oxford and through the Edwardian pictures of Henley and the swanneries. From here it winds to Westminster and holds a mirror to St Paul's and the Tower of London. It sweeps past the docklands whose steely shining towers suggest a future but look transplanted and tentative.

It crosses the meridian line at Greenwich, from which all time at sea is measured, and, flowing past Tilbury and Gravesend, opens out into Lower Hope Reach and the Yantlet Channel and Sea Reach and the Nore, the old naval anchorage where *Victory*, at last, surrendered the body of Nelson to a smaller vessel for the journey up the Thames. Beyond The Warp and Shivering Sands the tidal streams perform their endless dance, changing and swirling through the King's Channel and over Gunfleet Sand and through the Black Deep, forming their question marks as the estuary mingles with the old Narrow Sea, the European sea, the place of decision and, since ancient times, the point of departure.

Acknowledgements

My thanks to Wil Aaron, Fred Bridgland, Matthew Cocks, Gwyn Erfyl, Alan Hamilton, Graham Hutchings, John Edgar Mann, Mair Owen, Natasha Pakhomova, the Ridgway family; and Penny . . . without whom.

Index